The Venetian City Garden

For
Philip & Jane
And
Nubar & Pallina

Preface

Much more might be said of ... the most beautiful gardens in Venice, but I will leave something for other writers to tell.

Pietro Casola, 1494

There have been other books published on the Venetian city garden; notwithstanding, my own work on this topic over many years has usually been met with surprise that there are any gardens at all in Venice, let alone some that are worth writing about seriously. So a word seems in order by way of explaining the subject of this book.

I trace the genesis of this project to the time when I was researching materials for my book, *Garden and Grove*, published in 1986. That work, subtitled "The Italian Renaissance Garden in the English Imagination", dealt with the reception of Italian garden design by 17th- and 18th-century English gardenists (this useful term was coined by Horace Walpole to include all those interested in gardens as well as those who actually make them). That research involved the visitation of gardens in Italy by the English, the review of everything I could find on how they formulated their reactions to these gardens in both word and image, and ultimately on the translation of those Italian experiences into new, built forms back home in England. Ensconced in the small room at the British School in Rome that contained Thomas Ashby's collection of Italian guidebooks, I found a treasure trove of materials; there I was able to compile a virtually complete itinerary of garden visits, a full inventory of the elements of garden design that mattered to these visitors, and a profile of what I have come to term garden experience. Yet I was soon struck by one significant *lacuna* in the travel literature: there was absolutely nothing substantial on gardens in the city of Venice. (Another gap, of no significance in this context but worth remarking nonetheless, was the absence of any record of visits to Bomarzo, the so-called "monster garden" north of Rome, surely an important if not unique mid-16th-century garden and rather different (like the Venetian ones) from those usually visited by travellers on the Italian garden circuit.)

Especially odd was the silence of travellers to Venice who were either expert gardenists, like John Evelyn, or who elsewhere in Italy were quick to visit and report on gardens, like Richard Lassels. Other tourists remarked that while guidebooks to Venice mentioned gardens, nowhere were they to be found. I, too, knew –from reading Italian guidebooks, as well as from a general knowledge of such Venetian imagery as Jacopo de' Barbari's bird's-eye view, or from passing remarks by writers like Henry James and Thomas Mann –that Venice had always had gardens, in fact plenty of them. So I determined to find out more about the Venetian city garden itself, the history of both its design and its use, and about how and why it vanished (or could re-appear) in the discourse of what, translating an Italian neologism, I term Venicity (or Veniceness, from the Italian *Venezianità*).

The scope and framework of my study of Venetian gardens has come to include both the origins of the city– topographical, ecological, urbanistic and mythological– and its still unknown and ill-determined future; these therefore form two, unavoidable *termini* in Chapters Two and Nine. Then I look in detail at the moment when, in Jacopo de' Barbari's bird's-eye view of the city of c.1500, gardens became an acknowledged item in the city's self-fashioning. Upon this high point of Venetian garden culture I bring to bear in Chapter Three a cluster of other images and written accounts–the background of Venetian paintings come in particularly useful here, as do some literary observations.

At the very centre of the book, in Chapter Four, are gathered materials that can be used as reference and evidence throughout the study. These materials consist of a catalogue of selected key sites that can be known in some detail over a *longue durée* of history. That this section is situated towards the midpoint of the book, rather than constituting (as it might more conventionally do) an appendix, is meant to emphasize that the accumulation of materials on the topography, design and evolution of so many gardens is an ineluctable element of any discussion of and learning from them. The mapping of Venice from de' Barbari onwards, the subsequent cadastral surveys of the French, Austrian and later Italian authorities, then the surveys that underpinned the "primo impianto" (first master plan) of 1938 and culminated in the systematic aerial photography of *Venezia forma urbis* published in 1983–all these enable the identification of especially interesting sites and a mapping of their successive stages;

this in its turn can be augmented with archival documents, especially notarial surveys and plans made for purposes of inheritance, rental or sale.

Then follows a chapter on a variety of what, borrowing from Egle Trincanato, I want to call *giardini minori,* namely vernacular, productive and botanical gardens. Throughout the city there have been – and still are – small gardens and orchards (the distinction can be blurred) that contribute to the overall gardenist profile and therefore cannot be neglected. As for Venice's botanical gardens, the story begins with the earliest known private site in the 14th century, supported by the city elders, to the public one instituted by the Emperor Napoleon at San Giobbe in the early 19th century; in-between came various private gardens, including those of such distinguished 18th-century pharmaceutical specialists as Lorenzo and Francesco Rizzo Patarol, whose garden at the Madonna dell'Orto survives, though reworked in the picturesque vein the following century when it passed into the Correr family. This chapter also addresses the gardens of various religious foundations and establishments, since it was under their auspices that much practical and medical gardening was established in the lagoon.

I then turn (Chapter Six) to the garden in what is sometimes termed the "long" 18th century, stretching from the late 17th to the end of the Venetian Republic in 1797. It looks at the re-invention of the private garden in an age of extravagant, even wild, public activity across the city: this involved both the opening of private spaces for theatrical events and *feste* – we have evidence here of gardens reconfigured for balls and assemblies and of the intrusion into their spaces of the city's masquerades. Vital pieces of evidence here are Guardi's drawing of 1780 showing masked revellers in the gardens of the Palazzo Contarini dal Zaffo and his subsequent painting with the gardens being visited by different groups. Yet these 18th-century spaces also saw the construction of *casini*, gathering places for private groups and select societies of virtuosi who wanted to retreat from the theatrical medley of the city. If artists like Tiepolo only suggest the secluded gardens behind grilles and *claires-voies*, past which figures in *ridotto* and masquerade carelessly disport themselves, other evidence reveals in more detail how these gardens were laid out and how they were used.

Napoleon's strategic formulation of a non-Venetian garden type – characterized by wide open spaces of promenade, military parade grounds and public botanical gardens – is the subject of Chapter Seven. This *démarche* is documented in the urban histories, yet the significance of his imposition of a new garden type, while at the same time eliminating dozens of private gardens belonging to both individual citizens and religious communities, has not been explained. Furthermore it set a pattern for 19th-century urban "renewal" (not to say vandalism) that would radically change and diminish the garden quality of Venice. If it produced a series of public spaces like the Giardini Pubblici, the Giardini Reali and the semi-public Giardini Papadopoli, and further allowed in – following the tides of French and later Austrian taste – a whole world of European "picturesque" garden decor, it also saw the decline and ruination of much of the older garden culture that de' Barbari's view had celebrated.

These actual ruined palaces and gardens – the decay of a byzantine-gothic city – would provide the metaphor by which many in the 19th century came to discuss modern Venice. Ruskin among many others saw the city as a ruined garden, an abandoned and desecrated Eden. And the metaphor could only too easily be reified or registered around the city, as artists like Whistler or writers like Henry James and Thomas Mann testify. And if 19th-century Venice was a ruined paradise or garden, it came easily to the Englishman John Eden, brother-in-law of Gertrude Jekyll and no doubt happily aware of the aptness of his chosen surname (he was born Hyden), to recover an extensive old property on the Giudecca and rename it the Garden of Eden, an account of which he published in 1903. Yet Eden's was by no means the only effort to make gardens anew in the city, and we must counter the powerful myth of Venice's ruined gardens with some narrative of an important florescence of garden culture in the 19th and early 20th centuries.

However, the present scandalous inaccessibility and neglect of this Garden of Eden (guarded sometimes by Doberman pinschers rather than by angels with fiery swords), its inhospitable appearance and its uncertain future bring into sharp focus yet again the role of gardens in the continuing city. That topic will therefore feature as the inevitable and the necessary conclusion of my study, which must consider the often risible invocations of Venetian garden culture in the projections of an urban future and, in a more constructive vein, see whether a more nuanced and energetic understanding of Venetian garden experience can contribute to what is, undeniably, a hugely contested future for the city.

That Venice is unusual, not too say unique, in its urban formation and character does, then, make any study of its elements very particular. Yet the role that gardens have played in its development and in the social and political lives of both inhabitants and visitors – and the role that they could play in reshaping the future of the city – may still prove instructive when other cities are under consideration. That the Venetian garden was created and maintained against the very odds of its lagoon situation is not likely to afford ready comparisons with other cities (Amsterdam, or perhaps Mexico City [Tenochtitlán], notwithstanding, a comparison the Venetians were sometimes pleased to make); but the role of open spaces in an old and dense building fabric, rich with historical reference, and touching both the physical and imaginative economy of society, has enough parallels in other communities to make this one case study of more general interest.

One further word by way of orientation. My focus is upon gardens in the city of Venice and some of the lagoon islands, like the Giudecca and Murano. It does not treat of those created in Venetian territories on the *terra firma*, though occasionally some contrasts will be drawn between them. Some publications seem to offer to discuss the Venetian city garden; yet the term they use, *giardino veneto*, turns out (perfectly legitimately) to reference the landscape architecture of the mainland rather more than the city's. Thus, brief discussions of city gardens turn rapidly to examples outside the lagoon proper as part of an extended argument, a slippage that rather distorts the special features of those city gardens that were established (to quote a character of Henry James) "in the middle of the sea". Typical of this slippage is the extremely influential volume by Luigi Dami, *Il Giardino Italiano*: though early on he invokes, as I shall do, the illustrations for the *Hypnerotomachia Poliphili*, published in Venice in 1499, these are absorbed into his promotion of a generalizing account of the Italian garden; otherwise he references the "Venetian type" of villa garden exclusively by examples on the mainland, including two paintings of the Veronese school (plates CLV & CLVI in his book). It is clear that for Dami the only role for gardens in the Venetian city – including those represented by Jacopo de' Barbari, an engraving which, significantly, he does not reproduce – is to take their place in his larger understanding of an "Italian style" of garden-making and garden use. However, as should soon be clear, the Venetian city garden is in many respects *sui generis* and must be treated as such. Henry James was then surely correct to opine, in his travel writings, that "the gardens of Venice would deserve a page to themselves".

It is, then, rather obvious that we need – to start with – a somewhat different approach to the Venetian city garden than that adopted by narratives of gardens in other places and cultures. Venice's gardens pose a peculiar challenge to the garden historian, and this is therefore the topic of the first chapter. And one of the obligations that this particular garden culture seems to lay upon its historian is to bring a study of the past to bear upon a possible future. The earliest Venetian settlements found and literally created grounds for existence, solid places in the lagoon on which their citizens could be at home. The question then arises as to what role, if any, the garden might play in the wholly different future of those who still seek their grounds of being in "the middle of the sea".

IN AN OLD GARDEN

YOU think, perhaps, there are no gardens in Venice; that it is all a sweep of palace-front and shimmering sea; that save for the oleanders bursting into bloom near the Iron Bridge, and the great trees of the Public Gardens shading the flower-bordered walks, there are no half-neglected tangles where rose and vine run riot; where the plash of the fountain is heard in the stillness of the night, and tall cedars cast their black shadows at noonday.

Really, if you but knew it, almost every palace hides a garden, nestling beneath its balconies, and every high wall hems in a wealth of green, studded with broken statues, quaint arbors festooned with purple grapes, and white walks bordered by ancient box; while every roof that falls beneath a window, is made a hanging garden of potted plants and swinging vines.

41

I.1 F.Hopkinson Smith, *Venice of Today* (1902), opening page of the chapter "In an old garden".

A new approach to the Venetian city garden

Chapter One

Gardens are a unique human activity. They are a prime and highly valued part of that larger enterprise whereby human society establishes links with its physical environments. Unlike other arts, the garden involves both nature and art, thereby drawing into play a dual range of cultural concerns. Gardens are a prime expression of men's and women's involvement in the world, indeed of their formation and structuring of spaces, physical and metaphysical, within which to exist; these become the very grounds of being. As such they are likely to be contested as much as valued arenas, a fact that has become particularly evident with the late 20 th-century need to project plans for the future urban development of Venice. Furthermore, though material on the vernacular garden in all its forms is difficult to elicit, they – just as much as the elite garden – must be allowed to contribute to an adequate garden history, in a similar way as the *architettura minore* has filled out the spaces of the city that were not occupied by grand palaces and houses[2].

But gardens may also–though this is frequently neglected–shape human activities as well as give expression to them. Charles Burroughs has written of environmental process and reform in another Italian city, Rome: "All human societies occupy, utilize, and invest meaning in territory. The physical setting of settlement and husbandry, whether or not it undergoes extensive physical change through human agency, becomes the repository of symbols–or rather a privileged matrix and even medium of symbolization –through which patterns of belief, authority, and social structure *are realized* (not merely reflected)"[3]. Napoleon well knew, as we shall see, the directive if not coercive power of environmental forms when he tried to impose public gardens on Venice in the early 19 th century. There is also the eloquent incident, now on a different continent, narrated by Claude Lévi-Strauss: failing to convert native Indians to Christianity, Jesuit missionaries determined to demolish their villages built in concentric circles and re-align the housing along a grid of right-angled streets, with the result that conversion was rapidly accomplished[4]. What that story suggests is that, despite the usual perspective on gardens and urban design as expressions of human history and cul-

ture, they may also in their turn be seen as determining and shaping history and culture. And since the garden – by its reference to and invocation of so many human interests in arts, science, engineering and technology–is such a considerable conspectus, what the 17 th century liked to call a "theatre"[5], of human involvements, it repays study, not simply because it may confirm separate enquiries into each of those human involvements and interests, but also for the light it can throw upon their conjunction, a totality where the whole can be greater than the sum of its parts.

Gardens, especially when they are established in such a territorial situation as the Venetian lagoon, must be considered as an element of the larger landscape. "Landscape is a way of seeing that has its own history", writes Denis Cosgrove, "but a history that can be understood only as part of a wider history of economy and society, that has its own assumptions and consequences"[6]. He argued rightly that in the development of the "landscape idea", no city played such an important role as did Venice, with its commitments to "merchant capitalism, navigation, printing and cartography" (p.103). Yet Cosgrove's focus was almost wholly on the *terra firma* (the Venetian mainland) and upon its agricultural land, which was increasingly relied upon to supply the food needs of the metropolis, and he does not address the smaller units of garden, orchard and small holdings within the lagoon itself. Though he briefly discusses the de' Barbari view with its prominent display of gardens along the Giudecca (see below in Chapter Three), the role of the garden in both the city's cultural self-fashioning and in outsiders' perspectives is not taken up, even when mainland expansions in the 16 th century challenged (not always effectively) the symbolism of the city's own territorial character and development. Notwithstanding, the example of Cosgrove's discussion of the construction and meaning of cultural landscapes can usefully inform a more focused concern with gardens: "seeing the world as landscape and developing landscape as a metaphor for human relationships with fellow men and with nature was part of a more inclusive ideology" (p.140).

DIFFERING PERCEPTIONS

Now, with regard to Venice, nothing is more striking than the narrative of how its earliest settlers established themselves within the lagoon territory, a narrative that acquired quickly the thrust and aura of mythology, what Charles Tomlinson in another context has called "a history turning itself into fable"[7]. Indeed, so vital had been that human response to an extreme physical environment that elements of its story quickly enshrined themselves in Venice's self-fashioning or mythology. The very rudimentary act of settlement in the lagoon necessitated the separation of land from the waters, the creation of ground for inhabitation and sustenance. This was an act resonant with overtones of the biblical narrative of the Creation, as Venetians well realized. It is clear that the making of land, not to mention its enhancement and decoration as gardens, has been a central fact of Venetian existence and indeed survival. And it was a concern equally to patrician and ordinary citizen alike, as well as striking many visitors as endemic to the special quality or poetry of Venice, like the character in *The Aspern Papers* into whose mouth Henry James puts the exclamation – the very "idea of a garden in the middle of the sea!"[8]. Even in the mid-17th century a visitor could utter the unusual advice that houses in Venice were worth viewing, because they had "spacious Gardenes and other Stately walkes, *in the midst of the sea*"[9]. The strange relationship between dry land and the earth covered by waters is, furthermore, an inevitable and ongoing aspect of the modern city.

Yet not every visitor acknowledged the existence of gardens. One of the oddest features, on the face of it, of visitors' reactions to Venice has been a refusal to believe that gardens existed at all, or, confronted with some evidence to the contrary, the declaration that they were invisible, not to be seen[10]. Even early travellers, who elsewhere in Italy were fascinated by and devoted to gardens, found nothing to interest them in Venice: John Evelyn, that eminent and knowledgeable gardenist, could find only one garden to visit in the whole of Venice – that of San Giorgio Maggiore. It was, he wrote in his diary, "a rare thing"[11]. So, too, Richard Lassels, whose *The Voyage of Italy* (1670) is a fund of information on other Italian gardens, tells us that he looked down from the Campanile of San Marco and found only two places where there were

any trees; he concluded that gardens were as wonderful things as coaches in Venice. However, he did make one exception of the "neat Garden" of the Procuratore Giovanni Battista Nani on the Giudecca[12]. The Frenchman, Maximilian Misson, whose two-volume *New Voyage to Italy* was published in English in 1699, tells how he read in a guidebook that there were some 335 gardens in the city but that he simply did not believe it[13]. Edward Wright is blunter: many fine palaces in Venice "have no gardens at all belonging to them"[14].

There were obviously many reasons for this negative testimony. The Campanile is hardly the best place in the crowded centre of the city from which to scout for signs of gardens; other church towers on the edges of the city would have yielded more sightings, as they still do. But then it is clear that travellers, then as now, rarely spent long enough in Venice to penetrate to some of the less built-up areas where gardens would have been more in evidence. However and above all, as we shall see in Chapters Three and Six, Venetian gardens were private affairs, their presence and scope concealed behind high walls, and so they were rarely experienced by visitors (tourists) who generally had no access to private households. It is, however, one of the paradoxes of the Venetian city garden that its private nature would become a palpable element in the city's "self-fashioning" or in what we might nowadays call its public relations: how else would Misson have found a guidebook that boasted 335 gardens? And the occasional visitor seems to have registered that gardens were indeed but one element in Venice's boastful self-image: palaces on the Grand Canal, wrote A.D. Chancel in 1717, "seem to out rival one another. Adorn'd with fine courts, anticourts, delicious Gardens, Fountains, Grotto's, and all other Embellishments"[15].

Now, while the Venetian fashioning of their own special myths of origin is a staple ingredient in many accounts of Venicity[16], it is equally clear that gardens do not either enter substantially into many Venetian studies, a field dauntingly established by a host of distinguished experts. It is both a rare and a typical admission when Eugenio Miozzi in his *Venezia nei secoli* undertakes what he calls a "digression" for a few pages to look at Venetian gardens as an essential part of the city, "un elemento dell'abitazione incorporato nell'organizzazione della vita familiare..." (an element of habitation incorporated into the organization of family life)[17]. His excursus turns out, however, to be extremely sketchy, relying on a few familiar references and quotations. It is also something of an exception when Julia Cartwright's chapter on "The Gardens of Venice" remains firmly in the city before admitting that "even Murano could not satisfy the new passion for rural delights" and then devoting the remainder of her pages to the mainland[18].

Generally, the avoidance of any mention of garden spaces by most authors who address the cultural, political, commercial and artistic heritage of Venice is quite striking. In any number of major (and let it be said at once) excellent studies of Venice her gardens are conspicuous by their absence. Examples may be invidious, but if I select a couple of studies whose excellence on other grounds is evident and on which I have been able to rely for information and analysis of other Venetian matters, then their interesting *lacuna* – the absence of much attention, if any, to garden-making and use – can be demonstrated with less risk of severity. Alvise Zorzi's fine survey of the history, customs and activities of the Serenissima, *Venice 697–1797: A city, a republic, an Empire*[19], finds no room – no worthwhile purpose, perhaps – for introducing the topic of Venetian gardens at all. More puzzling perhaps is Patricia Fortini Brown's study of *Private Lives in Renaissance Venice*, a topic where one might expect private enclosures to feature, but where they receive a fairly cursory treatment[20]. Gardens, she rightly notes, reproducing a detail of Jacopo de' Barbari's bird's-eye view that shows gardens on the Giudecca, were "not all that unusual"; she also reminds the reader of Sansovino's list of garden sites in *Venetia città nobilissima* (see Chapter Three). But somewhat strangely she proposes that the gardens in de' Barbari's representation of c.1500 "must have resembled that of the Palazzo Nani-Luccheschi today", though the photograph by which she illustrates the latter is rife with horticultural profusion including a late 19th-century palm tree. One other familiar image, Guardi's drawing of the garden of the Palazzo Contarini dal Zaffo, is also adduced, now to show off the "grandiose proportions" that Venetian gardens achieved by the 18th century "in contrast to the kitchen plots of the Giudecca". Yet the overall size of the garden spaces on the Giudecca in de' Barbari and on the northern edge of the city in Guardi would, in fact, have been about equal, and

the distinction that is further drawn between them – "utility" in the former, "presentation and recreation" in the latter – seems too severe and is anyway a modern distinction of little use in this discussion see Figures III.2-4 and VI.3-4. But that is the extent of her garden discussions, and nowhere does Fortini Brown take up the role of gardens and garden usage in the domestic economy of the Venetian household. This is doubtless to be explained in that she structures her whole book upon Sebastiano Serlio's floor plan from the late 1540s of a palace expressively geared for a Venetian gentleman, a plan which does not indicate any exterior spaces, not even a rear *cortile* as a connecting link between the interior and exterior or garden spaces.

It seems as if gardens fall between the cracks of different disciplines, on the one hand, or, on the other, between the concerns of professional architectural and art history and – as we shall see below – amateur traditions of garden writing. Even explorations by urban historians are curiously reticent when it comes to gardens: detailed plans, photography and analysis of the urban fabric of one north-western district of Venice, where green space was and still is more conspicuous than in many other parts of the city, were undertaken by University of Venice students and faculty over several years and finally published in Giuseppe Cristinelli's *Cannaregio. Un sestiere di Venezia* of 1987. Yet it scarcely notices gardens and other open spaces – the text is virtually silent, while the otherwise useful large-scale plans leave gardens unmarked, white spaces without identification or annotation; and this is a study where the different kinds of open space might be considered a vital ingredient in the overall urban analysis.

There is, to be sure, a tradition of bellettristic, popular or what we'd now call coffee-table books on the topic of Venetian gardens, but this is strangely, indeed fascinatingly, self-contained, with no mission to link Venetian gardens with any other element of Venicity, just as those who explore aspects of the "big picture" rarely if at all make connections in the other direction and invoke the garden. The amateur and largely sentimental garden-writing starts, not surprisingly, in the early 19th century, when Pasquale Negri published *I Giardini di Venezia. Poemetto* (1818), an extravagant versified litany of mythological presences in the city. This was followed by Nicolò Bettoni's letters on *Venezia e I Suoi Giardini* (1826)[21], and by Francesco Dr. Gera,

I.2 Cover of Damerini's *Giardini di Venezia* (1931). Its design, more than its atavistic approach to the study of gardens, declares its modernist moment.

I Principali Giardini di Venezia (1847), a largely horticultural effusion. In the early 20th century Charlotte Elfriede Pauly, published her somewhat more scholarly *Der Venezianische Lustgarten* (1916) and then Gino Damerini issued first his *Giardini sulla laguna* (1927) and subsequently his *Giardini di Venezia* (1931 Figure I.2). While none of these discuss their subject in ways that the modern garden historian would probably follow, they did keep alive an interest in a distinctly local tradition of gardens and gardening as well as an anecdotal mode of commentary [22]. Their elegiac and self-indulgently lyrical tone may be guessed from another of Damerini's publications, subtitled "nostalgie del passato, malinconie di oggi e di domani" (past nostalgias, today's and tomorrow's melancolias) [23]. For these writers, the Venetian garden is, if not the site, then a symbol of the city's lost pre-eminence; but the connection between garden activities and socio-political events is not a theme upon which they elaborate. What is interesting to note, however, is that this line of commentary and celebration of Venetian garden history begins immediately after the Napoleonic im-

position of public gardens on the city, which thereby challenged (as I shall argue later in Chapter Seven) a long tradition of very different garden design and use throughout the Republic's earlier history. It is as if the sudden rise of writings on city gardens after the 1800s was a direct result of some need to compensate for the loss of—as well as to memorialize – a certain, authentic and endemic Venetian garden now threatened by foreign models introduced under French and Austrian rule. Damerini, indeed, makes this connection explicit when he castigates the urban destruction of "la brutale megalomania Napoleonica"[24], unleashed in particular upon traditional garden spaces in the city. Equally and significantly, the first serious attention to Venetian garden culture in modern scholarship also focuses on that same moment of Napoleonic interventions, most notably the work of Giandomenico Romanelli, *Venezia Ottocento. L'Architettura. L'Urbanistica* (1977;1988).

The 19th century mode of garden writing continued to cast its shadow over later publications. A typical if extravagant example is F. Hopkinson Smith's *Venice of Today*, a large folio volume of 1902, designed undoubtedly as a vehicle to display its author's artistic talents in both colour plates of his paintings (protected by tissue overlays) and a profusion of black and white in-text illustrations[25]. Gardens have one chapter dedicated to them Figure I.1, but along the way Smith's drawings play with seductive glimpses of private gardens "where oleanders hang over the wall", as one image is captioned (p.15), as well as an account of a visit to a canal-side garden after a picnic lunch in his gondola: "You soon discover that it is unlike any other [garden] you know. There are no flower-beds and gravel walks, and no brick fountains with the scantily-dressed cast-iron boy struggling with the green-painted dolphin, the water spurting from its open mouth. There is water, of course, but it is down a deep well with a great coping of marble, encircled by exquisite carvings and mellow with mould; and there are low trellises of grapes, and a tangle of climbing roses half-concealing a weather-stained Cupid with a broken arm. And there is an old-fashioned sun-dial, and sweet smelling-box cut into fantastic shapes, and a nest of an arbor so thickly matted with leaves and interlaced branches... And there are marble benches and stone steps, and at the farther end an old rusty gate..." (p.16).

The eye for detail is as acute in the prose as in his drawings; the obligatory nostalgia for ruined pastimes is emphatic; the recognition of the garden as an essential, hidden element of the Venetian *ambiente* is by now quite traditional, as its *identikit* of the Venetian garden is largely a-historical. When Smith comes to devote a whole chapter to one particular garden on the Giudecca, he uses it as the setting for an extended anecdote told by a French professor about some love-lorn countess after the fall of the Republic; the author's sentimental fantasy is displaced onto its narrator, but his investment in it is palpable. However, the garden is lovingly invoked, albeit a composite invention to judge from the drawings purporting to illustrate it, while the insertion of a rare black and white photograph – of "The Gardener's Daughter" Figure I.3 – seems designed to give credence at least to the existence and maintenance of an actual site.

There would be no need to dwell upon other examples of this approach to Venetian gardens – though it is extremely pervasive[26] – were it not for the extreme influence this strain of writing has generally exercised, particularly (but of course not exclusively) in accounts of Venice. It is easy to be dismissive of it, yet the kind of reception of gardens that it records and represents becomes an inescapable element in garden writing and cannot be ignored entirely. We also need to recognize that alongside this tradition of rather sentimental books on the garden (a 19th-century European phenomenon by no means confined to Venice) there was a parallel trickle of often very informative essays, memoranda and articles in Venetian reviews and periodicals during the 19th and early 20th centuries, where local historians and antiquarians took up episodes in the story of the Venetian garden, publishing isolated notices on specific sites and (in particular) beginning to chronicle the botanical gardens associated historically with the pharmaceutical industry of Venice. This resource offers a more promising documentation, partly because of its avowed aim to establish elements of a lost narrative, partly because of its specific focus, and partly because its authors often enjoyed access to sites long since lost or built over and saw them in the light of historical information.

The approach to gardens that Hopkinson Smith represents continues throughout the 20th and even into the 21st century, but seems to have enjoyed a particular flowering in the late 1980s. Gianni Berengo

I.3 F. Hopkinson Smith, *Venice of Today* (1902), *"The Gardener's Daughter"*.

Gardin's and others' *Giardini segreti a Venezia* (1988) extends the genre with a virtuoso elaboration of its salient repertoire: tone, focus and angle of vision are the same as Hopkinson Smith's, but now explored through photography and with a somewhat less self-indulgent prose. Wonderfully suggestive photographs offer glimpses of fragments – garden pillars, isolated sculptures, benches or pergolas; or they focus in close-up on some green moment, for this is the genre of writing that loves to invoke "I richiami reconditi del verde" (the recondite markings of green), all of which details stand in for a presentation of whole gardens; sites are rarely identified (most are anyway inaccessible because private), or are shot from aerial heights, though many literary references in the text to James, D'Annunzio and others are glossed in its margins. It is the best of today's coffee-table picturesque: delicious fragments, carefully framed by the camera's attention to confined and narrow sightlines, garnished with a few old engravings, and buttressed with a text that deserves a different context and a different linguistic register[27].

Hot on the heels of Gardin's *Giardini segreti*, came Alessandro Albrizzi and Mary Jane Pool, *The Gardens of Venice* (New York, 1989), and Mariapia Cunico, *Il Giardino Veneziano* (Venice, 1989). That by Cunico is especially useful for its listing and analysis of both lost and existing gardens, its author being a practising landscape architect with a strong interest in plants, who also teaches at the University of Venice. The book by Mary Jane Pool (texts) and Alessandro Albrizzi (photographs) is chronologically arranged but with minimal commentary on the images; it does, however, have an introduction by Ileana Chiappini di Sorio, which draws upon a variety of archival material, though her command of garden history and its terminology somewhat undermines the specifically Venetian narrative. Just when it seemed this florescence of Venetian garden books was exhausted, the publisher Flammarion issued *Venetian Gardens* in 2007, its text by Mariagrazia Dammicco and full colour illustrations by an experienced garden photographer, Marianne Majerus. Its approach is to distinguish between types of gardens – aristocratic, artistic, intimate, gardens of the soul, etc. – but without explaining or utilizing those typological discriminations. Its visual contributions are mostly printed to bleed off the page and thus leave the impression that the anthology of local moments, intimate close-ups and impressionistic details are but extracts from much larger wholes; this is somewhat misleading, given the often very small scale of Venetian gardens. The images of approach and invitation (steps, gateways) seem to make much of how these spaces are used, were it not for the endless sequence of empty chairs and garden tables uncluttered with the leavings of a meal or an abandoned newspaper: the solitary figure of a venerable Capuchin friar in the vegetable garden of the Redentore makes the other empty spaces even more conspicuous; even the hotel gardens (Cipriani, San Clemente Palace, Hotel des Bains, and Albergo Quattro Fontane) are deserted!

Nonetheless, I have found some incidental information and stimulation in all of these rather miscellaneous publications, and hope that throughout what follows my debts to their work are clearly acknowledged[28]. But it must be confessed that they barely address the historical and cultural meanings of what is, in fact, a very *longue durée* of garden-making and use in Venice. Nor do they focus upon any continuing role for gardens (other than being the objects of today's photography). Were more of the gardens exhibited by these four books open to the public, their logical afterlife could at least be in visits that would allow first-hand experience of the garden art of Venice. There is indeed a guidebook, *I Giardini Veneziani* (2003), directed at what it identifies as leisurely Venetians, enlightened foreigners and passionate gardeners ("Veneziani distratti, forestieri illuminati, giardinieri appassionati") issued by the Wigwam Club Giardini Storici Venezia, an organization that offers to conduct guided visits to a few sites, and which also has a website[29]. Visitation of gardens is certainly one way of opening up the gardenist culture of the city for visitors (and inhabitants), but informed interpretation needs to be part of such an experience. And it is only part of the wider topic to be addressed in the last chapter, namely the fresh deployment of open space and the possibilities of new design. A small contribution to this future perspective, grounded in adequate historical enquiry, is a publication by the University of Venice in 2000 of a much abridged version of the 1998 *tesi di laurea* of Leonardo Ruffo, *Il Giardino Storico Veneziano: una metodologia d'intervento*. His sub-title holds out the promise of what he claims is some ongoing usefulness of a historical study of the city's gardens for a viable and exciting programme of Venetian open space in the future.

IMAGINING AND INHABITING THE CITY

There is an intriguing connection between the increased interest in gardens and an important political *démarche* in Venetian history, namely, its loss of self-government to French and later Austrian rule and its absorption into other power entities during the 19th century. Not least, such a connection suggests ways in which the garden can usefully be inserted into larger issues in the history and future of Venice. There are, perhaps, three main opportunities to do this. But it should also be emphasized from the start that all three kinds of historical enquiry have immediate, if not always recognized, implications for the continuing life of the city and its gardens in the 21st century. One area, the most obvious, to which garden history might contribute is the urbanistic development of the city from the earliest strategies for inhabiting the lagoon to the 21st-century's attempts to maintain its existence in the face of being overwhelmed, variously, by

I.4 Painted map by Giovan Battista Arzenti, late 16th century, detail showing the Giudecca. On many maps of Venice the green areas of the city are prominently displayed.

environmental disasters and the *acqua alta* of tourism. Here the garden, along with its cognate open spaces of *campi* (squares) and *corti*[30] (courtyards), has played a considerable role; yet unlike, say, the *corti* , the role of this whole repertoire of open spaces has been paid little attention. Venice has performed so much of its civic existence on the public stage, as its tradition of large narrative paintings of political life testify[31], that the private realm and the smaller urban areas where the performance of state did not take place have been marginalized. Yet it is here that ordinary people lived and had their being, and here – in both hidden private spaces and communal courtyards – that we may track some of what may be called Venice's social infrastructure. And these largely unexplored zones shared with the world of elite gardening a conscious dedication to plants and their cultivation.

A second area of potential interest, closely related to the first at least in the early periods, involves the mythopoeic strategies of the Venetian state, what David Rosand in his *Myths of Venice: The figuration of a state* termed the "fictions or half-truths forming part of the ideology of a society"[32]. Two symbolic ways of suggesting the scope of this contribution are to note,

first, how almost every map of Venice takes pains to show off – even to exaggerate – the extent of green areas Figure I.4, and then to recall the incidence of gardens represented in unexpected places – on boats taking part in the annual regattas along the Grand Canal during the 18th century, or in table settings fabricated in Murano glass see Figure VI.7[33]. Venice also relied upon its gardens graphically to project ideas of its state, and it went out of its way to protect those local traditions of garden-making against alternative designs proposed during the 16th century[34], just as, conversely, it failed to maintain them in the face of Napoleon's interventions. It could enjoy the association of gardens with its maritime traditions, at the Arsenal with a garden of cannon balls see Figure III.15, or the ubiquitous veneration of Venus, sea-born goddess but equally the presiding deity of gardens. Nor should we think that this topic is only of historical interest[35]: the projections for a future Venice by modern-day planners are every bit as dedicated to a received or perhaps re-invented mythology as were, say, Tintoretto's or F.Sansovino's. The issue will be whether Venice can utilize both its many surviving garden spaces and the possibility of new landscape creations as serviceable "fictions or half-truths" in the decades to come.

A third area where gardens can profitably be involved in Venetian studies concerns the different ways in which Venice has been perceived and explained by its citizens and by its visitors. Gardens are one topic that seems to have divided the two categories of narrator, with some of the latter, visitors, opining that there were no gardens there at all, while many of the former, the residents, registered their presence in both daily circumstance and their publication of civic iconography. The reception by visitors of both the realities and the idea of Venice has sometimes coincided with local perspectives, but just as often has been against the grain of official or public representations of the Republic and its territory. Many 19th-century visitors, for instance, chose to see the city as a ruined paradise or a lost Eden, including those who lingered and sought to know the city intimately; yet the same period featured a thriving and expansive garden culture, open to fresh design ideas from the rest of Europe. Given that so much (too much?) of the lagoon city's survival seems now to depend upon the perceptions and demands of outsiders, maybe their perspectives will have a role to play in some future refashioning.

ON WRITING THE HISTORY OF THE VENETIAN CITY GARDEN

All three of these areas – the urbanistic narrative, the self-fashioning, and outsiders' contributions to the invention of Venice – are already well researched and published elements of Venicity. Yet it is my claim (ambition, if you like) that a study of her gardens may augment and even significantly help to reconsider the resources that her history offers for shaping her future. But that enterprise will also inevitably enhance the procedures of garden history, which in its turn has become a subsidiary yet important theme of this book. For it must be said that garden history itself is none too well-equipped to tackle whatever the Venetian city can produce by way of materials to work upon. Garden history habitually bases its narratives upon the careers of leading "name" designers and upon changes in styles of design, neither of which would really work here. There were few, if any, of the former in Venice: Gianantonio Selva, the Venetian architect responsible for creating the Giardini Pubblici under the Emperor Napoleon, is probably the biggest "name", yet one little known outside his native city. Further, both the distinction ritualistically invoked by all garden historians between "formal" and "informal" gardening [36] and the teleology that guides the narrative of "progress" from an autocratic and geometrical to a "natural", "unconstrained" and "free" style is even more than usually irrelevant to Venice; this is why, one suspects, such garden criticism as does exist quickly shifts its focus from the city to the mainland where such handles, though somewhat worn, can still seem plausible. In the different context of urban Venice, analytical-descriptive terms used in other contexts to describe gardens need adjustment before they can be deployed in a tougher analysis here: to start with, the stylistic "development" of Venetian gardens did not seem to keep pace with other European traditions, so that its conventional terminology and teleology seem useless; labels like baroque or picturesque so often serve as blinkers not magnifying glasses [37]. Then again, a design-orientated history, which is promoted by a focus upon "formal" and "informal" along with a concentration on name designers, always marginalizes a reception history of place-making, a narrative of use and garden experience that promises a more instructive approach to the Venetian scene.

The Venetian garden cannot easily if at all readily be subsumed into the modern narrative of the *giardino italiano*, a point made as early as 1931 in the *Rivista di Venezia*. Reviewing the huge 1931 garden show at the Palazzo Vecchio in Florence that promoted the idea of a self-defining "Italian" garden, the writer protested the hegemony of the umbrella term, and continued with a plea for the separate identification and display of local gardens:

"Venice would merit, we repeat, a treatment of more scope, more precision and more significance [than at the Palazzo Vecchio], and that it would not be difficult to put together on display a room that demonstrates that from the 15th century there was established a synthetic iconography at least until the gardens of Romanticism" [38].

My own enquiry hopes, therefore, to take up that challenge and offer an "exhibit" of city gardens and related open spaces in Venice; in so doing, it must also question and substantially revise the ways in which garden history itself is generally conceived and conducted. But the reverse is also at stake: what could this relatively new field of garden history contribute to the already well-cultivated landscape of Venetian studies? There would be – so at least a skeptical colleague pointed out to me – no point in elaborating a narrative of Venetian garden design and use if it could not augment what we already know about Venice. Whether gardens will prove, however, to be the open sesame to some fresh understandings of Venicity remains, obviously, to be seen.

Like so many others before me and in particular the poet Diego Valeri in his *Guida sentimentale di Venezia* of 1942, I have succumbed to the temptation to articulate, to give voice to, to translate, what he called this unsayable or unspeakable city ("indicibile città"). As Valeri notes, this is a temptation as potent as are the frustrations of the enterprise itself. He listed – and I can only echo him at this point – all the elements, already existing, which might offer "a key" (*chiave*) to our understanding of Venice, yet which seemingly fail to yield up its "mystery": "Storia e leggenda, verso e prosa, *spleen et idéal*, grandezza e decadenza, *Dichtung und Wahrheit*, tutto è gia stato messo a mano per tradurre [Venezia] in parola. Risultato di tanto travaglio: molte mirabili e memorabili pagine, ma non una pagina che vi dia la chiave del mistero". (History and myth, verse and prose, spleen and the ideal [in Baudelaire's phrase], grandeur and decadence, poetry and truth [in Goethe's phrase] – everything is ready and to hand for translating the city into words. And the results of all this endeavour: many marvellous and memorable pages, but not a single page that yields a key to the mystery) [39].

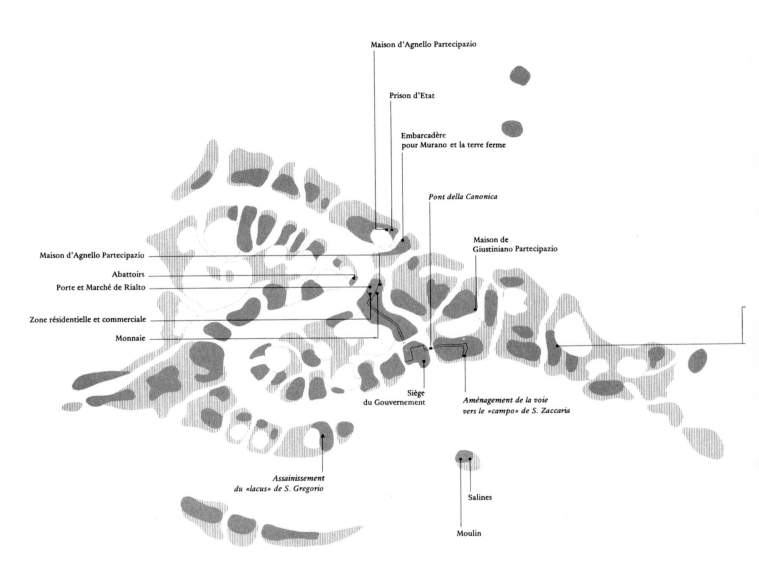

Maison d'Agnello Partecipazio

Prison d'Etat

Embarcadère
pour Murano et la terre ferme

Pont della Canonica

Maison de
Giustiniano Partecipazio

Maison d'Agnello Partecipazio

Abattoirs

Porte et Marché de Rialto

Zone résidentielle et commerciale

Monnaie

Siège
du Gouvernement

*Aménagement de la voie
vers le «campo» de S. Zaccaria*

*Assainissement
du «lacus» de S. Gregorio*

Salines

Moulin

II.1 A map of early Venetian settlements in the 8 [th] and 9 [th] centuries, from *Venise au fil du temps, atlas historique d'urbanisme et d'architecture* (1971). The hatched areas are mudflats, the dark ones consolidated land.

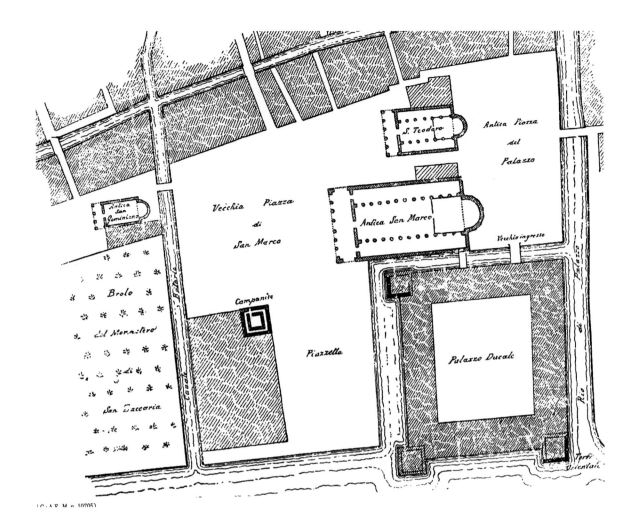

Labels within the plan: S. Teodoro · Antica Piazza del Palazzo · Antica San Dominico · Vecchia Piazza di San Marco · Antica San Marco · Vecchio ingresso · Brolo del Monastero di San Zaccaria · Campanile · Piazzetta · Palazzo Ducale · Rio · Canale · Porte Orientali

I.C.A.F. M. n. 10705)

II.16 Plan of San Marco, with the site of the *brolo* or *broglio*. Before the area around San Marco was developed, it included a *brolio* or open ground to which citizens could go and engage in debate and discussions. Once it was built over, the name of the *brolio* still survived, attached to an area beside the Doge's Palace where political and other business could be conducted.

16th-century visualization of an early urban settlement centred around a church and the open space in front of it see Figure II.4. And when that original *broglio* at San Marco was absorbed into and covered over by urban developments, its significance was still maintained, even commemorated, by the area, no longer a garden, but called by the same name of "Broglio", alongside the western flank of the Doge's Palace. It is so marked on 18th-century maps by Andrea Tirali (1726) and Antonio Codognato (1781)[46], and the *broglio* still earned its mention in a 1772 guidebook for foreigners, even though they would not have been able to visit its original location[47]. Furthermore, the word *broglio* has an interesting afterlife, bifurcating into a local word for gardens and into a more univer-

sal term for political intrigue. As a result of the original *broglio's* proximity to the political power base of San Marco and its use for political activity, the Latin *brolium* and Venetian *broglio* came to refer to reprehensible electoral intrigue[48], from which derives the anglosaxon usage of embroiled or getting tangled up in things. But *broglio* also retained its local significance of some open space, as when Sanudo reports that in the 11th century masons were brought from Ravenna to an area near San Teodoro to build "sopra un luoco piu ampio, quasi piazza, licet all'hora non fosse – ma si chiamava brolo" (on a larger site, almost an open space, not deemed a garden, but called a "brolo")[49]. Other *campi* or *brolia* throughout the city, in almost all cases attached to churches and used for various local

II.17 A detail of the foreground in Carpaccio, *Return of the Ambassadors*, Gallerie dell'Accademia, Venice, suggests how the unpaved Venetian *campi* must have looked.

events and communal activities, remained unpaved for much longer than the Piazza, so their field-like character and open-air opportunities gave Venetian inhabitants, especially those without their own plots of land, some recourse to a green or "natural" world in the midst of the sea. The Campo of Santi Giovanni e Paolo remained in grass until 1835[50], and that of San Giacomo dell'Orio had (as it still does) trees, some of which also remain in the Campo San Polo. That certain *campi* lived up to their designation may perhaps be judged by their appearance in Carpaccio's paintings where we glimpse meadow-like surfaces, decorated with wild flowers Figure II.17. Today, quite a few of them seem to be reverting to their original state Figure II.18!

The other contribution to open, green space in the city came from the ecclesiastical and monastic communities. Not only, as we have seen, did the local parish enjoy open space adjacent to its church for various communal activities, but the conventional layout and duties of monasteries ensured that cloisters and medicinal garden plots were established, especially around the fringes of the city by the pioneering efforts of the various orders (Dominicans, Franciscans, Carmelites, Augustinians and Benedictines). Cloisters were both courtyard and garden, or at least green space. The earliest surviving example of the ecclesiastical cloister, that of the tiny Sant' Apollonia (previously called Santa Scolastica) behind San Marco, despite its more recent modern paving Figure II.19, can remind us of how life in the city, crowded onto sandbanks and artificial foundations, cherished such open spaces for their greenery, their views of the sky, and the ubiquitous well head that gave access to the collected rainwater. Such developments obviously began early, but the continuing visual representation of ecclesiastical establish-

II.18 Grass growing in the Campo dell'Angelo Rafaele, 1980s, which seems to be reverting to the aspect that Carpaccio painted.

II.19 Cloister of Sant' Apollonia, an early surviving cloister in the city, once presumably grassed rather than paved.

ments, especially those located on islands in the lagoon, always shows them with a density of trees and associated hints of gardens. In his 1724 guide for foreign visitors, Coronelli, though primarily concerned to direct attention to the city's churches, specifically notes the incidence of such horticultural enclosures, specifically the *orti* of the Servite nuns, which still survive in the very middle of the Cannaregio see Figure V.13[51].

The realities of real estate for Venetians were intricately enmeshed with its symbolisms. The uncanny parallel between the early refugees from the mainland seeking safe haven and cultivatable space on dry land that rose above the waters and the biblical narrative of the Creation was not lost upon the Venetian settlers and their descendents. On the second day of Creation, as the first book of Genesis tells it, God divided the vault of the waters from the vault of the heavens: it only takes modern travellers to experience an *acqua alta* or to venture out into the lagoon on a stormy day Figure II.20 to register the ineluctable necessity – yet precariousness – of this division. Daniele Barbaro was surely alluding to this part of the Genesis story when, in his commentary on Vitruvius, he described the Venetian locality as "the sea and the earth, one of which seems to want to recede and the other to occupy the space of the lagoon"[52]. And in 1715 Bernardo Trevisan wrote, quoting the *Book of Job* 14, of what he termed "le naturali inclinazioni dell'acque" in the lagoon[53]. As the Genesis narrative has it, from the original windswept "abyss" of the waters, God drew the "dry land" and called it "earth", and he made the ground produce "plants bearing seed, fruit-trees bearing fruit": all of that on the third day. Such natural fecundity, marking the midpoint of the week-long Creation, gibed with the relatively slow establishment of productive plots by Venetians amidst their new, watery sites. As opposed to simply orchards, vegetable plots and quasi-agricultural land, all "bearing seed according to their kind", actual gardens came even later, as did the Garden of Eden itself. The lateness of gardening both in the biblical narrative ("eastward in Eden") and in the lagoon settlements to the east of the *terra firma* was another parallel that Venetian mythmakers must have found appealing, though it was perhaps left to John Eden at the end of the 19th century to realize that analogy explicitly on his ground in the Giudecca.

The Venetian propensity to refurbish their narratives of settlement in poetic and mythical terms is attested throughout their own writings, paintings and sculpture[54]. Myths are metaphors or ways of understanding reality and can be used to articulate meaning in historical events and places (they are, however, not necessarily falsehoods, as modern uses of the word "myth" often imply). They may be extravagant in their invention, but they can also remain or seem to remain very faithful to actuality – not least because mythmakers are in the business of providing believable explanations of real places and events. Thus when Petrarch described Venice as "another world" (*orbis alter*) and as "surrounded by salt waters", he was simply telling it as it was; but the poet's implicit reference to the Genesis myth and the emergence of usable land from saline wastes cannot be gainsaid, for he would have been drawing upon those "fictions or half-truths [that form] part of the ideology of a society"[55].

Gardens have, of course, frequently been justified as reiterations or recreations of the original Garden of Eden[56]. But other events from both Christian and classical mythology could be invoked to describe the Venetian garden (in all its forms and manifestations) and to understand its place in the city's culture. Most notably, the sea-born goddess Venus was readily appropriated by Venetian political discourse as is evident in various contexts – such as remarks by the Englishman James Howell, by the orator in 1577 who saw Venus and Venice as sisters, or by Giovanni Nicolò Doglioni's *Venetia triomfante et sempre libera* of 1613[57]. That Venice exploited the oceanic origins of the goddess should not, however, blind us to the parallel tradition in which Venus was also the goddess associated with gardens.

This chapter has assembled only preliminary identifications of early gardens and garden-like spaces, and it is hoped that other research will be able to add to the repertory of that history. And issues still remain. Above all, what might we understand by the word "garden"? It appears spasmodically and late in documents of Venetian urban developments, but even when the word is specifically used, in Latin, Italian or Venetian, we cannot be certain that it pertains to anything that today we would recognize as a garden. Put differently, it would not win its place in those modern publications on Venetian gardens reviewed in the first chapter that glory in green and flowery solitudes and retreats. It is just as likely to refer to an open space where edible plants or fruit or vines are grown along with herbs and possibly flowers; it would have been a space either destined for such cultivation or actually worked horticulturally or agriculturally – the small scale of Venetian lagoon agriculture, again, makes that particular distinction difficult[58].

Furthermore, the creation and un-creation (abandonment, alteration of use) of spaces that we'd call gardens always depended upon the changing needs of a property's owners or inhabitants, plus the availability of suitable spaces for those needs. Our modern assumptions of what constitutes a "garden", driven by suburban living and the services of the local garden-centre or commercial nursery, tend to limit a garden to a place of flowers, shrubs and general greenery, perhaps including trees. In the historical context of Venice, and indeed in many other situations too, this restricts our understanding of open space too severely and indeed may well exclude from consideration as "garden" many areas within the city. A case in point would be the Palazzo Giustinian-Pesaro: according to the detailed researches of its modern restoration architect, Giorgio Bellavitis, there were at various times in its history unbuilt areas to the left of the main pal-

II.20 Storm over the lagoon. The omnipresent, and here distinctly ominous, threats from the sea make the creation of gardens in Venice a somewhat defiant gesture.

ace – areas he designates as Corte Giustinian or simply *terra vacua* (empty but probably not unused space) that seem to increase in size by the early 19th century[59]. During the changing life of the building, it was the utilization of these areas down its long flank and ending at the edge of the Grand Canal that could offer the logical possibility of and indeed would eventually become a garden. The establishment of what we would now recognize as a garden, a space with no obvious utilitarian purpose, laid out with planting beds, trees and shrubs, and with places to sit, along with the ubiquitous and eventually only decorative well head, came in the 19th century, and it is this same area that is now occupied with Bellavitis's own new re-design of these elements in the 1960s and 1970s. So it is important to grasp the mediaeval and early Renaissance understanding of human control over the natural world. This mastery was valued first and foremost for its efficient and productive enterprise; it was what Cicero had called a "second nature"[60], by which he meant raw materials worked by the craft and labour of human hands in order to provide infrastructure and the wherewithal of sustenance. If it did that well, and

if the craft and labour that went into it were pleasing, then certain aesthetic qualities were attached to it. It has been noted above that urban developments in mediaeval Venice were occasionally argued on the basis of appeals to "beauty". Crouzet-Pavan states emphatically that "the first history of Venice demonstrated that from the beginning the city was constructed as a place of order, beauty, and urbanity"[61]. Craft and skill in horticulture could well involve the creation of structures such as shapely pergolas to support vines, handsome seats on which to rest, paths on which to traverse the lot, compartments to divide property into usable segments protected from the sea winds, and cisterns and troughs to hold and conduct water. It is via a special crafting of these primarily utilitarian elements that the art of gardening emerged from its merely practical phases. When it does come to so distinguish itself in the 16th century, as we shall see in the next chapter, it was accorded the designation of "third nature". What has been tracked in Venice so far are only those "gardens" existing in that indeterminate zone between mere practicality and some appreciation of their pleasures and delights.

III.1 Jacopo de' Barbari, detail of gardens on the Giudecca, from Bird's-Eye View of Venice.
De' Barbari draws the viewer's attention to the foreground or bottom of his view where the island of the Giudecca
is shown with a variety of gardens.

Venetian gardens in the year 1500

Various gardens... notable and famous... incredible to foreigners, who think that the salt water cannot accommodate human artifice.

Sansovino

Chapter Three

GARDENS IN JACOPO DE' BARBARI'S BIRD'S-EYE VIEW

Gardens in the Venetian city suddenly become an important visual item for the first time in the woodcut panorama (c.1500) by the Venetian painter and printmaker, Jacopo de' Barbari Figure 2 III.1&2. Details of this extraordinary, and most useful, document have already been invoked see Figures II.7-9 to help us understand some aspects of the mediaeval period, the continuing evidence of which de' Barbari records. But his panorama significantly extends an understanding of gardens in territorial, typological, and historical terms. The discussions of this wonderful image are many and learned[1]; it has often been used to document discussions of building sites and architectural developments, so accurate has proved to be its imagery. Such scholarly reliance on de' Barbari's record of his visual observations therefore endorses the use of his panorama here to document and analyse Venetian gardens.

Though striking and prominent examples of gardens are depicted along the Giudecca island towards the bottom of the view Figures III. 1, 3 & 4, and though their proximity to the viewer makes them particularly important and interesting, these gardens have not attracted serious scrutiny for their own sake, as have other elements of the urban fabric elucidated in architectural commentaries that rely upon his work.

De' Barbari produced his woodcut in the years before 1500. It consists of six sheets, each approximately 66 x 99 centimetres, making an overall image of 135 x 282 centimetres (three states of which are known)[2]. Three years went into its making, according to its German publisher, Anton Kolb, who felt that this justified his application to the city fathers for sole publication rights and exemption from export duties (the exemption was denied, but he was allowed exclusive rights for four years). He also argued that the printing was undertaken for the greater glory and fame of "this supreme city"[3]. The high cost of the woodcut,

III.2 Jacopo de' Barbari, Bird's-Eye View of Venice, c.1500. This astonishingly detailed woodcut has provided reliable visual evidence for many architectural discussions of the late 15th-century city.

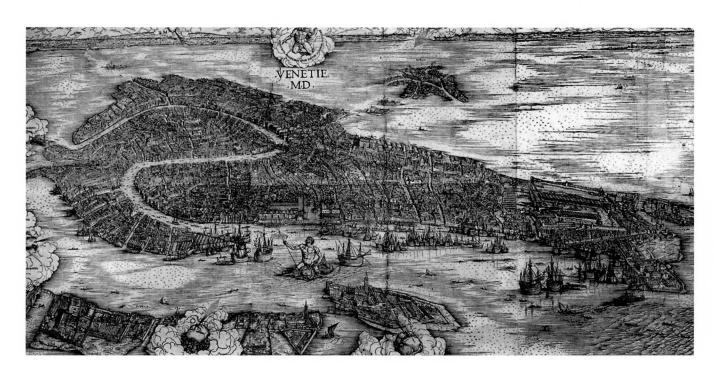

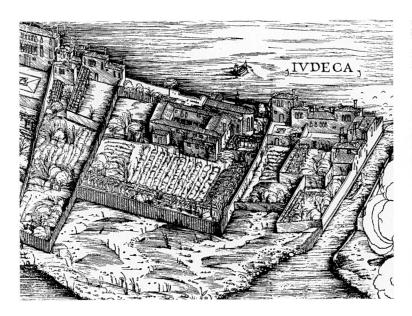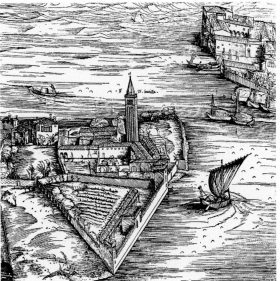

III.3 & 4 Jacopo de' Barbari, details of gardens on the Giudecca, from Bird's-Eye View of Venice.

for which a selling price of not less than three ducats was required, has also been explained as the desire to aim for a market among those with political and intellectual reasons for being interested in territorial representations.

The woodcut is at once panorama, map, bird's-eye view, and (as Martin Kemp usefully puts it) city "portrait". Like many Renaissance human portraits which display "attributes" that gloss the subject's character or career, this of the Venetian city also includes em-

blematic devices that tell us more about the "sitter". In this case, Mercury and Neptune figure prominently Figures III.5 & 6 – Mercury, the patron of commerce, Venice's central activity at this time; and Neptune, god of the sea through whose beneficent care Venice's trade could be accomplished; or as Kolb put it, Mercury and Neptune are the tutelary deities who preside over "this above all emporia" and make placid the waters of its port. And as with conventional portraits, where there is some assumption of a plausibly physical or

III.5 & 6 Mercury and Neptune are twin deities that preside over Venice's trade and the sea on which trade is conducted, from Jacopo de' Barbari, Bird's-Eye View of Venice.

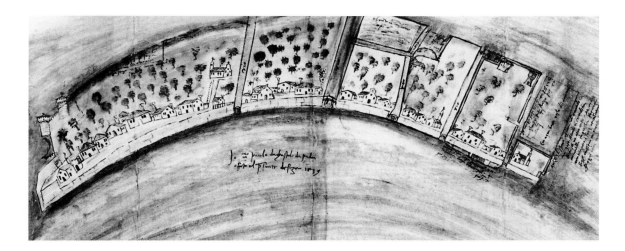

III.7 Paolo da Castello da Padova, map of Giudecca, signed and dated 1539. A rough sketch that nevertheless makes a point of indicating orchards and gardens along the Giudecca.

ideal "likeness" between sitter and his or her representation, de' Barbari's picture of the city has proven of exceptional accuracy, the result of his extraordinary topographical research and close attention to the urban fabric: though Schulz warns that it is "not a perfectly accurate record", he says nonetheless that de' Barbari's view "exhibits an extraordinary degree of fidelity to the complex geography and topography of Venice"[4]. We are therefore, I suggest, confronted with an ancillary question: what should we make of the Giudecca gardens so prominently displayed across the bottom of de' Barbari's "portrait"? If not "accurate" – in the sense that he represents specific gardens as they were actually in the years before the print's publication, along the lines of his representation of the Arsenal or San Marco – we would still have to read them in the same fashion as the figures of Mercury and Neptune, as emblems or attributes of the city's particular and peculiar character and prestige. Either way – as topographical precisions or allegorical *topoi* – they deserve careful and detailed analysis.

The first thing to be acknowledged, though it will go little way to answer our question, is that by 1500 cartographical conventions had established that north would be the top of a map and so usually at the head of a sheet[5]; accordingly de' Barbari orientates his Venice so that its southernmost aspect is towards

the viewer. But as his is also a perspectival representation, this southern portion is registered at the largest scale, with the gardens along the Giudecca brought into exceptional prominence (compared even with the administrative centre, San Marco, or the ship-building focus of the Arsenal). The Giudecca was always one of the prime gardenist locations in the city, along with Castello, the Cannaregio and the area redeveloped as the Fondamenta Nuove, the western ends of the city, and Murano; so the inevitable use of the Giudecca as foreground by de' Barbari makes much of the garden element in the urban fabric. (If, by chance, the convention had been reversed and Murano to the north been placed at the forefront of the view, gardens would still have featured conspicuously). Every subsequent cartographer followed by having to address the Giudecca as the prominent foreground of his city view. In the late 16th century Giovan Battista Arzenti painted the panorama that now hangs in the Danieli Hotel see Figure I.4, and while he seems far less absorbed than de' Barbari by the demands of topographical accuracy he still honours the Giudecca garden world with conspicuous area of green groves, which are obviously his shorthand for "gardens", across the bottom of his canvas. The high bird's-eye view of Venice painted by Ignazio Danti during the same period marks the Giudecca brilliantly in a green crescent, while the city it-

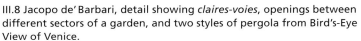

III.8 Jacopo de' Barbari, detail showing *claires-voies*, openings between different sectors of a garden, and two styles of pergola from Bird's-Eye View of Venice.

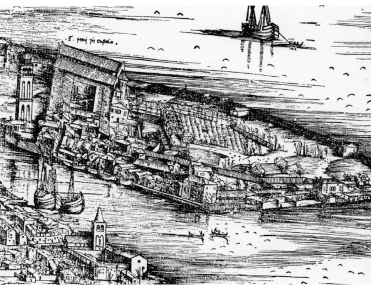

III.9 Jacopo de' Barbari, detail of area by San Pietro di Castello, from Bird's-Eye View of Venice. Behind the Venetian cathedral church are gardens and pergolas.

self is depicted in the red colour of buildings with only its edges touched with green[6]. Similarly, the map of the Giudecca by Paolo da Castello da Padova, signed and dated 1539 Figure II.7, barely attempts any real topographical accuracy, but does nonetheless indicate what are mainly sections of tree-studded ground (perhaps orchards) stretching behind the houses. At least this sketch confirms the reputation or association of the Giudecca with "gardens", using one of many shorthands that artists adopted to designate spaces of Venetian "gardens"; we shall encounter other such shorthand notations in later mappings of the city, specifically that of Ughi see Figure VI.22.

However, it is not clear that de' Barbari's representation of gardens relies merely on some graphic shorthand. Rather, the half-dozen gardens that he depicts in detail are by no means homogeneous, a fact that goes some further way to support my hypothesis that he chose to record things as they were (or, at the very least, that he had an eye for subtle differences in the forms of Venetian gardens and deployed them accordingly when he came to depict the Giudecca). Yet, and perhaps more importantly, the various gardens do share a certain typology, and this structure itself may be shown to have additional significance. It is totally inadequate to describe them as "The fancy gardens

depicted by Jacopo de' Barbari", and misleading on many counts to say further that such gardens were "reproduced into the early nineteenth century, long after they had disappeared"[7].

The northern façades of the houses front the Giudecca Canal, so we cannot see them. Immediately behind the buildings is, first, a courtyard, depictions of at least three of which sport the well head that gave access to the cistern beneath, where was collected precious rainwater from the adjacent roofs – de' Barbari even shows the runnels that fed these cisterns. Beyond this paved area are spaces which we might call indifferently gardens, orchards, vegetable plots, even fields, which are again represented with some detailed variety and indications of fecund plant growth: some garden sectors have pergolas with elegantly carved arches, while other pergolas, adjacent to what seem more utilitarian plots, have flat cross-beams; but both are devices for raising plants towards the sunshine in confined areas. Beyond the cultivated spaces lie scrub, wasteland, mudflats and finally the seawater. The garden segments are separated sometimes by walls pierced by doorways that give access to succeeding sectors, but also in one case Figure III.8 by a pair of *claires-voies*, openings cross-hatched in the woodcut to indicate grilles that permit glimpses from one seg-

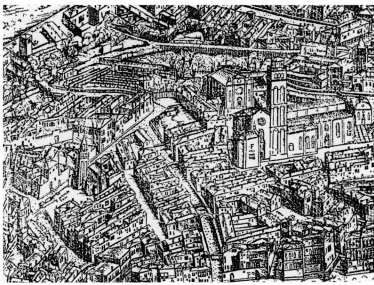

III.10 Jacopo de' Barbari, detail of the island of San Giorgio, from Bird's-Eye View of Venice.

III.11 Jacopo de' Barbari, detail of the area around the church of the Frari, from Bird's-Eye View of Venice, showing open land around the church, including fields for drying woolens.

ment of the garden to another. Finally, on the edge of the cultivated land were buildings: Figure III.4 shows one clearly and another, more extensive, hides behind the wooden fencing in Figure III.1; the first certainly is a pavilion from which views of the lagoon could be taken. As we shall see (section II below), this basic typology of the Giudecca garden can be supported and augmented from a variety of other visual sources.

The separation of cultivated land from mudflats (as of land from water) is conspicuous in de' Barbari's image, and it suggests further meanings for his portrait of Venice. Gardens were certainly created on "high ground" wherever that was available above water level; but, as we have seen, such elevations were too precious for them not to be annexed for building, so that gardens and orchards were also established on ground made artificially higher by dredgings from the channels and waterways. Being the essential thoroughfares of this city, canals were carefully maintained, but on the principle of 'waste not, want not' the mud taken from these canals was used to bulk up low-lying land, forming ground for construction or agricultural terrain, including orchards and gardens. This activity was strictly regulated by the authorities. In the years following de' Barbari, the archives of the Savio ed Esecutori alle Acque (The Wise Ones and Ad-

ministrators of the Waters) are full of site inspections and permissions to infill, enlarge and enclose with walls land hitherto unusable. One of the busiest and most visible inspectors in this line of work was one Paolo di Ponte, and in 1575 he gave permission for one landowner on the Rio di Sant' Andrea to bring in a staggering 50 boatloads of *fango* (mud) to create an "orto Grande"[8]. And over the 20 years after 1572, the northern edge of the lagoon was infilled with dumped spoils brought to the site, after which a stone embankment, the Fondamenta Nuove, was begun[9].

It would therefore be hard not to read de' Barbari's Giudecca landscape as demonstrating a significant concept of Venice's foundation and development, which was known to be established on land partly found, partly augmented or even created (in the case of gardens especially) from the very detritus of the city's waterways. But there is more to it. The sequence of spaces that he depicts may be read as the chronological story of Venice's own physical emergence from the waters, coloured as well by the mythical aura that surrounded this narrative. If her substantial buildings are the final product of urban settlement and architectural culture, then the rescue of cultivable land from the lagoon and the establishment on it of subsistence

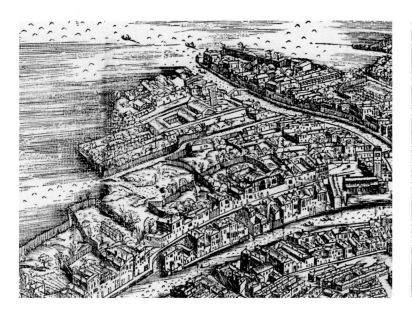

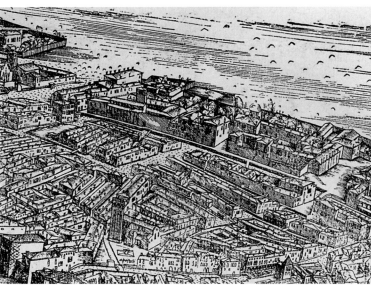

III.12 Jacopo de' Barbari's detail of the north-eastern edge of the city, where there was less construction and so more space available for gardens and open plots at the edges of the lagoon, from Bird's-Eye View of Venice.

III.13 Jacopo de' Barbari, detail of area at the Sacca della Misericordia, from Bird's-Eye View of Venice. Tell-tale trees emerge from courtyards, and in the top left the land that would eventually become the gardens of the Palazzo Contarini dal Zaffo.

crops and fruit were the first necessities and achievements of the lagoon settlers. As life become more secure, more sophisticated spaces were developed, until the domestic complexes that de' Barbari shows as occupying the Giudecca were achieved. What may seem simply a mix of outdoor spaces takes on a symbolic because historical meaning [10].

From the *palazzo* or house, its inhabitants or visitors could stroll through a series of what amounted to chapters of the city's history. A central pergola in the most elaborate Giudecca garden (depicted in Figure III.1) extends the tunnel-like hallway or *androne* of the house into the open air; the *androne* and the pergola conduct the visitor from the waters of the Giudecca canal, through the house, across its paved courtyard, then past furrows that suggest agrarian activity, to fallow land with trees (perhaps an orchard, but anyhow less worked than the previous sectors) and finally to the very edge of the colonized area. Turning back, the visitor could walk the stages of Venice's own emergence and triumph over the lagoon from mudflat to cultivated land to stone courtyard and finally to palace. And details in other parts of de' Barbari's panorama suggest the same physical facts: in land behind San Pietro di Castello Figure III.9 elaborate and arched pergolas extend outwards from the rear of the cathedral and lead

towards land cultivated in rows, which itself peters out into untilled earth, at the lagoon edge of which are two buildings, maybe a boathouse to the north and a dwelling or waterside pavilion to its south.

What is visible on the Giudecca is repeated using more abbreviated signs elsewhere on the woodcut [11]. Inevitably, given his perspectival position, de' Barbari brings elements in the southern parts of the city closer to the viewer and into sharper focus than those, say, in the Cannaregio to the north. Thus on the island of San Giorgio Figure III.10 gardens are clearly marked or indicated: a cluster of cypresses to the left of the tall tower betrays the presence of one, and immediately south of it another in a small courtyard is signalled by trees or bushes and overlooked by five lancet windows, while in the more expansive territories are worked fields – a series of ridges indicates cultivation of a fairly extensive kind – orchards, pergolas (both flat-topped and rounded), and another pavilion overlooking the lagoon; two persons are seen walking under the arch of the rounded pergola. A personification of the south wind blows across the whole cultivated area.

The clear images by which de' Barbari registers gardens nearer to the viewer can be used as keys to interpret the shorthand signs in more northern areas. Given that lesser detail is expended in the representa-

III.14 Jacopo de'Barbari, detail of area near San Francesco della Vigna, from Bird's-Eye View of Venice. Even at this distant edge of the city de'Barbari can show the gardens of two monastic institutions with some details.

tion of distant areas of the city, and given, too, that the sharp printing of his woodcutting even in the southern areas does not lend itself to great enlargement, it is still worth combing the six sheets of the overall view for further evidence of garden spaces and structures. These are, indeed, visible everywhere[12] . In the middle distance is the church of the Frari Figure III.11, with considerable open ground behind it, partly filled with trees and also with extensive rails for drying woollens[13]; uncultivated ground with a small hut is also shown. In the bottom left corner of the detail a well head appears on open ground beside a canal and the church of San Pantalon, while another one peeps out of the space designated as the Campo San Tomà. Further away still, now along the northern edges of the city, there is considerable open ground to the west of where the Cannaregio canal enters the lagoon Figure III.12; much here seems uncultivated, but even these spaces often have pergolas, and all are shown as already enclosed; San Giobbe is depicted with a cloister between the church and a large orchard, also divided down the centre with a pergola, while the canal (nowadays filled as the *Rio Terà* Lista di Spagna) boasts several houses with rear gardens, the main one of which has a walled courtyard surrounded on three sides by other cultivated land with a rounded pergola.

Further east Figure III.13 around the Sacca della Misericordia tell-tale trees shoot up in many places; the Campo Santi Apostoli has its well head set on a platform above the cistern; while the site of what would become the famous garden of the Contarini da Zaffo in the 18th century is still a safely fenced and tree-d protrusion into the lagoon. The detail of Figure III.14 focuses on the area of San Francesco della Vigna and Santa Maria Celeste (now lost): many courtyards appear among the buildings, some even arcaded like the Celestia's cloister; there is considerable uncultivated land along the lagoon, but orchards and pergolas are shown within the monastic compounds, and perhaps espaliered fruit along the south-facing wall at the Celestia.

As one penetrates further into the city and the angle of our vision becomes more oblique, the woodcut still shows tree tops above the ubiquitous walls, filling such tiny areas of the print that the detail scarcely seems necessary, except that it hints at courtyards and open ground. De'Barbari delineates different materials forming the enclosures – mostly wooden palings, but also masonry and even a suggestion of brick see Figure III.4. He shows the criss-cross pattern of a trellis and many spots where plants have been trained or grown against south-facing walls. All in all, this city portrait confirms that the very late 15th century continued to show, as did the mediaeval period, that gardens were an ineluctable part of its urban character.

This notion that a landscaped site could encapsulate or represent the history of its creation and of the cultural forces that ensured its maintenance and success was nothing new. It was also a commonplace that a building was the external reflection of the mind of its owner[14], so that the representation of buildings and their sites, above all in a map with claims to be useful as political propaganda, would have carried the same kind of significance and value. A Venetian handbook for merchants of 1458 by Benedetto Cotrugli Raguseo had made the same declaration about the visible statement of character and identity[15]. Perhaps more significantly, some years before de'Barbari, Leon Battista Alberti had argued in his treatise on building that gardens needed to draw upon the materials and opportunities of their 'locality'; further, that the 'areas' specifically chosen for such sites would represent an intensification of the features of that locality[16]. Alberti's argument about the relation of building or

III.15 The "iron garden" at the Venetian Arsenal, from *Artiglieria Veneta* (Venice, 1779). Cannon balls contrive a topiary effect inside the heart of the Venetian shipbuilding and naval complex.

garden sites to the surrounding territory may be seen in its turn to have sustained reflections on what came to be termed the "third nature" of gardens.

This term (*terza natura*) would be coined later in the 16th century, as practical interventions upon the land were evoking more conceptual formulations[17]. It could well have been applied to de'Barbari's representation of the Giudecca, which provides an excellent illustration of the concept *avant la lettre*. This third nature had a double significance for the two humanists who, independently, coined the phrase: in aesthetic terms it announced that gardens were an ornamental extension of agricultural work and civic infrastructure, a development of what Cicero had named second nature (*alteram naturam*) in his treatise *De natura deorum* (On the nature of the gods), an early edition of which was published in Venice in 1508. We may deduce that Cicero thought the first nature, which he names only by implication in the word *alteram* (the other, or second), was the unmediated world before humans took it variously in hand. In cultural terms the third nature helped to make palpable and explain a history of human progress from a wild and savage state, through cultural landscapes of settlement like roads and bridges and ports, to the finer world of gardens and villas.

Both cultural and aesthetic readings of land as second, then as third, nature constituted a sequence of "natures" both historical and, on the ground, also topographical. This is what, I suggest, we can also see in de'Barbari. He envisages the significance of the gardens strung out along the island of the Giudecca in the years immediately before 1500 as an epitome or abstract of Venice's colonization of the primal or first nature of lagoon territory. The gods whom Cicero also identified with his implied first *natura* are also here – Neptune, and the gods of the winds – while the commercial Mercury is a deity who presides over Cicero's "second nature".

However we choose to read the details of the gardens that de'Barbari shows, they form a complex characterization – along with Neptune, Mercury and the winds blowing from different directions on the city – of a certain mythology or self-fashioning. Venice without gardens, as without trade and the fortunes of the sea, was simply not Venice. The paradox or wonderful impossibility of gardens, the very "idea of [them] in the middle of the sea", made their creation and sustenance the more miraculous. Even the Arsenal – that other focus of Venetian identity in de'Barbari's perspective, and represented as a series of compounds and encircled with courtyards – would later install its own "garden" of cannonballs piled in pyramidal heaps, like metallic topiary and known as the "iron garden"[18], to celebrate the visit by a dignitary in the 18th century Figure III.15.

The presence of gardens in the de'Barbari view, then, signalled many things: an advanced state of civilization and settlement, when time and space allowed the cultivation and maintenance of such areas; evidence of the Venetian skill in turning the disadvantage of the watery habitation to spectacular profit and display; perhaps also, given the strong pharmaceutical reputation of the city (for which see Chapter Five), gardens represented the site of the cultivation of plants for medicinal purposes – and an illustrated herbal, which we will examine closely later in this chapter, certainly seems to register that magnificent gardens went hand in hand with the collection and utilisation of plants of all sorts.

GARDEN LAYOUT AND DESIGN ELEMENTS: DESCRIPTIONS BY 16TH-CENTURY PAINTERS AND WRITERS

De'Barbari's representation of garden spaces can be augmented from other sources, mainly but not exclusively in the century that follows, which either confirm at least the formal accuracy of his observations or cast some additional light on the Venetian idea of the garden. These include archival documents showing the layouts of houses and gardens, later mappings of the city, literary descriptions, illustrated books from Venetian printing houses, like the famous *Hypnerotomachia Poliphili,* backgrounds of some Venetian paintings, and one particularly interesting 16th-century herbal that depicts a few garden spaces. None of these sources is unproblematical, except perhaps the archival plans that often were executed for purposes of property inheritance, purchase or other legal business; but in its own way each kind of material furnishes ancillary evidence for a certain kind of Venetian garden layout and design elements. This layout responds both to physical factors – the conditions of garden-making and available space in the Venetian city – and, perhaps, to mythopoeic perspectives.

Even as early as 1494 the Milanese Pietro Casola had expressed his surprise at "the many beautiful gardens which are to be seen here, especially, I must say, those belonging to the different religious orders"[19].

A canon himself, he doubtless had more access to these religious enclaves, such as the orchards of the eponymous Madonna, than to gardens of private citizens during his two weeks in the city. But much other testimony, albeit patchy and often annoyingly general, would support his recognition of the incidence of gardens. Sanudo's diary for February 1514 records garden visits by a group of "gardeners", like any modern club of horticultural enthusiasts. And by 1581 the first edition of Francesco Sansovino's guide counts, in its eighth book, "diversi Giardini" throughout the city's different *sestieri*, and without taking into consideration the "things of Murano". His list is at once precise, naming owners and locations, and also rhetorical ("con straordinaria vaghezza & dilicatura" [with extraordinary attractions and delights]):

"There are also various gardens, besides those with common herbs, notable and famous for noble and rare plants, incredible to foreigners, who think that the salt water cannot accommodate human artifice. And among other memorable ones, can be seen that of Gasparo Erizo at San Cantiano [Canciano], ornamented with buildings that have statues [*figure*] and paintings. That of Andrea Michieli at San Geraso [Trovaso] with singular plants, set out in fine order with important statues and a beautiful fountain that spurts sweet water, and likewise that of Francesco Bono. A similar one is situated at Sant'Angelo, at the house of Cesare Ziliolo, deputy Chancellor of the Doge, from which great delight is taken, having rare plants from the Levant that are new to these parts. Noteworthy also is that of Pietro Bosello, besides its buildings and singular courtyards, for being graced with various shaped [topiary] local trees and with all the herbs that have been identified. And Francesco Testa's garden is equally wonderful. Furthermore, a visit is urged to the orchard (*Horto*) at Santa Maria, the garden of Tomaso Contarini, Procurator of San Marco. At San Antonio, Santo Moro's. At Santa Caterina, the Grimani's. At San Basilio, Andrea Pasqualigo's. At San Gerolamo, Leonardo Moro's. At San Samuele, Iacomo Contarini's. In the Cannaregio, Maffei Medico's. At Santa Croce, Agostino Amadi's. At the Pietà, Alessandro Vittoria's. On the Giudecca, the garden of the Gritti is delicious, and famous for its plants (*semplici*), its buildings and for sculpture and paintings. In addition to those, other notable sites on that island are the gardens of Andrea Dandolo on the point opposite San Giorgio Maggiore,

III.16 Elaborate pergola and bench, *Hypnerotomachia Poliphili*, 1499. Several woodcuts published to illustrate this strange and wonderful romance show gardens and garden features; arguably the artist drew upon local garden work in an effort to make more believable the author's narrative.

of the Mocenigos, the Vendramini, the Cornaros, and many others on this island, as well as, throughout the whole body of the city (not forgetting for a moment those on Murano), are copiously spread with extraordinary beauty and delicacy *(vaghezza & dilicatura)*. With the variety of the entertainments and with the ornamentation of the greenery, paintings and sculpture, with fountains and other delicious and gratifying discoveries, you are pleased with everything that you see, all consoling and pleasing."[20]

This succinct survey of Venetian gardens ("worthy of memory") was published first in 1581 in Sansovino's *Venetia città nobilissima et singolare*, then augmented in 1604 by Stringa and finally supplemented by the Abbé Giustiniani Martinioni in an edition of 1663. By the late 17th century the updated list of fine gardens by Martinioni maintains Sansovino's focus on planting and, now especially, on sculpture, fountains created with great naturalism, and work done by garden owners themselves *(fatte ad lui da sua propria mano)*. Most of this is offered in very general terms, with the exception of a detailed description of the garden of Signore Cataneo (for which see Gazetteer in Chapter Four).

Yet slipped into his survey are some contributions towards a catalogue of garden elements: there are courtyards ornamented with local trees ("corti sin-

III.17 Vernacular pergola and trellis, supporting vines, *Hypnerotomachia Poliphili*.

III.41 Studio of Benedetto Caliari, *Susannah and the Elders*, Museo Civico, Treviso. Another Veneto artist draws upon various elements of the local garden repertory in his depiction of an event that is generally shown in an outdoor setting.

This selection of paintings certainly contains elements that are also especially visible in the construction and layout of actual Venetian gardens, many determined by the evolution of palaces and the exigencies of their exterior spaces. The two most ubiquitous features are the *corti* themselves and the different means of dividing spaces; this latter device makes the available territory seem more various and – given that the individual spaces were often quite tight – allows views from one to another, often framed in a pergola or arch. In Bonifacio de' Pitati's *Dives and Lazarus* the spaces are probably too extensive for a Venetian city site[42], but what seems a courtyard adjacent to the pillared portico of a house is divided into squares of what appear to be turf, on which are set one shrub growing in a pot and a statue, an effective design strategy in floodable territory; furthermore the courtyard is walled or hedged only to shoulder height and its two openings are made the more conspicuous as the artist has represented figures moving through them. While grilles are a useful feature to mitigate any sense of confinement in small, enclosed gardens, they are also perhaps an element that Venice made its own from eastern examples: Carpaccio's *Annunciation* in the Cà d'Oro displays them conspicuously, and modern visitors to Venice, as to modern Istanbul, find them everywhere. The Venetian contacts with eastern gardens are hard to pin down, but another Carpaccio, his *Reception of the Venetian Ambassadors in Damascus* (Louvre, Paris), which includes many other garden features – crenellated garden walls, vine-draped pergolas on roofs, hints of several garden courtyards and even an "oriental" *altana* or roof terrace[43] – may be either a Venetian projection of its own garden habits onto a foreign location or some acknowledgement of actual eastern practices.

Written and literary references to actual garden design are probably even more rhetorically camouflaged than painterly examples – the *Hypnerotomachia* would be the extreme example, and accordingly serves as an important *caveat*. Yet the medium of writing can cast its own special light upon gardens and has its own interest. We might begin with some scattered references that emerge from the world of a painter, Titian, who from 1531 came to occupy a new, four-year-old house with a garden on the northern edge of the city (where are now the Fondamenta Nuove), having previously lived in the *sestiere* of San Polo[44]. Although the garden was expanded considerably by Titian in 1549 when he leased adjoining land, it is hard to deduce much of what it would have looked like; we have only a 19th-century engraving of the site Figure III.42.

But we do have a glowing commendation of it a decade earlier from Francesco Priscianese, the Florentine printer and humanist, written sometime before 1540 to recount a "Bacchanalian feast" to which he was invited. The description is conventional and very general: the August holiday was hot, but the guests spent the time before eating "in discussing the rare beauty and charm of the garden ["rara belleza, & vagheza"] with singular pleasure and note of admiration... It is situated in the extreme part of Venice, upon the sea, and from it one sees the pretty little island of Murano

III.42 A 19ᵗʰ-century engraving of Titian's house. Titian's house and garden were famous in their day, and their memory, if not their spaces, are preserved in both this 19ᵗʰ-century view and in a modern plaque on the site near the Fondamenta Nuove.

and other beautiful places... The garden ... was so well laid out ["tanto bene ordinato"] and so beautiful, and consequently much praised, that the resemblance it offered to the delicious retreat of St Agata refreshed my memory..."

This is infuriatingly barren of useful detail, except that it shows how this northern edge of the city was being exploited for quality houses and well-laid out gardens and that the garden in particular (more than the paintings that guests also viewed inside the house) was striking enough to impress a Florentine who came with experience of a different Tuscan garden culture.

Not much more is known about the lodgings of the writer, Pietro Aretino, whom Priscianese mentioned among the guests of Titian on that hot and happy

ferragosto. But in his case we have a few extra hints in his writings (however ambiguous their tone) to expand somewhat upon the garden culture that he knew, including the information Juergen Schulz has gathered about his lodgings in Venice[45]. Aretino came to Venice first in 1527 and took various billets, in one of which he got Tintoretto to paint his bedroom ceiling. In a letter to his landlord of 1537 he describes the view from his lodgings and his sight of "vines on the boats", "orti" in the streets, and water covered like meadows with every kind of produce in season[46]. But in 1551 he settled on the Riva del Carbon in a spacious apartment, reached by an outside staircase from a side courtyard of the palace; it enjoyed an outdoor terrace (*liagò*) at the rear.

But other people's gardens, as did the city's horticultural bounty, attracted Aretino's attention. In his *Sei giornate* he compares favourably the *orto* of a local courtesan, with its vine-covered pergola, rosemary hedges around flower beds that have urns at their corners planted with boxwood, with Agostino Chigi's garden on the Quirinal Hill in Rome[47]. He praised the meadows and the shades around Benedetto Cornaro's house, and the smells and sounds in the garden of Francesco Marcolini, both on the Giudecca[48]. It was in the garden of this publisher that Aretino set his famous attack on princely courts, the *Ragionamento delle corti* of 1538[49]. While, once again, we derive little more than generalized notations of this garden (its breezes, its green shadows, the sweetness of its flowers, and its "Petrarchan" birdsong), it functions throughout as a site with specific meaning and authority: a place, exclusively and essentially Venetian, where those who oppose the hegemony of court and church can discuss privately and safely their alternative visions. So it is, perhaps, a typically Aretinesque gesture to set his attack on courts and courtiers in a Venetian garden that presumably was an extension of a *corte*. The printer and publisher Marcolini himself, absent from his garden throughout Aretino's dialogue, issued at least one book whose authorship he acknowledged, significantly entitled *Le (ingeniose) sorti intitulate giardino di pensieri* (1540); here, too, the "garden", metaphorical as it is, reaffirms a particularly Venetian virtue of space characterized for its combination of happy social exchange with the opportunity for practical intellectuality.

Aretino's interest in the significance rather than the physical properties of Venetian dwellings also emerges in a letter of 1537, where he compliments Andrea Odoni on his house and gardens that contained, in the latter especially, a considerable sculpture collection ("such carvings and castings" that would have graced ancient Greece "had she not let herself be deprived" of them)[50]. The tone, as often with Aretino, is deliberately ambiguous, but his implication is certainly suggestive of an excess and self-importance that may seem un-Venetian; yet it also supports much other evidence that, in the first place, gardens were used for the display of sculptural items – what Schmitter calls a garden *all'antica* and what the English traveller Peter Mundy witnessed in one Cannaregio garden in the 1620s ("a curious garden full of fine devises and marble images")[51] – and that, secondly, what happened behind garden walls was increasingly a matter of private ostentation not countenanced in the public and political realm.

Not surprisingly, much literary testimony on gardens comes in reference to Murano, where "country estates" or *villeggiature* could be enjoyed in more extended spaces than the city itself permitted[52]. Indeed, the palpable opportunities of this island even promoted the commonplace error that in comparison with it there was no green space in the city at all – so Triffon Gabriele, who owned a villa on Murano as well as on the mainland, desired country quiet and not the "noise and tumult and bustle" of cities, the "life of the Rialto, San Marco, and the squares of Venice"[53]. In the 16th century Cornelio Castaldi composed a Latin poem on the Villa Priuli, entitled "Priolani ruris ad Murianum delitiae"[54]: rhetorical in the extreme, it nonetheless celebrates the profusion and manipulation of fresh water, woodland, an aviary and, above all, a repertoire of foreign plants. By the 19th century, when Vincenzo Zanetti publishes his *Guida di Murano* in 1866, he laments that all that survives of this once famous site are a cottage and vegetable plot[55].

Zanetti offers a roll call of other famous 16th-century Muranese gardens, along with commentary on their subsequent fate: Bernardo Giustinian's 15th-century will left his property including a garden and gardener's lodgings with the instructions that his descendents keep "ben coltivato il giardino"; Palazzo Soranzo had a huge garden in the 16th century later turned into a commercial or truck garden (*ortaglia*); Palazzo

Trevisan had gardens no longer recognizable; Caterina Cornaro enjoyed two palaces, on which Scamozzi claimed to have intervened[56], with two gardens and orchards joined by a gallery and with a field for sporting activity and with fountains. Many of the urban nobility owned orchards that are recorded from the early 14th century, like the Badoer, Mocenigo, Querini and the Grimani ("due palazzo [sic] con giardino").

And above all there were the gardens of Andrea Navagero, whose absence on diplomatic duty in Spain and France caused him to write in detail to those friends who were looking after his beloved garden on Murano[57]. From these we have glimpses of a well-stocked botanical collection, with espaliered fruit, trellis-work, roses, laurels, cypresses (some also espaliered), woodland that Navagero wanted to be made denser ("un bosco foltissimo"), pergolas, topiary work, and a boundary wall. Overall it evinced a "delicious and beautiful arrangement", but details of its layout do not survive. A few more useful glimpses come, not from Navagero who was his own garden designer and had no need to describe it when he wrote to his friends about its maintenance during his absences, but from visitors like the Frenchman, Christophe Longueil, who was welcomed to the garden in 1520. His Latin description was sent in a letter to a fellow humanist, Pietro Bembo[58]:

"The garden belonging to this villa was a very pleasant sight, since all the trees in the orchard and plantations are laid out in the form of a quincunx ["ordines in quincuncem dirigentur"], with lines of exquisite topiary each side of a path ["exquisitissimo ambulationum topiario opera latera ejus"] and a walkway ["decumanus"] covered by vaulted arches ["limitis camerae convestiantur"] . ... The apple trees are all planted in regular rows, at discreet intervals, and have grown with amazing rapidity, since they were put in the ground by our Navagero himself, only a few months ago. Nothing could be more beautiful in shape and colour, nothing sweeter in smell or taste, or more excellent in size and variety than the fruit which the orchard produces."

The letter suggests, unsurprisingly, much regularity. Though *quincunx* probably refers simply to planting in lines (rather than in the strictest sense of the term, a recurring five-point pattern), it is clear that order is imposed throughout, especially down the main axis (decumanus, or *decimanus,* is a Roman term con-

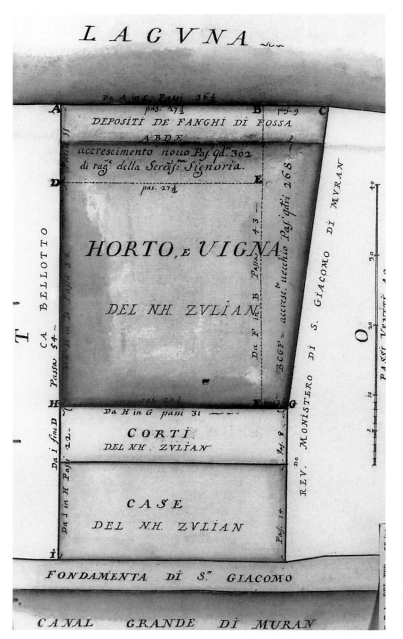

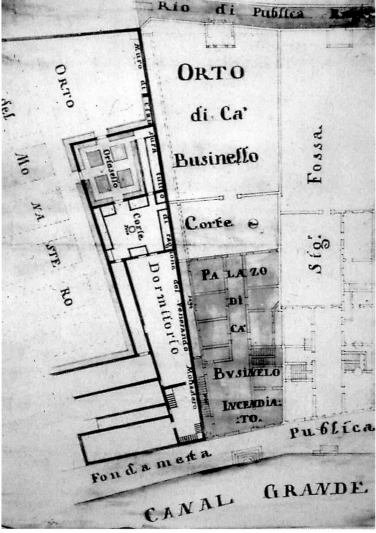

III.43 This plan of the Zulian house on Murano shows the standard layout of house, courtyard and garden and orchard or vineyard.

III.44 The plan of Cà Businello is similar to that of the previous figure, though the various elements have been shaped differently by the contingencies of the urban space.

nected with farming but also with a city gateway, and so a straight street), and that this central vista is covered with a long pergola, as de' Barbari shows in Giudecca gardens. The testimony of Filiasi in the early 19th century describes an exceptionally regulated arrangement of botanical specimens, beds alternating with allées of lemon and myrtle trees[59]. Yet the emphasis on order and delight in regularity coexist with a fond acknowledgement of an abundantly sensuous experience.

A TYPOLOGY OF THE VENETIAN GARDEN

The urban panorama of Jacopo de' Barbari graphically records, and these other verbal and visual sources confirm, that by the early 16th-century a pattern or typology of garden-making had been established that would be tenaciously maintained till modern times. Basically this envisaged the Venetian garden as a series of finite spaces, in an increasing scale of human

64

control from the edge of the lagoon (or sometimes a back canal) right up to the *palazzo*, a pattern that seemed to symbolize the very history of the city's rising and self-formation from the sea. This typology, however, cannot be absolute or claimed as exclusively Venetian, even if its symbolic reverberations can be understood as unique to the city. In formal terms, the Venetian city garden's handling of garden spaces may not always differ from Tuscan 15 th– and 16 th-century gardening or even the layouts suggested in the writings of Pietro de' Crescenzi, with their sequences of differently handled spaces, their division by walls and trellis-work, displays of sculpture, or the provision of pavilions. But it is the Venetian skilful and creative adaptation of such common practices and the fresh meaning they derive from being sited within the lagoon city and its often compressed scale that nevertheless typifies the garden in Venice.

We are therefore extremely fortunate in having de' Barbari's careful "description" of some typical Venetian gardens by which to orientate ourselves through other, much more fuzzy evidence. Even the graphic materials are sometimes infuriatingly blank: such is the archival plan of the Zulian house on the Grand Canal of Murano Figure III.43, where the basic features of the site are simply blocked in and their measurements recorded without any further details; there is a courtyard and then a garden and vineyard, but their internal disposition was of no interest to the surveyor and remains simply as a coloured rectangle. Indeed, it may be precisely because of this continuing and predictable pattern (house + courtyard + garden + orchard or vineyard) that draughtsmen could be relieved of any responsibility to record specific details. A later, 18 th-century plan of the Cà Businello on the Venetian Grand Canal Figure III.44 has very little more detail than the Murano plan of the previous century: the disposition of rooms within the *palazzo* itself is shown, as are the courtyard, its well head and the opening from it into the *orto*, which appears to have a small pavilion at the end giving on to the *rio*. Otherwise the layout or content of the *orto* is not depicted, although the large monastic property alongside does have the beds of its *orto* indicated as well as the wellhead in a small courtyard and the quadrangular beds in a small *ortesello*. But both the Cà Businello and indeed the neighbouring dormitory evince the same, basic sequence of spaces that de' Barbari first delineated.

We have a striking instance of how tenacious was the Venetian hold upon its own forms and spatial controls. In 1566 Alvise Cornaro proposed to the city fathers some radical revisions to the Venetian topography involving gardens that were not at all faithful to the typology clearly encoded by de' Barbari's view [60]. One was a circuit of protective walls encircling the city's islands, with public parks and gardens along them. But this offended the well-established myth that the sea was the city's best defense, or, to paraphrase the words of Bernardo Giustinian's *De origine urbis gentisque Venetorum historiae* [61], the city needed neither gates nor walls but only the inaccessible marsh and unconquerable passage of the sea, both well-tested, what the inscription by G.B.Ignazio put succinctly as "acquis pro muro munitur" (waters provide the walls).

Another of Cornaro's projects was for an ideally naturalistic island at the mouth of the Grand Canal between the Piazzetta and San Giorgio Maggiore; this radically departed from the design of contemporary Venetian gardens in favour of a piece of pan-European garden design, and consequently must have offended the cherished view of Venice's unique topography. Similarly, a plan of Fra Giocondo's for rebuilding the market area after a fire at the Rialto in 1514 was rejected because "he failed to understand the place" [62].

Venetians are, by many accounts, a conservative people, and architecturally they have consistently moved towards "original and exclusively Venetian" forms and details [63]. We may therefore assume, too, that the exterior spaces as much as the architecture were another local response to environmental and social imperatives. The gardens discussed at some length here, based on and related to the prototype recorded in de' Barbari's view of Venice, had a long life, in part due to the inherently conservative attitudes of Venetians but also because, as discussed, they responded to and declared the fact of what Juergen Schulz calls "local imperatives, both environmental and social" [64]. The next chapters document and analyse what we know about how these imperatives determined specific sites at various periods.

Chapter Four

This section of the book is devoted to the documentation of some specific Venetian gardens, to which other parts of the book will be able to refer. Its "Gazetteer" is not intended to be exhaustive, but simply representative of the range of Venetians gardens – a range over different historical periods, through the different *sestieri* (the six districts into which the city is divided for administrative purposes), of formal layouts, of many uses and receptions, and (inevitably) a record of alteration, decay or disappearance. It has drawn upon many sources: on graphic evidence for Venetian gardens – plans, maps, aerial views; on verbal commentary in both historical documents and modern scholarship and publications; and on direct observation. Many buildings in Venice are so much the result of multiple and diverse interventions and have patchy architectural histories[1] that narrative coherence is often impossible; it is often far worse for their gardens. But fragmentary evidence does gain some coherence by being stockpiled.

The selection of specific sites is designed to address a couple of basic issues. The first is simply to counter the familiar response that "there are no gardens in Venice" by setting out the distribution, extent, character and scope of a selection of them. It is also hoped that this catalogue may serve later as the basis for others to extend and establish a fuller repertory of Venetian gardens. The second aim is to flesh out the typology of Venetian gardens established in the previous chapter; for the basic format of gardens that we can discern in de' Barbari's representation of the Giudecca island was adapted – necessarily, inevitably, and endlessly – both to the topographical exigencies of available spaces throughout the city and to the constraints of garden use and property inheritance. It was, nonetheless, a formal layout that often persisted at least until the 19th century, when some of the larger sites were adapted to the new and so-called "English" style. Specific examples, then, will help to characterize the Venetian city garden with more precision.

Many gardens have simply been lost to everything but passing remarks, hearsay or reminiscence; since they cannot be reconstructed in even a rudimentary fashion, only a bare selection of these lost sites is included; their mention does, however, help to register the once important presence of sites that have now disappeared. It also serves to suggest that gardens have been presences in all periods, even though many have survived neither physically nor with detailed archival reference. It follows that the "Gazetteer" has an inevitable bias towards sites that still survive in some form on the ground or for which a useful documentation exists. Some interesting gardens succumbed to various urban developments, of which the most dramatic have been Napoleon's remodelling of the urban structure (mainly in the east beyond the Arsenal), the later construction (in the west) of the railway station during the 19th century and of Piazzale Roma during the 20th, along with the cutting of the Rio Nuovo and the making of the Strada Nuova, both in the 20th century.

The "Gazetteer" or catalogue of examples is divided by *sestiere*, with final sections devoted to the two prime garden islands of the Giudecca and Murano. A chronological order, otherwise desirable, makes little sense in the *longue durée* of a garden and given the varying fortunes of Venetian sites under different owners; otherwise, it might make sense to highlight a given historical moment in a garden's existence – the garden of the Palazzo Contarini dal Zaffo is important in the 18th century because of the rare visual documentation that Guardi provides; the Giardino Papadopoli is important in the 19th century, though in both cases there had been earlier gardens or orchards, including monastic grounds on the latter.

Each entry comprises five elements:
1. The name or names of the site, whether palace / house / garden.
2. Its location by current street address (if applicable), using the anagraphical numbering by *sestiere*[2]. Square brackets [ ] around an address signify the approximate location of a now lost site.
3. A bibliography of major references to the site in chronological order (often these will inevitably concern the building as much as the garden attached to it).
4. Some iconography, where this is useful and available: either a plan of its formal layout, or a selection

of other archival or modern imagery; sometimes the garden is no more than a glimpse above a high wall or otherwise surrounded by buildings that prevent photography.

5. A brief commentary on significant aspects and uses of the site; or cross reference to its discussion elsewhere in these chapters. For this last section in particular I have relied on both an array of published sources and on my own explorations in archives and throughout the modern city itself. I would acknowledge here my particular debt to Mariapia Cunico (notably her own gazetteer in *Il Giardino Veneziano*, pp.147-86), which my bibliographical entries make clear has been of invaluable use to me; her plans primarily record current plantings, with which I am generally less concerned.

The Gazetteer does not include entries for monastic properties, although these have been (and some still are) a major element in the city's horticultural profile. In a few cases listed here, private gardens came into being on sites that were originally ecclesiastical or monastic. However, the ecclesiastical and monastic gardens are treated elsewhere in this book, especially in Chapter Five.

CANNAREGIO

The *sestiere* was always a prime site for gardens and is still, in both aerial photography and by ground-level observation, filled with gardens and sports grounds (football pitches and baseball courts), and industrial open areas, many of which have a somewhat neglected appearance. Many properties originally stretched and still do, though fragmented and built over, between the series of parallel canals that run the length of Cannaregio (Rii dei Riformati/Sant'Alvise, della Sensa, di San Gerolomo/della Misericordia). Many plots have loggias or *casini* at the rear of the site, overlooking a canal, obviously reworked for (and sometimes therefore destroyed by) commercial use; some plots still contain significant treescapes and even, in one case, the rear turrets of a brick neo-gothic pavilion at the Palazzo Arrigoni, Cannaregio 3535-6.

Palazzo of Chiara Pisani Moretta
Santa Chiara [Piazzale Roma]

BIBLIO: Chiappini di Sorio, *Palazzo Pisani Moretta* (Milan, 1983).

Between the convent of Santa Chiara and the church of Sant'Andrea; suppressed in 1806 and the whole area lost to Piazzale Roma in the1930s. Not in Cannaregio (it is in the area of the Piazzale Roma garages), the site is accomodated here as part of the series of sites lost to the modern developments of railway and road access into the city.

Figure IV.1.

Palazzo Rezzonico
[Cannaregio 50] adjacent to the Church of the Scalzi

BIBLIO: Bassi, p.368.

This site had a relatively short life, being established by the 1730s with vineyards and orchards, and a casino. Destroyed in 1846–47 for the railway station.

Palazzo Lion Cavazza
Santa Lucia [on site of railway station]

BIBLIO: Martinioni.

Destroyed to make way for the railway station, but memorialized by Martinioni in 1663 for its hexagonal well head of Verona marble in a courtyard surrounded

Figure 10a: A winding pathway in the Patarol garden.

Palazzo Contarini dal Zaffo

(now a Cottolengo hospice), Fondamenta Gasparo Contarini, Cannaregio 3539

BIBLIO: Martinioni; Cartwright, pp.113-4; Damerini, photographs of the Johnson's garden between pp.92 & 97; Ruffo, p.51; Protti: *Giardini Veneziani*, p.60-6; Cunico, pp.8, 130-3; Albrizzi/Pool, p.37; Dammicco, pp.28-31; pp. 118 –120 below.

Like many garden sites, this has a long history as cultivated open space, and is listed by Francesco Sansovino in his chapter on gardens: but its fame rests upon both its Casino degli Spiriti (commemorating wits or "spirited" people rather than ghosts, the meeting place in the 16th century for folk like Aretino, Sansovino and Titian), and its 18th-century representation by Francesco Guardi in both drawings and a painting (discussed in Chapter Six). The Casino was constructed right at the corner of the property, rather than on any central axis from the palace, presumably to take advantage of a variety of views over the water. The

gardens have been much modified since Guardi: the wall with arch and niches alongside the garden has disappeared, and a later wall, built down the garden on roughly the near edge of his painting, separates the Contarini garden from that of the adjacent Palazzo Minelli (this is discussed at length, with diagram, in Hunt 2009). Both gardens were progressively filled up with sheds and rubbish dumps during the 19th century and thirty years ago still contained much rubble and bits of statuary. It inspired D'Annunzio's novel, *La Leda senza Cigno* (1913), (quoted by both Albrizzi/ Pool, p.37 and Cunico, p.130). Subsequently restored by the Johnson family, for whom the French garden designer Ferdinand Bac worked between 1923 and 1938: over a dozen photographs and nine designs by Bac, along with letters to Mrs Johnson, are held at the Bibliothèque de l'Arsenal, Paris. Today the two much-dislocated sites are occupied by nursing homes.

See Figures VI.3 & 4.

Palazzo Rubini

Rio della Sensa, Fondamenta dell'Abbazia
Cannaregio 3554A

BIBLIO: Bassi, p.471.

Built on land of the Scuola della Misericordia in the late 16th century; later remodelled; it overlooks a small Abbazia garden at right.

Figure IV.11.

IV.11 The entry to the garden of the Palazzo Rubini.

Palazzo Lezze
alla Misericordia, Cannaregio 3597

BIBLIO: Bassi, p.282.

The Palazzo is by Longhena; there is a drawing by Visentini of its casino, which still survives on the canal see Figure VI.14. According to Fontana 1865, p.307, there was a fountain in its *corte* later transferred to the garden, the spaces of which no longer survive encroachment by the adjacent buildings.

Palazzo Antelini (Tiepolo)
alla Misericordia, Cannaregio 3604

BIBLIO: Bassi, p.286; Zorzi, pp. 304-5.

Clearly visible between the Rio San Felice and the Rio di Noale, the garden was created on the basement remains after demolition of the palace in 1798–1800 (Zorzi) or 1812 (Bassi).
Figure IV.12.

Palazzo Giustinian Pesaro
Cannaregio 3935

BIBLIO: Giorgio Bellavitis, *Palazzo Giustinian Pesaro*, Vicenza, 1975; p. 36 above.

IV.12 Garden of Palazzo Antelini.

IV.17 View of the restored garden of the Palazzo Soranzo (2007).

with undisguised bitterness that it was here Napoleon Bonaparte "lodged during the short hours which he needed to destroy the Serene Republic"!
Figure IV.17.

Cà Tron
(now Istituto Universitario Architettura Venezia)
San Stae, Santa Croce 1947

BIBLIO: Fontana; Bassi, pp.190-1; Cunico, pp.113-6; *Giardini Veneziani*, pp.50-3.

The garden was presumably established in the 16th century following the building programme which pushed two wings out into the garden space and established an elaborate casino; the site of a reception of Emperor Joseph II in 1775. The casino, pulled down after the last of the Trons died in 1828, was on axis to the grand portal giving access directly to the garden from the calle (Santa Croce 1954). By the middle of the 19th century the gardens were ruined and abandoned ground (see Austrian *catasto* and Combatti); a

statue of Saint George and a pilastered niche are presumably remnants of this edifice. Other fragments were removed to the Palazzo Gradenigo garden during the 19th century.
See Figure II.12.

Cà Pesaro (Galleria Internazionale d'Arte Moderna)
San Stae (Eustachio), Santa Croce 2076

BIBLIO: Bassi 174.

A building with interventions by different architects; the inner courtyard is overlooked by a series of loggias and contains a colossal, arched well head by Danese Cattaneo from the courtyard of Jacopo Sansovino's Mint, as well as an elegant *pavimento* in the form of flower beds, attributed to Longhena.

DORSODURO

This part of Venice, stretching westwards from the Salute church along a ridge of sandbank (hence its name, "hard back"), offered sites for many gardens, small and large. Today several fine sites, mostly private, still exist, though the garden of the Guggenheim Collection is a welcome public amenity and others, like the Armenian College (Palazzo Zenobio), are sometimes open.

Cà Pozzo, now gardens of Patriarchal Seminary at the Salute
Dorsoduro 1

BIBLIO: G.A.Moschini, *Chiesa e Seminario di Santa Maria della Salute* (Venice, 1842); Albrizzi/Pool, p.43.

Gardens designed by Alberto Parolini in 1817 at time of their transfer to seminary; they stretch behind the Salute church.

Palazzo Dario
Dorsoduro 352

BIBLIO: Pool, p.24.

A late15[th]-century palace, with a small rear, enclosed garden, obviously raised; this presents a typical Venetian garden view – concentrated planting in a restricted space appearing exotically over the walls on three sides.
Figure IV.18.

Palazzo Venier dei Leoni
(now Peggy Guggenheim Collection)
Dorsoduro 701

BIBLIO: *Giardini Veneziani*, pp.62-5; pp. 184 ff. below.

Gardened by Miss Holland and redesigned by Giorgio Bellavitis in 1983, completed in 1995.
See Figures IX 14, 15 & 17.

Palazzo Venier delle Torreselle
Fondamenta San Vio, Dorsoduro 737

BIBLIO: Bassi, pp.356-6.

The site dates to the 14th century; it once had a long garden stretching to Sant'Agnese. The palace, now destroyed, shows as vacant space on the Combatti map; a modern building and garden space are visible from the Fondamenta.

Palazzo Basadonna
San Trovaso, Rio di San Trovaso, Dorsoduro 1012

BIBLIO: Bassi, pp.354-5.

A 17th-century garden, done over, possibly by Jappelli (or in his style), in the 19th century with hillocks and wandering paths (Jappelli was probably apprenticed in Selva's office). Bassi recorded it in poor shape, though earmarked for restoration, which a plaque now says was accomplished in 2005. Its being part of a school is not perhaps best designed to keep it in good shape: ugly litter baskets dot the space. A drawing of an archway or garden gateway that exists at the RIBA (F 6/26) may be one that marked an entrance into the garden from the Rio della Carità at the rear.
Figure IV.19

IV.18 Rear of the Palazzo Dario.

82

IV.19 Rear garden of the Palazzo Basadonna, San Trovaso.

Palazzo Contarini degli Scrigni
Fondamenta Sangiantoffetti, Dorsoduro 1057

Composed of two buildings on the side of the Rio di San Trovaso, a later portion by Scamozzi; the former enjoyed a small garden with an engaging change of level at midpoint.

Figure IV.20.

Palazzo Bellani
San Trovaso, Fondamenta Sangiantoffetti, Dorsoduro 1073

BIBLIO: Bassi, p. 510.

Visible on de'Barbari and on Combatti (Bassi, fig. 512), with gardens and *orto* stretching to the Sacca della Toletta. The *androne* and *corte* have a pavement of white and red marbles. Now a school.

Palazzo Sangiantoffetti
Dorsoduro 1075

BIBLIO: Bassi, p.507; Pool, p.34; Ridolfi, *Meraviglie dell'Arte*, p.310

Once the biggest and best kept gardens in the city – the area signalled as one huge green space on maps; this was the main target of the municipality's take-over in 1970s for a *sestiere* park (see p.188f.); its "boundaries intact" but the whole now "wild", according to Pool, the palace itself part of the University. Tintoretto painted its façade with Ovidian fables.

Palazzo Priuli-Bon-Clary
(formerly French Consulate)
San Trovaso, Dorsoduro 1397

BIBIO: Martinioni; Cunico, pp.13-4, 17, 21-2; Albrizzi/Pool, pp.25-6; see also Visentini, *Orto Botanico*, pp.15, 21, 106, 110 etc

Palazzo Priuli-Bon-Clary (its present name) rises on the site of the famous garden of the botanist Pier Antonio Michiel; we know nothing of its layout, but various testimony acknowledges the rich compendium of plants contained there – Sansovino also reported a "beautiful fountain spouting sweet water"; the curator of the Orto Botanico at Padua, Luigi Anguillara, in

IV.20 Garden of Palazzo Contarini degli Scrigni.

his 1561 *Pareri de' semplici* noted its "vaghissimo giardino", and Bauhin and Cherler's *Historia Plantarum Universalis* (1651) cited it for the rarity of its plants. Presumably some of the depictions of plants in Michiel's herbal (discussed above pp. 54 ff.) were taken from specimens there, so we might speculate whether the few images in the herbal of garden layouts and architecture might not also record some features of this lost site. At present the rear of the palace has a courtyard garden giving onto the rio, as do several other palaces that front the Zattere with gardens on the rear like this.

Figure IV.21.

Cà Zenobio
(Armenian College)
Fondamenta del Soccorso Dorsoduro 2597

BIBLIO : Damerini, photograph of a picturesque meandering path, facing p.72; Fontana 1967; Bassi, p.348; Albrizzi/Pool, pp.39, 138-41; Cunico, pp.92-5 ; *Giardini Veneziani*, pp.46-9; pp. 129–131 below.

The Zenobio family remodelled a 14th-century palace at the start of the 18th century at which time (1703) Carlevarijs engraved its rear façade and garden showing an elaborately worked *broderie* parterre; walls down either side, pots of citrus bushes along them, with an ornate iron grille between *corte* and garden (later moved backwards into the courtyard space, as now); currently only the sites of a pair of wellheads survive. In 1767 Temanza designed a casino modelled on that in the nearby garden library of Foscarini at the Carmini (q.v.), with another courtyard behind it giving onto the Rio di San Barnaba where it takes a right-angle bend. Under new owners after 1840, probably, the parterres were removed and a romantic

IV.21 Rear view of the Palazzo Priuli-Bon-Clary.

garden installed with mounds (incorporating an ice-house?) linked by an iron bridge (Cunico thinks once in Chinese taste) over a small "valley" between them. Some remains of possibly 18th-century statuary and a greenhouse.

See Figures VI. 13,18-21.

Cà Rezzonico
(Museo del Settecento), Dorsoduro 3136

BIBLIO: Bassi, p.114 with no mention of garden; *Giardini Veneziani*, pp.54-9.

The area behind the museum has been redesigned by Giorgio Bellavitis, making an entry courtyard and then a garden. In this last he gestures to the museum's 18th-century focus by lining the far wall with bas-reliefs, inscriptions, busts and other antique pieces, a practice known in much earlier gardens and courtyards. There is now a small area for kids to play, a pergola down one side with benches in its shade, and the central area is set out in a pattern of box-hedges that mimic

the Istrian stone patterns of the entry courtyard. The garden honours its Venetian site, without allowing any pastiche.

Figure IV.22.

Palazzo Nani Bernardo Lucheschi
at San Barnaba, Dorsoduro 3197-8

BIBLIO: Cunico, pp.90-1.

A 19th-century creation (1840s) after demolition of some buildings, with magnificent wisteria spanning entry into garden from pergola and palms from the very early 20th century. A well head survives from the earlier complex.

Figure IV.23.

IV.22 Garden of the Cà Rezzonico, redesigned by Giorgio Bellavitis.

Palazzo Giustinian, now Brandolini d'Adda at San Barnaba, Dorsoduro 3228

BIBLIO: Albrizzi/Pool, p.24; Cunico, pp.89-90; *Giardini Veneziani*, pp.14-9.

Twin palaces constructed at the end of the 15th century fronting the Grand Canal, with two symmetrical courtyards at rear. Now one garden with a pair of prisoner statues marking steps up into raised garden from courtyard. End of garden remodelled in the early 20th century into a heart-shaped box form. Chiappini di Sorio (in Albrizzi/Pool) says the 15th-century garden has survived the palace's modernization; but the garden shows evidence of the impact of Russell Page who designed the family's park on the mainland and may have influenced this one too; its dominant and elaborate boxwood parterres certainly betray his influence.

Figure IV.24.

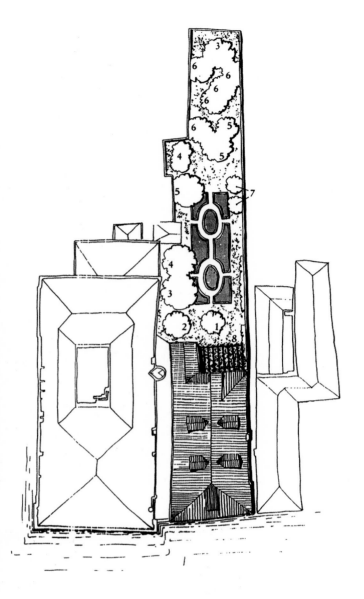

IV.23 Plan of the garden at Palazzo Nai.

IV.24 Palazzo Giustinian, now Brandolini d'Adda, at San Barnaba.

Palazzi Foscarini and Vendramin
at the Carmini, Dorsoduro 3463 & 3464 (Foscarini) and 3462 (Vendramin)

BIBLIO: de Régnier, pp.158-170; Damerini 1931 photograph facing, p.70; Bassi, p.342; Cunico, p.37; *Giardini Veneziani*, pp.38-41.

The most important of several Foscarini properties in the city, this site holds interest over many periods. Praised in the 18th century for an extensive garden "fornito di molte anticaglie" (antiquities), rare plants and the site of many *feste*. A library-casino was built at the end of the garden during the 18th century to house the collection of Marco Foscarini; this still exists, though separated from the garden by recent parcelling of the site. The extensive grounds have also been divided: near the buildings are separate garden units and at the far end modern housing apartments. Yet the main area is open across the whole site, accessed from the rear of Vendramin (now belonging to the University), scattered with a few rather forlorn 18th-century statues; there are some youngish cypresses trees, and some signs of respect for this wonderfully huge space and of modest gardening (vases, pergolas, etc.). Probably now in a better state of preservation than when Henri de Régnier lodged in the palaces and found the garden very ruined. Perhaps the most intriguing aspect of the garden was that, according to older inhabitants who talked to Bassi (p.342), in the early 20th century it was thrown open to neighbouring gardens to create a huge public, communal space, with stables and horse-riding.

Figure IV. 25 & 26.

Modern office building, now housing part of the University, known as Cà Foscari University
Dorsoduro 3449

BIBLIO: p.182 below.

Along the Rio di Santa Margherita, within a modern complex of office buildings is a garden courtyard, visible both from the side (Calle Nuova) and through the main glass doors of the University building along the Fondamenta Malcanton.

See Figure IX.13.

IV.25 The Foscarini Library-Casino across the gardens of the Palazzo Vendramin.

IV.26 Looking through the *androne* of Palazzo Foscarini ai Carmini.

SAN MARCO

San Marco is a densely packed urban area with few opportunities then or now for gardens. The original, important and large *broglio* near Saint Mark's see Figure II.15 and p. 31 was built over very early.

Giardini Reali (Royal Gardens)
San Marco

BIBLIO: *Giardini Veneziani,* pp.96-101; pp. 153 ff. below.

See Figures VII.19-23.

Palazzo Corner della Cà Grande
(now the Prefecture)
San Maurizio, San Marco 2662

BIBLIO: Bassi, p.88; *Architectural Review* (Venice issue), p.292.

The courtyard by Sansovino (still existing) has a labyrinth traced in pink stone where the family members used to play. A *squero* (boathouse) to its left was later transformed into a garden on the Grand Canal.

Palazzo Ponte (later Giustinian)
Calle del Dose, San Marco 2745

BIBLIO: Bassi, p.252.

After a fire in 1801, the site was reworked by Selva who added a "giardino pensile" overlooking an existing courtyard.

Palazzo Cappello Malipiero
Campo San Samuele, San Marco 3198/3201

BIBLIO: G.Damerini, *La Ca' Grande dei Cappello e dei Malipiero ora Barnabò* (Castelfranco Veneto, 1962), pp.93, 184, 197, 202; Bassi, p.110; Cunico, pp.137-9; Albrizzi/Pool, p.42; *Giardini Veneziani,* pp.42-7.

The present garden space to the right of the canal façade was created before 1631 when the owners acquired that land, demolished the buildings on it and made a garden. This is unusually aligned at right-angles to the palace, with a courtyard linking the two. The present garden, with its Neptune in a niche on the garden wall facing the palace and 18th-century statues of the four seasons by Antonio Bonazza, dates from 1890 when the palace was restored. Originally walled off (as shown in Moretti's view), it now boasts railings open to the Canal.

Figure IV.27.

Palazzo Mocenigo
Calle Mocenigo, near San Samuele, San Marco 3348

BIBLIO: Pool, pp.112-7; Howells, p.124.

Byron lodged here in the late 1810s, but its importance in garden history dates from earlier, when the courtyard was frescoed with Roman figures, as celebrated by Marco Boschini, *La carta del navegar pitoresco,* 1660. The modern garden dates from the 1930s.

IV.27 The gardens of the Palazzo Cappello Malipiero. The niche with Neptune is in the rear of the garden on the right.

SAN POLO

It is possible to spot a variety of open spaces, apparently gardens, in the *sestiere* today: at the junction of Rio de San Giacomo and the Rio de Sant'Agostin (no.2297); another at the juncture of Rio di San Polo and Rio di Sant'Antonio (no.2188, marked on current maps as commercial space but clearly now a garden). Cunico lists others, pp.162-4.

Palazzo Papadopoli
San Polo 1364-5

BIBLIO: Bassi, p.140; *Architectural Review* (Venice issue), p.292; Cunico, p.163.

One garden is on the Grand Canal, created by the Papadopoli in 1874–75 in an area to the left of the palace after the demolition of small adjacent house. Another considerable open space, grassed, with a well head and trees, is at the rear of the palace. A drawing for a garden loggia attributed to Scamozzi is in the RIBA F6/59. Figure IV.28.

Palazzo Albrizzi
San Polo 1940

BIBLIO: Hopkinson Smith; Bassi, p.325; Cunico, p.36; Albrizi/Pool, pp.41-2 & 189-95.

The Albrizzi came to Venice and bought property in the 17th century, including land on the other side of the rear canal, which is where the garden was eventually formed. Until 1810 that site was occupied by the Teatro Nuovo di San Cassiano, owned by the Trons, with an adjacent casino that still survives, though now within its own walled enclosure to the northeast of what is now the garden (and no longer part of it). Once the theatre was destroyed, a fruit and vegetable plot occupied the site, and then in 1820 a garden, joined to the palace's *piano nobile* by an iron bridge, still existing Figure IV.29; on the garden side of the canal the bridge meets a gothic brick tower down which stairs lead into the garden. Its space is made more intricate by an irregular layout, following Hirschfeld's advice never to let the whole be visible at first sight. This idea presumably derives from an Italian follower of Hirschfeld, the independent garden theorist Pindemonte, who was a frequenter of an Albrizzi salon. The garden (says Pool) is typical of a Venetian craze for irregular, romantic gardens in the first half of the 19th century. There is an iron pergola ending in a circular, open pavilion, all covered with ivy, a small streamlet descending through two rustic basins, and some extravagant planting, augmented in 1985 by Bruce Kelly when the ruined garden was redesigned. The level of the garden furthest from the canal rises appreciably into a small hillock, being the location of the stage of the former theatre see Figure VIII.22. During the Second World War the family kept a cow and a pig in the garden. During the summer it is filled with bird song.

Palazzo Contarini
[San Polo 2093]

BIBLIO: Bassi, pp.484-5; Cunico, p.163.

Destroyed before 1840, but foundation walls remain. After use as an open-air cinema during the First World War, a garden with an open pergola/conservatory has been built on it.
Figure IV.30.

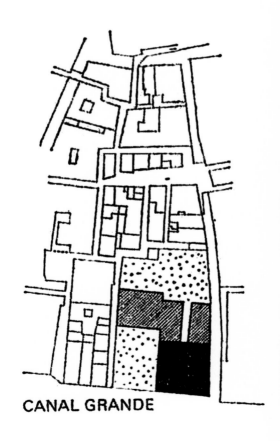

IV.28 Diagram of the gardens (dotted) at the Palazzo Papadopoli.

CANAL GRANDE

IV.29 The bridge into the Albrizzi garden.

IV.30 Palazzo Contarini seen from the Ponte San Polo.

IV.31 Plan showing the encroachment of buildings on the grounds of the Palazzo Zane.

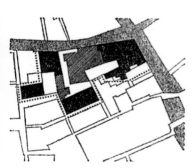

Palazzo Zane
(now a school)
San Stin, Rio de Sant'Agostin, San Polo 2360

BIBLIO: Bassi 1961; Bassi, pp.317-21; Cunico, p.162; *Architectural Review* (Venice issue), pp.291-2; Ruffo.

The site, dating from the 14th century, and is recognizable in de' Barbari's view, but was remodelled in the 17th century. The long, interior garden beside the Rio Marin is subsequently shown in a plan by Gaspari (Museo Correr). The casino (from 1695-6) and adjacent library, both remodelled early in the next century, were illustrated by Carlevarijs in 1703 see Figure VI.21; a Gaspari drawing shows a statue of Flora facing the garden. Both Gaspari and Carlevarijs make clear how the character and scope of garden façades were of importance at this date (Bassi, p.161). The whole site is now largely filled with school buildings, though a few relics of the library remain; the absorption of the site by buildings is diagrammed by Bellavitis in the *Architectural Review* article. Figure IV.31

Palazzo Molin

San Polo 2514.

BIBLIO: Cunico, p.162.

Old maps show a small temple at the end of the garden, and this is still there, languishing at the end of an overgrown garden in what is now an office of the Regional Health Authority.

Figure IV.32.

IV.32 Garden temple in the garden of the Palazzo Molin.

GIUDECCA

The Giudecca once boasted many more gardens and orchards (a Calle degli Orti still exists) than have survived or whose locations can with certainty be identified (as with the last listed below); see Basaldella, pp.33-7 for a brief survey. Many of their spaces were taken over by industry and modern boatyards, and even later in the early and late 20th century by new housing; throughout some of these new estates gardens and small parks have been established. A community park on the side of the lagoon also exists behind the gardens of the Redentore friars. De' Barbari's view, however, shows what some of them were like – the curved pergola and *claires-voies* of the Palazzo Trevisan, for example, now an industrial site (see Basaldella, pp.99-110). It was on the Giudecca that the printer and publisher Francesco Marcolini had his garden (see Cunico, p.23), which is the setting of Pietro Aretino's *Ragionamento delle Corti*; in Marcolini's *Il Giardino dei Pensieri* (1540) he asks where else he could find "ombra cosi densa e fresca, dei fiori cosi profumati? Dove altro puoi ascoltare i canti di innumerevoli uccelli, che con la loro musica petrarchesca ristorano l'anima" (such deep and fresh shade, such fragrant flowers? Where else can one listen to the songs of innumerable birds, whose petrarchan music uplifts the spirit...?). For other Giudecca gardens see Chapter Six, both for the drawings that survive of a "ridotto privato e giardino" in the Palazzo Sagredo and for the itemized inventory of the Casino delle Delizie of Marc Antonio Giustinian at its sale to Gerolamo Corner in 1745/6 (see Pool, p.38, citing Correr MS P.D.C2502/11).

San Giorgio Maggiore

BIBLIO: Toursaint de Limojon, *La ville et republique de Venise* (Paris, 1680), Albrizzi/Pool, pp.53-7.

Though not technically part of the Giudecca, the gardens on the adjacent island of San Giorgio Maggiore have been among the most visible gardens in the city (for some visitors, the only visible and visitable gardens). Alexandre Toursaint de Limojon, the Sieur de Saint-Didier, spoke for many when he cited its gardens as "la plus charmante promenade de Venise ... environné de terrasses revêtues en formes de ramparts" (p.65). Now with two cloisters, the first by Palladio redesigned after 18th-century patterns, and a modern open-air theatre with white marble seating interspersed with planting.

See Figure III.10.

Palazzo Dandolo-Nani
Fondamenta San Giovanni, Giudecca 10

BIBLIO: Zorzi, pp.302-3; Bassi, p.514; Basaldella, pp.63-6; Albrizzi/Pool, pp.27-8.

Partly demolished in later 18th century, it was cleared in the 19th century, the only surviving feature being the doorway numbered 10 that is now a land entrance to the Hotel Cipriani, which has its own newly laid out grounds (Albrizzi/Pool, pp.65-8; *Giardini Veneziani*, pp.132-7). De' Barbari shows the site before its development. From 1755 is a painting by the Longhi school (*Convito in Casa Nani*, reproduced Basaldella, fig. 37) showing a banquet for the Duke of Bavaria in a loggia overlooking the gardens. It was the seat of the 15th-century Accademia di Filosofia and the 17th-century Accademia dei Filateti.

See Figure VI.15.

Palazzo Mocenigo
Fondamenta San Giovanni [Giudecca 20-21]

BIBLIO: Bassi, p.524; Albrizzi/Pool, pp.28-9; Basaldella, pp.70-3.

Barbari shows it beside an open bridge see Figure III.1 before it was extensively enlarged as a summer retreat for Doge Alvise I Mocenigo and his wife, an accomplished botanist to whom Michiel dedicated his five-volume herbal (q.v.). Mocenigo's will (quoted Basaldella) both notes that he purchased the property expressly for his wife and that he lays down careful instructions for it continuing in his family. Already industrialized by 1846, it contained a warehouse in 1910 (photo of its courtyard in Basaldella, fig. 423). After 1976 it was turned into a condominium.

Casa Frollo
Fondamenta delle Zitelle, Giudecca 50

BIBLIO: Basaldella 1991, p.74 (1931 showing rear of building).

Originally a 17th-century palace, but a pensione at beginning of 20th century. Recently (late 2007) undergoing restoration, but with glimpses of courtyard, portico leading to a garden space and then a large iron gateway beyond.

Garden of Eden
Fondamenta al Rio de la Croce, Giudecca 138

BIBLIO: Eden; de Régnier, pp.192-6; Damerini 1931, photographs between pp.90 & 91; Rhodes, pp.103-4; Basaldella, pp.33-52; Rainer Maria Rilke, *Selected Letters 1902–1926* (London, 1988), pp.303-4; Albrizzi/Pool, p.44; Cunico, pp.98-102; John Hall, "The Garden of Eden in Venice", *Hortus* 17/3 (2003), pp.62-75; Basaldella 1991, p.114 (1922 painting of statues and pergolas by M. Corradini); Charles Quest-Ritson, *The English Garden Abroad* (London, 1992) pp. 93–96; pp.168–172 below.

Damerini thinks (mistakenly) that this was the site of the extraordinary garden of Sante Cattaneo (q.v.). Orchards, with a casino belonging to Caterina Sagredo Barbarigo, in the 18th century, were the site of festivities and horse-riding. In the 19th century the site was leased to a market gardener, until in 1884 the property, comprising orchards and a *brolo*, was bought by Frederic Eden (his actual name was Hyden). It was much visited and reported, and in 1906 hosted a gathering to celebrate the work of John Ruskin (see John Dixon Hunt, *The Wider Sea* [1982], p.413). In 1928 it became the property of Princess Aspasia of Greece. Ravaged by the 1966 flood, it was rented to Elizabeth Gardner who restored its "Moorish" kiosk in the very heart of overgrown vegetation. From 1979 it was owned by the Austrian painter Hundertwasser (and subsequently by his Foundation), under whom the gardens have by all accounts deteriorated. Access is denied. Glimpses of this important garden may be had from the Fondamenta. See Figures VIII. 17-21.

Palazzo Cornaro
Fondamenta al Rio della Croce
Giudecca 140 (Cà del Leone) and 149 (Casino Cornaro, former hospital).

BIBLIO: Cunico, pp.96-7 & fig. 3 (pergola); Basaldella, pp.73-97 (with photographs of Hospital and the gardens of the Casa del Leone); Basaldella 1991, p.75 (photo of 1936).

Now two properties, both with handsome gardens, but once a single and large holding of the famous Cornaro family, containing orchards and gardens, with impressive botanical collections, and a casino; Aretino was a guest there in 1549, as were other famous figures like Pietro Bembo. Both properties have their land entrances opposite that of the Eden garden.

An inventory of plants from 1745 survives in the Correr (MSS.P.D.2502); see Chapter Six. About 1900 the property was divided, one part (n.149) becoming Lady

IV.33 Aerial view of the Giudecca, showing the Eden Garden (top), and the gardens of the Cà del Leone and the Casino Cornaro.

Layard's Ospedale Internazionale o Cosmopolitano, after the First World War renamed the English and American Hospital, and the other (no.140), the Cà del Leone: both can be seen in the aerial photograph Figure IV.33. The former, the larger segment, was bought by Princess Aspasia, who also had the Eden garden (q.v.) on the other side of the rio, and this was later redesigned by Giorgio Bellavitis.

Villa Heriott
Calle Michelangelo, Giudecca 54/N

BIBLIO: Damerini 1931, photographs between pp.98 & 99 and between pp.100 & 101 showing it densely planted and well maintained; Basaldella, pp.36-7.

Originally the property of a German, Herion. Since 1914 a villa belonging to an Englishman Whittaker, then a factory and warehouse; finally in 1926 sold to a Frenchman Heriott. A school from 1947, still in part of its grounds, with other academic institutions. Extensive grounds exist overlooking the lagoon.

Accademia dei Nobili
[Giudecca 607-8]

A 16th-century *palazzo* where sons of poorer families were schooled, giving its name to the adjacent Calle Lunga dell'Accademia dei Nobili. To its rear and to the right is still quite an extensive space containing gardens alongside the Calle del Pistor with many bricked-up *claires-voies*.

Casino on Rio di Sant'Eufemia alla Giudecca
Giudecca 683

BIBLIO: Cunico, fig 25; Basaldella 1991, pp.126-7.

Invisible behind high walls, the garden sporting dense shrubbery and tall cypresses.

Palace of Alvise Grimani

No longer extant or its exact location even known, except that it was adjacent to the Vendramin property. Included here for the surviving 16th-century sketch plan in the State Archives.

Figure IV.34.

Palazzo Vendramin
Fondamenta San Biagio, [Giudecca 797-800]

BIBLIO: Zorzi , pp.305-6; Bassi, p.520; Rosella Mamoli Zorzi, *Letterre del palazzo Barbaro* (Milano, 1989); Basaldella, pp.117-123; Cunico, pp.29-30.

Largely destroyed in 1882 to make way for the industrial complex of Stucky and Fortuny factories and a beer manufactory, to which *magazzini* it gave its name. It had been a huge and immensely famous garden and is still shown as such on the Combatti map. The garden was finally wholly lost to construction work in 1970s, but it had contained several buildings, including a Rotunda, traditionally attributed to Palladio, destroyed in the early 19th century that still gives its name to the Rio della Rotunda and a Fondamenta della Rotunda; a drawing for/of another, Tuscan temple in the grounds is held at the RIBA (F 6/61; reproduced Basaldella, fig. 84). There are many references in Sanudo's diaries to *feste* held there by the Campanie della Calza: June 1512, September 1513, May 1533.

House of Sante Cattaneo
[near Convertite Monastery on Giudecca, Fondamenta de le Convertite]

BIBLIO: Martinioni; F.Mutinelli, *Annali Urbani di Venezia*, 1871, pp.564-5; Cartwright, pp.109-10; Damerini; Albrizzi/Pool, pp.34-5; Cunico, p.98.

Garden no longer exists, though Damerini thought it was where the Eden garden is. Wherever, it was described by Stringa in 1604 as having a courtyard with grottoes and fountains using pumice stone and Murano glass (Chiappini di Sorio in Pool suggests influence of Pratolino, but the mannerist vocabulary, though unusual in Venice, is not particularly reminiscent of the Medici property). Cartwright says the "stately columns and marble hall" were "after the style represented in Bonifazio's well-known painting of *L'Epulone*". A colonnade led to the courtyard that gave onto a large, lengthy garden, apparently with extensive trees, and ended in some loggia, decorated with painted landscapes, overlooking the lagoon. Bought in 1671 by Cardinal Giovanni Dolfin – the deed of sale survives in Correr Museum (P.D. C.2500/X).

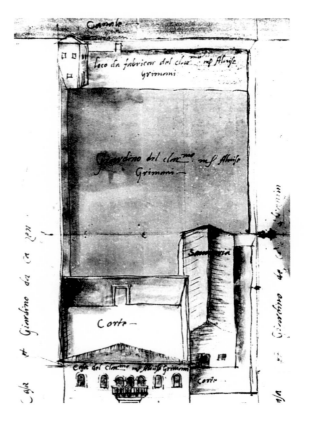

IV.34 Plan of Alvise Grimani's house and grounds on the Giudecca, 16th century.

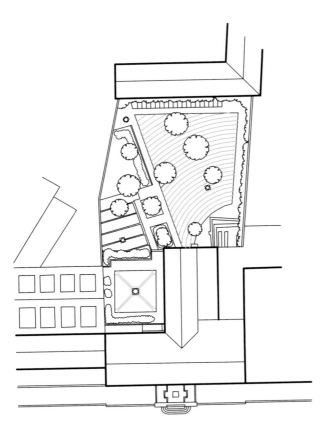

Canale di San Donato

IV.35 Plan of the modern reworking of the courtyard and gardens of the Palazzo Giustiniani, Murano, now the glass museum.

IV.36 The Mocenigo Casino, Murano, after restoration, seen from the water.

MURANO

The island of Murano, a short but significant distance away from the busy city was the site, at an early date, of both pleasure and productive gardens, often combined: for notes on these, see Zanetti, pp.176-8 and 278-87, and his 1880 supplement, p.95. Today it is largely focused upon the famous Venetian glass manufactory, but curious visitors may still wander further afield and discover hints of the old, pastoral and agricultural island.

Palazzo Giustiniani
Fondamenta Giustinian, since 1861 the Museo Vetrario di Murano (Glass Museum)

BIBLIO: Zanetti, p.120 (and p.129 for a garden with fountain "patiently worked in glass"); *Studi Veneziani* 8 (1966), p.454, for Paolo Giustiniani; Albrizzi/Pool, pp.68-73; *Giardini Veneziani*, pp.126-31.

Rebuilt in the late 17th century on the site of a 15th-century gothic building, a courtyard with well heads, an arcade and grille-work survive, but the space has been reconfigured in modernist forms.
Figure IV.35.

Gardens of Andrea Navagero
Fondamenta Navagero

BIBLIO: Giacomo Filiasi, *Memorie storiche de' Veneti* (Venice, 1813), pp.225-6; Zanetti, p.280-2; Cartwright, pp.115-23; Cunico, pp.15-6, 23; Pastore, pp.237-51; p.106 below.

The gardens stretched from the Fondamenta to the lagoon's edge, the site now partly occupied by a public park; these and the gardens of the Palazzo Trevisan (q.v.) would have dominated this end of Murano's eastern spur. The gardens were wooded (Navagero wanted more trees planted to create "thick woods"), with pergolas and bowers, fountains and a profusion of flowers, shrubs and trees. Arguably one of the early private botanical collections, enriched by Navagero's travels. His experience of other countries (like Spain and through Spain the New World) is typical of the wide reach of Venetian botany, yet it is unlikely that its layout aped those foreign models.

Casino Mocenigo
off Fondamenta Daniel Manin

BIBLIO: Zanetti, pp.50-3; Pool, p.24.

The restored casino overlooking the water remains inside the Fabbrica Marietti, its frescoed rooms celebrating music, poetry and *amore*. Many plants were lovingly cultivated in its gardens and in 1866 cedars still remained. Figure IV.36.

Palazzo Corner
San Bernardo

BIBLIO: Zanetti, pp.283-4; Pool, p.24; Zorzi, pp.293-4.

Corner had four palaces on Murano in all, with big gardens and orchards; destroyed in the 18th century. Caterina Cornaro entertained Beatrice D'Este here in 1494. Today the area is partly occupied by the campo San Bernardo.

Palazzo Corner-Dolfin
San Pietro Martire

BIBLIO: Zanetti 1866; Cartwright (on Trifone), pp.123-4; Zorzi, p.294.

Supposedly the site of the early garden of the learned Trifone Gabriele, with *orti* and *grotto*, to which members of the Aldine Academy often came.

Palazzo Trevisan
Fondamenta Navagero 34

BIBLIO: Zanetti, pp.157-9; G.M.Urbani de Gheltof, *Il Palazzo di Camillo Trevisan a Murano* (1890); *Arte Veneta* (1968), pp.47-59; Bassi, pp.528-43 ; Visentini 1988 (2), pp.102-3.

Jacopo Sansovino had finished this palace by 1562, building it on the site of demolished courts and small houses. His son Francesco writes of "un giardino e... una fontana alla Romana di eccessiva bellezza" (*Cose notabili Venezia*, 1562), referring to hydraulic water effects new to Venice (hence "alla Romana"). These were in the loggia that divided the large garden into two; the loggia has been attributed to Palladio: the garden façade of the loggia was frescoed (see Bassi, fig. 754) and inside were tufa niches, figures and *giochi d'acqua*. By the early 18th century these were not properly working (the cistern uncared for), but in 1712 the figures of Venus and Adonis still existed in the garden, though soon afterwards the garden was

given over to vines and vegetables. Matters were worse by the 19th century; in 1848–49 it was used as a barracks and soldiers practised shooting at the statues. Derelict by the time Urbani de Gheltof was writing. The site is now given over to industrial glassworks. A huge literature exists on this very famous palace and garden, attributed variously to Palladio or Daniele Barbaro or both.

Palazzo Benzon-Manin
Riva Lunga

BIBLIO: Paoletti, p.158; Zanetti, pp. 120 & 284; Zorzi, p.445.

Destroyed in 1866, this had a "deliziosissimo giardino" as late as 1837 (Paoletti). Zanetti notes a document written by Benzon instructing his gardner, who (as did others) lived adjacent to the *orti* that he cultivated. One of several sites that Zanetti lists as "in parte sussistenti e in parte demoliti" (1880 supplement, p.81).

Palazzo of Bernardo Giustinian
San Matteo

BIBLIO: Zanetti, pp.65 & 90-91; Zorzi, p.296.

Only the house remained after its garden went in 1819. Bernardo Giustinian asking in his will that the garden be maintained is quoted by Zanetti and Zorzi.

Palazzo Soranzo
Fondamenta Colleoni

BIBLIO: Zanetti, pp.63-64 & 65.

It once possessed two gardens, the second a big one, "con bellissima e vasta ortaglia ch'era l'antico giardino", implying that an earlier "garden" had been transformed into a more practical growing area.

Palazzo Priuli

BIBLIO: Castaldi; F. Mutinelli, *Annali urbani di Venezia* (1838); Zanetti, p.280; *Diario di Murano di Francesco Luna 1625– 1631*, ed. Vincenzo Zanetti (Venice, 1873), p.60.

At end of the 15th century the Priuli family owned property that was called hyperbolically a "terrestrial paradise... a place of nymphs and demigods" by Andrea Calmo (quoted by Zanetti); it was highly elaborated with sculpture, fountains, groves (described as "woods and forests"), an aviary with rare birds, and fruit and flowers.

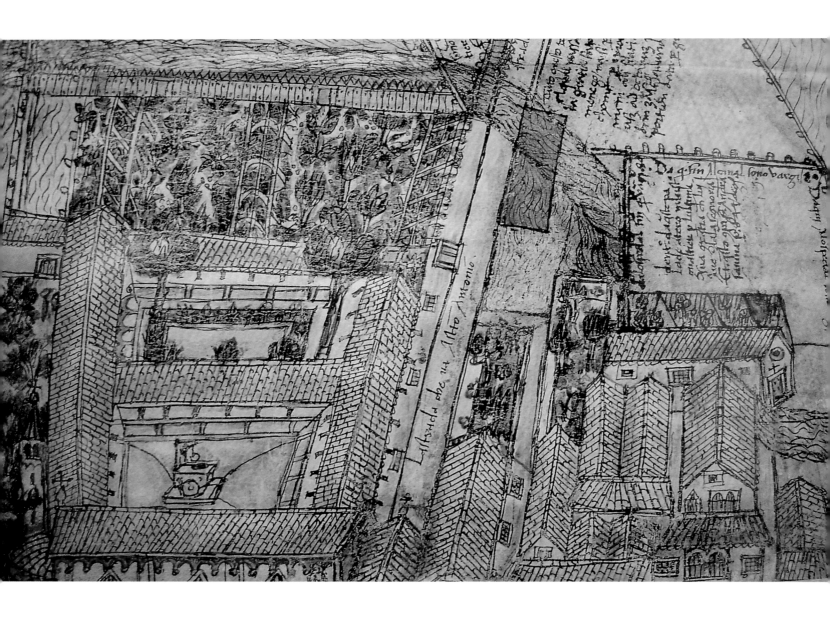

V.I View of churches and convents at San Domenico di Castello, showing the sequence of courtyard, cloister and garden with pergola. A 15th-century drawing on parchment.

Giardini minori

Ground, you may imagine, in their watery situation is
the thing that they must most want; so they seldom lose an inch of it.

Joseph Spence

Chapter Five

The gardens opened most conspicuously to our view by de' Barbari's map and Sansovino's list are those of the well-to-do. Yet the former's hints of small enclosures also alert us to the presence of much more modest plots that nonetheless contributed to the overall idea and conspectus of city gardens and open spaces. In Wladimiro Dorigo's detailed surveys of territorial holdings before and after 1300 there are innumerable references to all sorts of open ground, variously annotated in the archives as "vineam" or "vigna", "horto", "orto sive terra vacua" – indeed many refer to "terra vacua" – "pecia[m] di terra"(parcels of ground), and occasionally to a domicile "cum suo orto"[1]; a collection, in other words, of plots of ground established and valued enough to be classified in different kinds of documents, but not always assigned to a specific use. An archival drawing of the land along the Rio della Sensa Figure V.2 indicates a whole line of five differently sized orchards, typical of plots that are part of this larger urban situation. Similarly, although Egle Trincanato's book on *Venezia minore* focuses essentially upon smaller building complexes, her sketches and ground plans often reveal the continuing existence of areas where trees and bushes still grow[2]. And as her book so persuasively maintains, while this

"lesser" Venice does not relate to the picture postcard city or that of the international tourist, it is nonetheless essential for the fullest understanding of it[3]. It is these "giardini minori" that we must briefly study, not for their specific contents so much as for their role in the culture of Venetian gardens. For often they were a major element in the scientific life of the city: John Evelyn was impressed by the number of pharmaceutical shops he saw[4], and this trade for which the city was indeed renowned was supplied both by local gardens and by an extensive foreign commerce in medicinal plants. There were also productive or market gardens and orchards throughout the city and the islands, while within monastic institutions (many of which, too, were scattered among the lagoon islands) there existed a variety of productive and pleasure grounds. Marc Antonio Sabellico walks the reader of his book, *Del sito di Venezia città*, first published in 1502, through the different *sestieri*, noting reclaimed land, green spaces including an "erboso campo" (grassy meadow) near San Francesco della Vigna, and everywhere orchards: in the Cannaregio, "lieti orti" (pleasant orchards) near Santa Chiara and Sant' Andrea, and monasteries on the Giudecca with "mirabile amenità di orti" (marvellous amenity of orchards)[5].

V.2 Archival drawing of small orchards along Rio della Sensa.

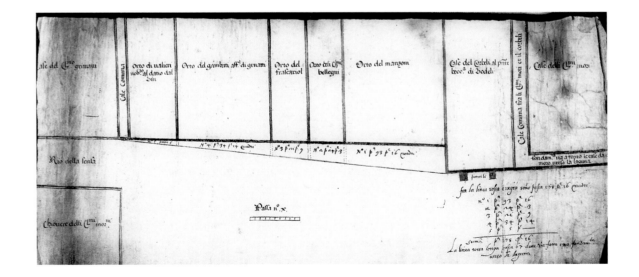

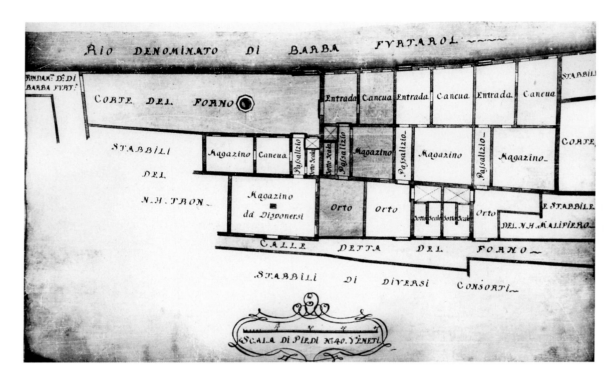

V.3 Mainly commercial buildings and two small *orti* along the Rio Terà di Barba Fruttarol, 18th century.

The Venetian archives, that rich depository of an exigent and long-lived bureaucracy, reveal how much the small open space was an intricate element in the overall urban fabric and well regarded even under threat. An anonymous drawing of the properties of Santi Domenico, Antonio and Servolo in the 15th century is a wonderful conspectus of different open spaces, mostly green: a cloister with its well, probably paved, then another cloister with a border of herbs, an orchard with a rounded pergola leading across it; smaller areas of garden plots appear in the other sites Figure V.I. A plan of a house at Santa Ternita in 1764, drawn up in connection with the division of property, notes what "remains" of an "orto" along with its owner's name[6]. Another contemporary document mapping houses along the Rio Terà Barba Fruttarol shows three small *orti* surviving amidst the proliferating commercial properties Figure V.3, while along the Rio di San Daniele, after the suppression of the eponymous monastery, a plan shows a "typical house and *orticello*", in the corner of which is located the oven Figure V.4. Church and monastery properties were clearly larger, in size of overall holdings and usually composed of at least one specific parcel.

Thus on the Giudecca the property of the monastery and church of San Giacomo extended all the way from the Fondamenta to the lagoon, and the plan marks the gardener's house ("casa Ortolani") at the water's edge Figure V.5. In the 17th century a rough sketch of a small area along what was the Rio delle Turchette in the Dorsoduro marks two garden areas, one of which, formerly a private property, is "newly attached to the Monastery of the Eremite"[7].

It is this very mix and distribution of open spaces within the city that gives significance to these "lesser" gardens. The uses to which these "gardens" were put, however, are more difficult to determine. The property of one Francesco Testa in 1589 labels a huge, coloured area, otherwise undifferentiated, as his "Horto sive Vigna" (orchard or vineyard), while a late 15th-century map of San Giorgio Maggiore signals the whole island area as dotted with regularly spaced trees[8]. A similar shorthand—perhaps for orchards—occurs on a very crude map of Murano Figure V.6. A plan of San Giorgio in Alga from 1688 distinguishes five large areas marked "Horto" from others recorded as "Campo" and "Prato" Figure V.7 A more formally drawn legal document of 1794, otherwise undetailed, shows a series of

time the Milanese Pietro Casola expressed his surprise at "the many beautiful gardens which are to be seen here, especially, I must say, those belonging to the different religious orders"[44]; a canon himself, he doubtless had reason and opportunity to see some of these for himself. An engraved map of Murano from the 15th century shows the trees, pergolas and gardens on the small islands of San Michele and San Cristoforo, to which these visitors would have been referring[45].

Another map of the whole lagoon and its islands by Benedetto Bordoni was drawn up in the 1510s and published in 1538 Figure 5.14. The iconography shows clearly how many islands were occupied by various ecclesiastical or monastic communities; the map-maker's graphic shorthand also implies that most of these communities possessed orchards or gardens. The same is true of a rather charming drawing from 1755 in the State Archives which depicts some, maybe merely generic, island as densely tree-d Figure V.15. A century and a half after Bordoni, when Vincenzo Coronelli published his illustrated survey, *Isolario dell'Atlante Veneto* in 1696, he calculated that there were 138 islands that made up the "crown" of the Venetian lagoon[46]. All of his views depict the islands as if seen from the water with inviting canopies of trees and tall shrubs Figure V.17 & 18.

Today two islands survive as formerly: the monks on San Francesco del Deserto tend an ample vegetable garden; there is a vineyard and what might be called "parkland" for strolling and meditation down alleys lined with cypresses. Coronelli's rather awkward engraving of the same island Figure V.18 shows many shade trees, the walled vegetable garden lined with cypresses and having a system of pergolas. Old photographs Figure V.16 show a huge umbrella pine rising from the edge of the vegetable plots. It is indeed remote, but the refuge is green and hospitable. The other island that still retains its monastic role is San Lazzaro degli Armeni, also with gardens and a productive culture of fruit and vegetables, which the engraving by G.Zucchi displays as a series of neat compartments protected from the lagoon by a thick "hedge" of fruit trees Figure V.19. Old photographs here reveal a thick and extensive spread of trees Figure V. 20.

Outside Murano, Torcello, Burano and of course the Giudecca, the modern tourist has no familiarity with the islands of the lagoon, nor is more than barely aware of the role that islands have historically played. The remainder are for the most part – with one extraordinary exception, the cemetery of San Michele – abandoned, ruined and unvisited. Gone are the days when Lord Byron would frequent the Armenian island in an effort to learn the language; he was probably an exception, for the majority of visitors would have been, as was Beckford, simply rowed past under the monastery walls but never visiting the gardens

V.15 Anonymous drawing of a lagoon island with its dense plantation of trees, 1755.

V.16 View of the island of San Francesco del Deserto, c.1920, which about 200 years after Coronelli (V.17), shows the treescape that exists there to this day.

V.17 *San Giacomo di Palude*, from Coronelli, *Isolario dell'Atlante Veneto* (1696). Coronelli depicts many of the lagoon's islands, all with their different indications of orchard, grove or garden.

V.18 Coronelli's *San Francesco del Deserto* celebrates its tranquil groves and gardens.

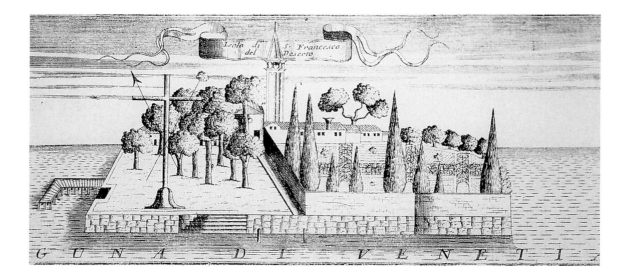

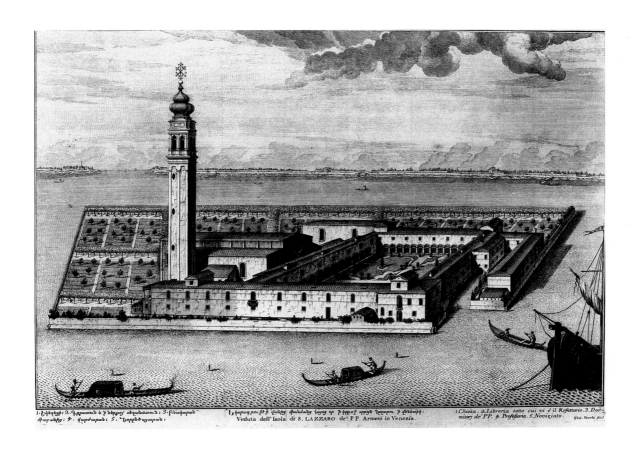

Veduta dell' Isola di S. LAZZARO de' P.P. Armeni in Venezia.

V.19 G.Zucchi, engraving of the island of San Lazzaro degli Armeni, with its plantations and denser orchards.

V.20 View of San Lazzaro degli Armeni, c.1920–1930, showing its later and denser treescape.

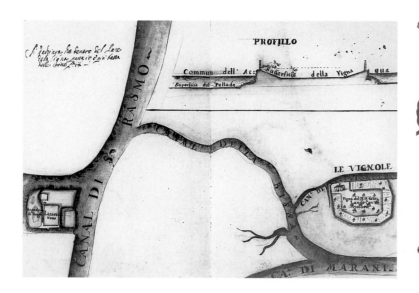

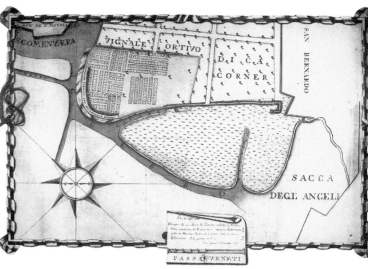

V.21 Detail of a map of the island of Le Vignole, showing in both plan and section the dyking to protect vineyards from the lagoon waters, 1691.

V.22 Archival map of a *vignale ortivo* alongside a market garden on land owned by the Monastery of San Mattia.

which he observed rising above them. A somewhat more eccentric later visitor, Frederick Rolfe, would get himself rowed through the lagoon and, landing on the deserted shoreline of some unnamed island, observe the snakes slithering through the eye sockets of skulls in the abandoned ossuary [47]. His experience there may be taken as an extreme but not implausible emblem of the fate of many islands by the end of the 19th century.

The first and major threat to their existence came when Napoleon suppressed religious institutions which had been the *raison d'être* of much island inhabitation. Abandonment and erosion then worked their own destructions, as later did the repercussions of a whole cluster of modern amenities like a proper cemetery on San Michele, civic hospitals in the city and on the mainland, and industrial production of vegetables, fruit and wine. Some islands – Mazzorbo and Poveglia in particular, but also Le Vignole which enjoyed fresh well water – continue to have fairly extensive market gardens; various documents Figure V.21 acknowledge Le Vignole's historical dedication to commercial gardening. But otherwise the tale is one of a gradual, saddening diminishment; by 1844 only 62 islands could be counted, and in 1978 an exhibition focused on just 16 abandoned islands. Yet prior to Napoleon and the subsequent erosion of abandoned sites, the islands were well attested in both writings and in engraved views. Especially useful in recalling how they boasted extensive and well-maintained gardens are Coronel-

li's engravings, along with other imagery by Antonio Visentini (1777) and Antonio Sandi after Francesco Tironi (1779), almost all of which register how these sites were well planted with trees. Occasional post-Napoleonic views, like Chevalier's, suggest less garden-scape, or at least less interest in recording it.

Vineyards and orchards abound from very early on and were frequently mapped [48]. The Benedictines on San Giorgio Maggiore enjoyed extensive land, as the Cini Foundation now occupying the island still does: a walled vineyard was established there by 1090, and olive oil was in production by the 14th century [49]. The Augustinian canons were attached to the Madonna dell'Orto, growing apple and quince trees in the eponymous orchard, as well as occupying the island of San Cristoforo where they manufactured white wax candles. An early 16th-century map shows the monks' orchard on Poveglia (A35), while another of 1530, now on the Lido edge facing Malamocco (B74), is notable for its care in distinguishing different kinds of ground and is also annotated with notes on the many trees that one segment contains. On Murano in 1777 Figure V.22 there is a large orchard (called a "vignale ortivo", so presumably a mixture of fruit trees and vines) and a considerable section laid out in beds for cultivation; this last sector is protected from erosion by what an inscription says is a "barrier formed of rubbish and mud". The property on Torcello of the monks of San Gerolamo in Venice included a "vigna

Ughi's map of 1729 offers indications in plan of several buildings erected in spaces that would be either orchards or gardens – for instance, he marks the Casino degli Spiriti at the end of the garden that Guardi painted (and is still visible from the water today Figures VI. 16 & 17, and see Figure VI.22, and the space at the Palazzo Zenobio where a *casino* would eventuelly be built Figure VI.18, both of which are examples of how reasonably large garden areas were augmented with secluded buildings that could cater to the various pleasures, intellectual, scholarly, or political, of like-minded persons who wanted to escape the mad whirl of the city's endless carnival, as well as to the private, amorous and illicit[60].

VI.16 View from the water of the garden of the Palazzo Contarini dal Zaffo and its Casino degli Spiriti, the site drawn and painted by Guardi in Figures VI.3 & 4.

VI.17 Aerial view of the garden of the Palazzo Contarini dal Zaffo. In the foreground are the grounds of the Scuola Vecchia della Misericordia.

LAYOUT OF GARDEN SPACES

One element of these 18th-century Venetian gardens poses a particular problem: the formal shapes and layouts of the ground between palace and *casino*. Sometimes these are shown as simple, rectangular or square plots of grass, sometimes elaborated in *broderie* patterns, while other seem to have opted for a reasonable compromise yet nonetheless tending towards a more conservative formula. The question, therefore, is to what extent, and why, did European fashions, albeit old-fashioned by the time of their imitation in late 18th-century Venice, get invoked in the interests of public or private garden display? Granted that we

cannot rely upon a draughtsman's topographical accuracy when it comes to indicating the existence of gardens in the city, especially when these occupy such a small area of an overall panorama, we can nevertheless be struck with the very different ways in which, by the 18th century, these gardens are graphically represented. Even the same garden is seen both in extreme simplicity and in baroque complexity.

Take, for example, the gardens behind the Palazzo Zenobio, built at the end of the 17th century and nowadays housing the Armenian brothers. One engraved view from 1703 Figure VI.19 fills the whole width of the gardens with curvilinear forms, perhaps laid out in coloured earths (gardeners who are working on

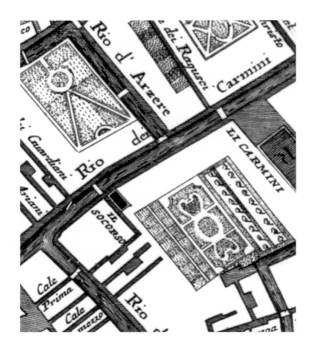

VI.18 Map by Ughi showing the Palazzo Zenobio gardens in bottom right, along with neighbouring gardens across the Rio dei Carmini, a neighbourhood that still retains several generous garden spaces.

VI.19 L.Carlevarijs, Palazzo Zenobio gardens, depicted with an extravagant and busy baroque parterre, engraving, c.1703.

them seem to be tidying the material within each arabesque), while potted plants are ranged around the edges where more gardeners are at work. A later plan of the same space Figure VI.20, probably drawn at the time the handsome *casino* by Tommaso Temanza (1705–89) was installed at the end of the main stretch of garden, shows a completely different layout: now it has four simple beds around a small central and circular pool, each quadrant taking the form of probably a grassed area, with a bush or small tree at its centre, and surrounded by beds or low hedges broken elegantly on each side to allow access to the middle. The *casino* itself, which still survives, had a back entrance from the little canal, and on the plan is labelled only as "Luogo Nobile per trattenimento" (Noble [or main] place for entertainments); the adjacent structure that faced down the orchard-like garden to the side is what is labelled "Casino for the use of the gardener". The site today Figure VI.13 (p.116 above), modified in the 19th-century with some picturesque interventions (see below, Chapter Eight), retains some of those on one side, while the other is left in neat serviceable grass squares; so it offers no clues as to how we should understand the different 18th-century layouts. Even if neither 18th-century image accurately represents what was on the ground, their very different delineations of the site make of it either a showpiece of very un-Venetian forms, seemingly inaccessible to

people who might want to walk in the gardens, or it becomes a simpler prelude to the striking portico of the *casino*, a design that, nevertheless, by breaking up the long garden into segments, makes the approach seem longer and gives more weight to the serene invitation of the pavilion.

One Zenobio image gibes with an image of Venice that is the busy, dizzy and enticing forum of festivity and luxury, self-consciously fashionable, a destination for visitors from many other nations; the other offers a private, more restrained, quieter and reticent Venice. These rival versions of how space is designed, and used, recall the debates of the second half of the 16th century between Alvise Cornaro and Cristoforo Sabbadino [61]. The former proposed elaborate parks along new city walls and an artificially naturalistic island in the Bacino, the other insisting upon the indigenous circumstances of the lagoon, its "sacrale naturalità". Now in the 18th-century garden, this debate seems to be revisited, though for different reasons: on one hand, simple forms, more organized and amplified to be sure than de' Barbari depicted in 1500, but still observing certain Venetian codes of propriety and decorum, as in the engraving of the garden in front of the *casino* and library of the Palazzo Zane Figure VI.21; on the other, a conspectus of elaborate, playful, even fanciful, parterres that invoked a world of recently fashionable European design.

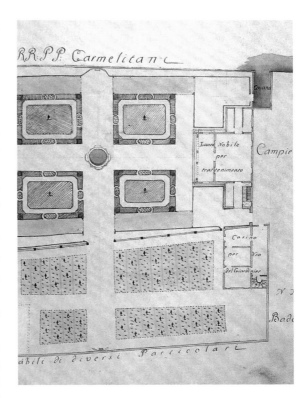

VI.20 Plan of the Palazzo Zenobio gardens after the design of its *casino*; now the gardens are shown in a much simpler format.

VI.21 Carlevarijs, *casino* and library of Palazzo Zane, engraving, c.1703. Here, too, the garden is laid out in simple, rectangular beds, interspersed with statues. Gardeners are at work.

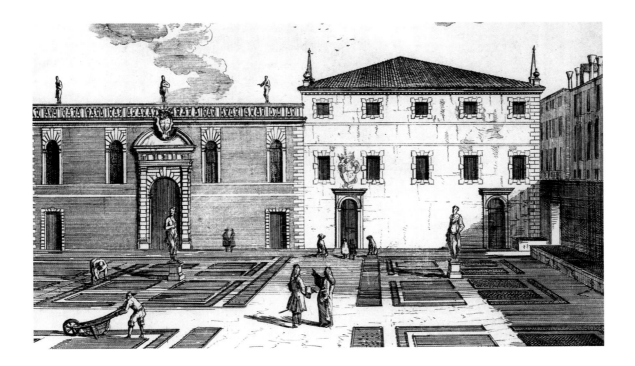

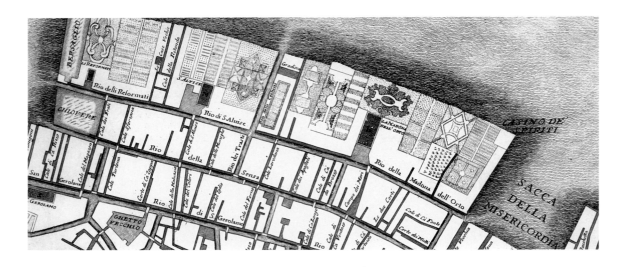

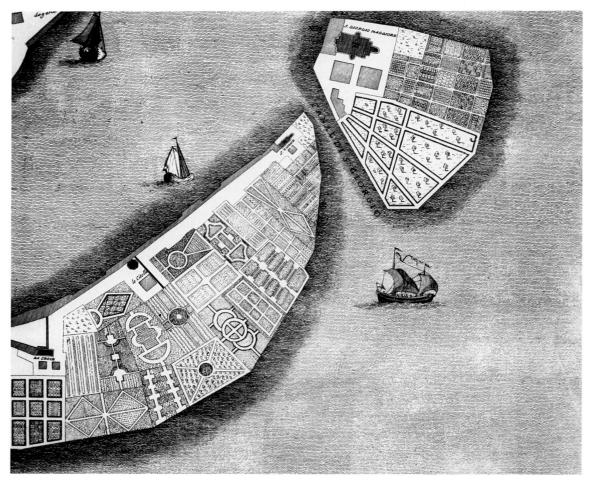

VI.22 Two details from the map by Ughi showing gardens on the Giudecca and in Cannaregio (top). Ughi generally shows the city gardens in elaborate and highly wrought patterns, that may rather be his way of indicating garden spaces than accurate records of their precise forms.

It is in this light that we might read the representation of gardens throughout the city in Ughi's 1729 map of Venice Figure VI.22 [62]. They feature exactly where one knows they would be – along the Giudecca, the northern edge of the Cannaregio, and at the western and eastern ends of the city, with virtually none indicated in the large central areas. It confirms the judgment of Giorgio Bellavitis and Giandomenico Romanelli that Ughi's map is the first to show "with great precision the relationship between buildings and open spaces" [63]. But there is something rather odd about Ughi's graphic language: almost every space that is indicated as being a garden is depicted in elaborate geometric parterres. Circles, ovals, interlocking forms, rectangles with cross-paths, trapezoidal lozenges, and some layouts that defy linguistic description – it is in fact a repertoire of pan-European designs for baroque parterres; the occasional indication of a plainer *boschetto*, quincunx or field/orchard with dotted trees alone punctures this rhythm of fanciful intervention. It seems, however, wholly implausible that all Venetian gardens would have been remade during the 17th century in this dizzy profusion of similar forms; so it seems doubtful, to say the least, that "particular attention has been reserved for gardens, documented with abundant details including their internal designs" ("Documentati con dovizia di particolari anche nel disegno interno"), as Bellavitis and Romanelli also write. Rather, what I think we have here is Ughi's reliance upon a graphic shorthand for gardens that borrows what most purchasers of his map in the 1720s and 1730s would immediately recognize as signs for gardens. Indeed, the forms he invokes would even by then be considered a touch *retardataire* elsewhere in Europe, and so a serviceable and familiar code by which to signal gardens on his map; an engraved register of map signs in the Correr suggests that the depiction of gardens did require its own shorthand [64]. Equally, the inventive manipulation of them throughout the garden spaces of the city does show off Ughi's drawing skills; at the same time it makes its appeal to those who value Venice for its theatre and festivities, along the same lines as the Murano glass table settings, or the Piranesi and Bettini gondola designs. The plainer layouts may, then, in contrast reflect the taste of conservative elements in the city who complained of luxury and vice and enforced sumptuary laws (keeping women in black, for instance) or of those like Goldoni who would stress nature, simplicity and propriety.

Perhaps, if we have taken de' Barbari's cartography as our model for descriptive accuracy in Venice, Ughi's would be annoyingly imprecise and unhelpful, beyond signalling the location of gardens. But that may not be the whole story. Careful scrutiny of the map suggests not only that the location of gardens is indeed often accurate enough but that in representing differences between adjacent sites Ughi is alert to some design changes in the city without necessarily characterizing each garden layout with precision. In the sequence of gardens along the northern edge of the Cannaregio, for instance, Ughi uses signs that would seem to distinguish between functional layouts (strips of planting beds), orchards, gardens compartmentalized in older Venetian ways as well as four or five elaborately swirled and intricate; while there is no evidence that this records layouts on the ground, it does gibe with other visual evidence of how the spaces of Venetian gardens were generally handled. Yet when Ughi depicts what is clearly the garden of Palazzo Zenobio see Figure VI.18, with a central, segment divided into three zones, each treated very "naturally", this bears no relation to either of the other layouts we have discussed above; however, he does indicate the lateral strips of garden laid out in a more utilitarian mode.

Archival evidence suggests the continuing existence of a much simpler, more conservative layout of garden spaces: along the Fondamenta Nuove, as recorded in April 1756 Figure VI.23, the garden is an elongated rectangle subdivided into four simple quadrants (of course, for bureaucratic purposes the outlined shapes may not have needed filling in). Another archival drawing (c.1750) of a Pisani palace at Sant'Andrea also shows a squared garden see Figure IV.1, with one segment cut off by the long and segmented *orto*, and here the main cultivated areas are shaded to distinguish them from the pathways and adjacent *cortile*. Again, the 1709 engraving by Vincenzo Coronelli of the garden façade of the Palazzo Soranzo on the Rio Marin is somewhat crudely drawn Figure VI.24: nonetheless, it indicates a wide central alley lined with statues that leads away from the walled courtyard immediately behind the *palazzo*; more lightly drawn in on either side of this pathway are four parterres formed in scrolls and whirls. (Ughi, incidentally, gives no indication of such a sculpture garden on his map).

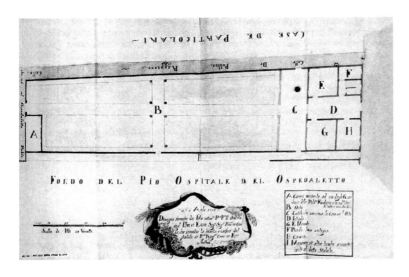

VI.23 This plan of a property on the Fondamenta Nuove suggests another fairly simple regular layout, 18th century.

Again, we may have here simply a draughtsman's shorthand for flowerbeds, a shorthand summoned either out of boredom or incapacity (in other details of the screen between courtyard and garden the image is not accurately rendered[65]); but the elaboration of the flower beds does seem more in keeping with the elaborate statuary – Roman emperors in niches along each side of the courtyard – and the classical loggia, with six pilasters and portico, that ends the garden (all of which still exist and have been restored in the early 21st century).

It is now worth returning to the exceptional views of an 18th-century Venetian garden see Figures VI.3 & 4, Guardi's images of that at the Palazzo Contarini dal Zaffo[66]. Yet, here too, I think there are some as yet unnoticed problems that perhaps suggest Guardi's manipulation (or interpretation) of the actual site. As customarily annotated[67], both Guardi views show the garden façade of the 16th-century palazzo on the right and, closing the view on the left, the Casino degli Spiriti (the tall building with upstanding chimney), famous for its gatherings of literati, artists and scholars. That means that we must be looking roughly south-eastwards across the Sacca della Misericordia (these days clogged with a marina) that is presumably unseen behind the further wall of niches, and then beyond that to a line of buildings with another tall chimney marking the end of the distant Fondamenta Nuove. There is nothing wrong with all of that except

that the garden layout has therefore been distorted in two ways: the length of the actual site from *palazzo* to *casino* has been considerably compressed and, more crucially, the rectangular parterre swivelled 90 degrees so that we now see what we'd surely observe if we were looking *down* its north/south length rather than across towards the Sacca (the proportions of the beds Guardi has drawn seem to make that clear). That Guardi may have been exploring how best to depict the garden, given the determination to view it across its width, is suggested by his unfinished drawing in the Boymans-van Beuningen Collection in Rotterdam: here the artist has drawn on two sheets joined together, which give him the required length for the garden, yet he has not filled in any of its details[68].

The painting has more clarity than the zesty, but somewhat fuzzy, preparatory drawing in the Ashmolean, and from it we can recognize a grassy area on the left, divided from the geometrical parterre by a line of bushes, an area which indeed would logically have succeeded the parterre as visitors proceeded down the gardens towards the *casino* on the lagoon edge; the painting has two figures looking into this segment. Ughi's plan see Figure VI.22 also confirms a change in handling between a squared parterre near the *palazzo* and the block of the *casino* at the far corner of the property. Furthermore, the painting also reveals what the drawing barely, if at all, discloses, namely that behind the garden wall, elegantly set with three niches containing statues on either side of its central doorway, is what appears to be a meadow; it contains another portico or tempietto whose pediment peeps over and to the right of the arched doorway in the first wall, and beside which half a dozen people appear to be at work scything grass. Guardi has again distorted the width of this meadow, allowing us thereby the better to notice that it is there. If this analysis is correct, the various elements of the property and its location have been accurately recorded, but the overall proportions and correlations have been somewhat adjusted – I can only assume – to better convey both the extent of the geometrical garden and its two adjacent grassy meadows.

What plans and mappings, and indeed Guardi's two views, do not have any chance of communicating in any detail are the actual plantings of these gardens. Yet clearly the opportunity was taken to enhance them with the usual Venetian dedication and appetite for flowers. A rental agreement for a "casino" on the Giudecca in 1709 itemizes the contents of each room, and finally "In Giardin appres a la Casa" is listed a collection of different urns, vases and pots containing various sized plants including small oranges, a "fountain" and its water spouts, and a vine of some sort trained up a tree, while also noting among missing items both a pergola and 34 plants[69]. In Paolo Clarici's book, published in Venice in 1726, on how plants may adorn gardens through the whole year, he specifically singles out "li vasi [che] in un giardino son il più bel ornamento che vi campeggi. Siano distribute nelle ajette o alzati in piramidi o disposti ad anfiteatro" (vases in a garden are the most beautiful ornament to exhibit. They may be distributed in the flowerbeds or stacked in pyramids or displayed in an amphitheatre)[70].

Another, now more extensive inventory in 1690 for the rental by Ferigo Corner of a house with garden, orchard and *casino* ("casa con Giardino, Orto, e Casino"), also on the Giudecca near Sant' Eufemia, provides a wonderfully more complete picture; it exists in both manuscript and a printed version.[71] There were three "wells", two with stone basins – one in the house, the other in the *casino*; a fountain with lead plumbing in good order, shells and divers stones that formed a grotto. While the agreement simply states that the contents of the house must be kept in good condition, it specifically sets out the items to be found in the garden, in the orchard and in the "garden at the top [or end] of the orchard": these include a four-part flower bed with roses, a feature noted as being in each of the gardens, and elsewhere many espaliered plants, fruit trees (pears, figs, pomegranate), cypress trees, along with items simply noted as "2 plants called small" or "2 Piante Verdazzi grande", and so on. The collection is both considerable and, clearly, valued sufficiently for it to be carefully, if in some cases vaguely, inventoried.

On the Giudecca again, this time in the year 1746, the gardener of Marc Antonio Giustinian, one Francesco Milliani, prepared an annotated inventory of the whole property, room by room, that was used four years later at the time of its sale to Gerolamo Cornaro[72]. One "camera detta a fiori" overlooks the courtyard and is painted with vases of flowers above the doors. There are garden storage rooms, a well in the courtyard recently renovated to increase and improve the water supply; a loggia open towards the garden lets the sun

VI.24 Coronelli, garden façade of Palazzo Soranzo, 1709. The very crude rendering nonetheless shows the alley of statues that lined the main garden axis behind the rear courtyard of the palace.

get to the plants underneath it and is decorated with statues (the busts painted bronze); a "boschetto" follows the garden, and a "balcony" of stone and iron terminates the site at the edge of the lagoon. Plants kept in the house are listed first, then exterior plants in pots (of which some measurements are given), and these are followed by lists of those in the ground (many espaliered). A further section reviews the plantings of a lawn and some sort of mount[73].

The contribution, then, of flowers to the world of private gardens was significant. Sometimes terminated by loggias or casinos, and used variously for activities that ranged from the wholly private to the conspicuously public, from learned gatherings to lewd encounters, from theatrical to floral displays, the 18th-century Venetian garden saw an extension of practices that had been hitherto sporadic. That they intrude only rarely into public discussions of Venice at this time does not lessen their significance, and indeed their continued graphic representation on city maps suggests how much the private garden was still invoked in the larger promotion of the city. This was to change. For the invention and imposition on Venice of truly public gardens by the Emperor Napoleon, which is the subject of the next chapter, had consequences across the whole urban plan and profoundly affected how the garden and related open spaces were designed, used, neglected or marginalized in the following two centuries.

Figure VII.1: In the Public Gardens, with sculptural celebrations of Italian worthies.

The invention of public gardens for the modern city

The Gardens ... made by Napoleon... are pleasant enough, and not gardens at all ...

W.D.Howells

Chapter Seven

The Republic fell in May 1797, and Venice thereafter endured a chequered existence, a pawn in the hands of European superpowers, until absorbed finally into the Kingdom of Italy in 1866. In that interim, it was conquered, bartered, plundered and its urban forms severely challenged and reformulated, along with its politics and cultural life, first by the French under Napoleon, then in 1798 by the Austrians, to whom France traded the city and her territories in exchange for Belgium and Lombardy. The Austrians retained Venice as part of the Hapsburg Empire for seven years, at which point Napoleon, after the Battle of Austerlitz, forced the return of Venice and other territories, appointing Eugène de Beauharnais as "Prince of Venice" and launching an all-out reformation of, or (depending on your point of view) assault upon, Venetian institutions. Monasteries and convents were suppressed by the dozens, as were the charitable institutions (the *scuole*), and churches were closed and some destroyed, while others were converted to secular uses [1].

What concerns this book is the role that gardens were called upon to play in the French transformation of the conquered city after 1806. When the Republic fell to the French in May 1797 there was an immediate move to bring – indeed to push – the city into line with French revolutionary ways: these included the adoption of the Revolutionary calendar with its gardenist and agricultural nomenclature, the dispatch of public orators to every *campo* to preach democracy, and the manipulation of the libretti and presentation of theatrical performances at the new Fenice Theatre to restructure Venice's mythical self-image and champion more egalitarian values [2]. Artworks – like the four bronze horses of St. Mark's – were seized and whisked off to Paris. Even the "garden" of cannon balls at the Arsenal see Figure III.15 was confiscated. But what the new and busy, but short-lived Committee of Public Instruction could not do very quickly was change the permanent fabric of the city. This required, to start with, the removal of major complexes of some institu-

VII.2 Liberty Tree in Piazza, 1797. This famous French Revolutionary symbol signals the newly established regime after the French occupation, but sits somewhat uncomfortably in a city with different ideas of gardens.

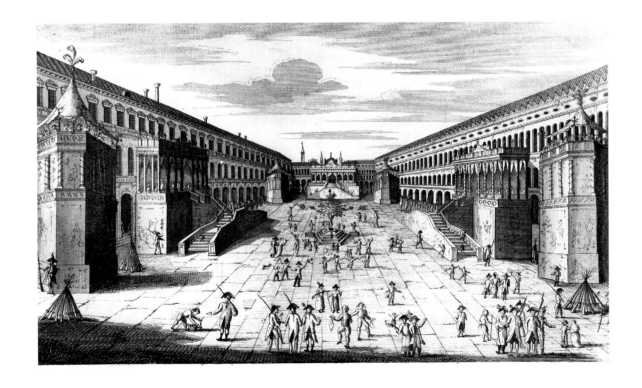

tional buildings (mainly convents and churches), and the determination of what urban forms would best take their place, thereby announcing and sustaining a new and non-elitist regime. Since patrician Venice had never seen the need for public gardens, these were clearly one amenity that could be introduced as a means of demonstrating that private privilege had given way to public awareness and popular responsibility. Liberty Trees could, of course, be readily displayed on the stage of the Fenice Theatre with many hortatory slogans, or quickly erected in the Piazza Figure VII.2, where their symbolic horticultural values were trumpeted as the replanting of Venice's "native species"–this in a city long dedicated to botanical science! But actual gardens took longer to establish. Nonetheless, they arrived with remarkable speed.

When Napoleon paid his only visit to Venice at the end of 1807 (he spent a hectic ten days there[3]), one of the groups who met with him were the architects engaged in re-structuring the city: among the projects assigned to them were the creation of a municipal cemetery on the island of San Cristoforo towards Murano; the strengthening of sea defences or *murazzi* between Chioggia and Malamocco; the creation of new public gardens at the eastern end of the city and another to replace the now demolished granaries of Terranova that lined the edge of the Bacino behind the Procuratie Nuove, and the establishment of new public promenades and parks on the Giudecca. Chief among the planners and architects working for Napoleon was Giannantonio Selva, the designer some time earlier of the Fenice Theatre, and now the chief architect of these fresh urban initiatives.

John Julius Norwich thinks that the provision of the public gardens has proved "of lasting benefit", since a "large green space was urgently needed"[4]. This echoes the claim of Romanelli for "l'unico apprezzabile verde pubblico veneziano" (the only appreciable public green [space] in Venice)[5]. I am not so sure. Our modern assumptions about the provision of open, green spaces in urban planning, shaped (ironically in this context) by what Napoleon III achieved for Paris in the 1860s under the direction of Baron Haussmann, are not the best criteria for judging the Venetian city in 1800 or even later. It is not, however, a question of the wholesale destruction of existing cityscape, which Romanelli identifies as the main objection of those who dislike the public gardens: certainly their creation

involved the elimination of much existing urban fabric – the clearance of the eastern sector, including the removal of a gothic and a renaissance church, an old sailors' home, a convent, a seminary and a monastery[6]; the demolition of granaries near Saint Mark's; or the proposed destruction of much existing urban fabric if the Giudecca project of a wide promenade were to have been realized. No, it is rather that both the formal vocabulary and the cultural aptness of the French proposals were totally at odds with Venice then or even perhaps later. That Napoleon's vision for the city was one that he sought to impose more successfully elsewhere in northern Italy makes its implementation in Venice the more insensitive[7].

But what Napoleon and his adjutants had in mind was to subdue an old and proud republic, however fallen upon sad and diminished days, and that necessitated a brisk, brutal and altogether radical *démarche*. Even before the decisive and permanent French and Austrian interventions, the brief "Democratic Republic" of 1797 had proposed the total reorganization of the administrative sectors of the city, renaming the communes or *sestieri* "Educazione", "Marina", "Legge", "Spettacoli", etc. in ways that would also have declared and determined the specific activities within each[8]. It is strikingly reminiscent of other impositions of a sovereign will upon a conquered population. Claude Levi-Strauss recounts an analogous manoeuvre by French Jesuits in Brazil in the 17th century, who reformulated the native population's dwellings into a pattern of rectangular streets the better to convert them[9]. And Venice herself had behaved similarly, when in 1204 Enrico Dandolo had reorganized the imperial structure of Constantinople along western feudal lines with elections conducted by Venetians and crusaders[10].

NAPOLEON'S GARDEN INTERVENTIONS

So now in Venice itself, after the fall of the Republic, along with new parish boundaries, new penal and civic codes, and a reorganized judiciary, were proposed some public open spaces unlike any *campo* or *corte* existing in the city, to be laid out in large gestures as an axial promenade. It was assumed that parade grounds, where conquering troops would train, and new planting evocative of other European cities would surely bring Venetians to accept if not appre-

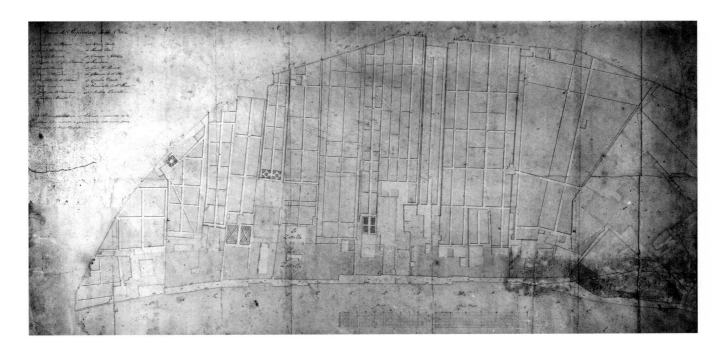

VII.3 Selva's record of the existing urban fabric on the Giudecca prior to his proposed changes.

ciate their new rulers. Along with the removal of all lions of St . Mark's throughout the city and the erection of a liberty tree in the Piazza **Figure VII. 2** [11], the public gardens and promenades which would be such a total transformation of the established idea of a Venetian garden, so deeply involved in the mapping and self-fashioning of Venice's myths, seemed both a symbolic gesture and an efficient urban reconstruction. Napoleon brought to the city what it had until then neither possessed nor thought that it needed – public gardens, along with the urban spaces, familiar elsewhere in Europe, of social promenade and military parade. But its subversive agenda challenged the very idea of the traditional Venetian garden and would have repercussions beyond any Napoleonic agenda for public spaces.

There are four specific garden interventions to consider, of which one (the transformation of the Giudecca) remained on paper, which is nonetheless where we can begin [12]. What were projected there were a "grandiosa passeggiata" or promenade, and a vast "piazza d'armi" or *champ de Mars*, a military parade ground. Various ways of accommodating these were put forward by different architects during a somewhat bungled and drawn-out bureaucratic process, but a

proposal by Selva was ultimately submitted in August 1811. Demolitions to clear the necessary space for his interventions would have been even more extensive than those actually effected in the Castello for the Public Gardens: this is immediately clear if we compare the new proposal with Selva's record of the existing urban situation, its plan showing a familiar pattern of elongated plots, in some of which Ughi-like garden forms are indicated **Figures VII. 3 & 4** [13].

The site, according to Selva's own verbal description, contained, as well as a furnace and a wax factory, many orchards and gardens with their accompanying buildings: "la coltura degli orti è ad erbaggi, viti e frutta, e somma industria usano quegli esperti coltivatori per avere i prodotti primaticci onde ritrarne maggior guadagno" (the cultivation of orchards is given over to vegetables, vines and fruit, and a considerable industry relies on these expert cultivators to obtain early produce on which a good profit is made). There was also, Selva noted, a special garden termed "botanical" that furnished the market for medicinal herbs [14]. These careful assessments of the existing urban landscape, valuable now as an indication of what was there, were required at least in part to calculate the costs of the whole re-development that the ad-

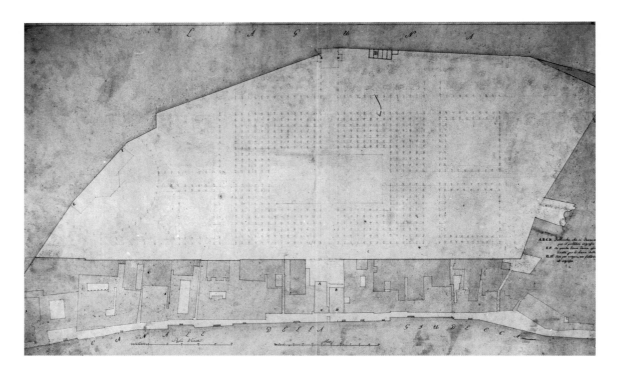

VII.4 Selva's proposal for the Giudecca involved eliminating large areas of private property and replacing them with plantations, a piazza where soldiers might drill, and other public amenities.

ministration would have to assume. It was lack of funds that eventually doomed the project.

Selva's proposed design was, of course, wholly out of keeping with the scale and the forms of the traditional, existing landscape of the Giudecca. A detail of Paganuzzi's 1821 map of the Giudecca Figure VII.5 suggests the kind of urban fabric that would have to have been removed as a prelude to its successful implementation (the detail shown here is somewhat to the west of the proposed Napoleonic intervention). The new site would have taken over all the hinterland of the eastern Giudecca, pushing against the rear of the existing buildings that fronted the canal; the absolutely rigid, northern edge of the proposed development followed a straight line, honouring by paralleling the proposed interior layout, yet it cuts through (and often truncates) the open spaces that stretched behind those palaces and houses. If the plan had ever been realized those buildings along the canal frontage would have presented a thin but familiar Venetian façade that hid the extended insertion of the new landscape; this retention of the existing house fronts was mandated in the Napoleonic decree; it is "façade-ism" *avant la lettre*[15]. A segment of the buildings is

indicated (bottom middle) to be demolished for a formal entry into the new development; an embarkation quay for troops is marked at the upper left, and a lagoon entry is planned at the top. On that far, lagoon side of the new landscape there was to be an enormous terrace, the length of which was closed with a wall, decorated with a loggia and columns (similar, as will be seen, to some of Selva's architectural proposals for the Castello site). A "passegiata" or promenade was, furthermore, a distinctly French urban form[16], needing considerable space to be effective, on the one hand, and encouraging a mode of public gatherings and promenading, on the other, that was in form and spirit very different from that hitherto accommodated by the local *campi* and the central Piazza. Regularly spaced trees (a modified quincunx) marked out and defined the surrounding groves in a manner, once again, distinctly reminiscent of ancient French estate design and formerly royal sites like the Tuileries or the Luxembourg gardens, all opened to the French public since the Revolution. And the groves proposed for the Giudecca framed vast open areas, avenues (*viale*) and squares, the latter to be utilized when necessary for the training and marshalling of soldiers. Two sections on the

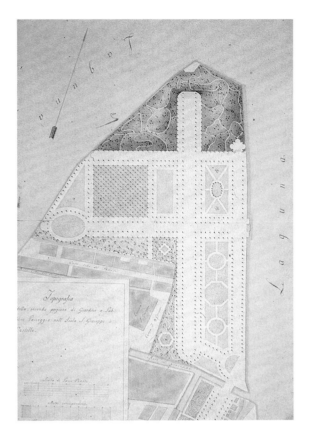

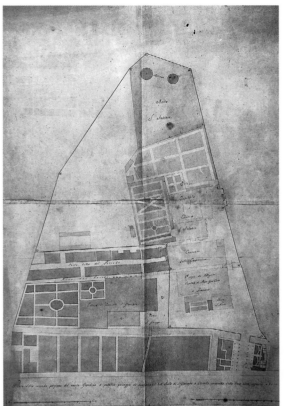

VII. 12 Selva's signed plan of the gardens, with slightly different adjudications of the spaces that would be laid out.

VII.13 Selva's signed plan of the existing land holdings with lines drawn around the proposed site of the Public Gardens.

more gardenesque segment out of the previously axial promenade, but the scheme does not in the end seem to have been laid out. The cabinet in the quincunx towards the top left stays in one, but is eliminated in the other, which also removes the one curved corner to regularize the bosco as a perfect square. In the second plan, the segment of the gardens abutting the un-parked urban zone has been given a more decisive organization: two interesting insertions have now been made—a thin triangle alongside the promenade has been enlarged and a rectangle inserted at its far left end, in both of which a regular shape (hexagon inside the triangle, square inside the square) is surrounded by a whirl of meandering paths; the straight edge of the promenade from the main entry to the gardens has been manipulated in one plan where it bumps into some buildings on the lagoon side before the bridge leading into the next zone.

Shortage of funds and other administrative hiccups prevented the planned gardenscape from being established as Selva had originally designed. Yet, with the elimination of some of the larger buildings, the site's essential layout, in part determined by the shape of available land, was accomplished: a long, formal avenue led from the Via Eugenia, and was lined with regularly spaced trees, its mid-point pulled apart into a square clearing (a trace of which still survives). The axis then took a 45 degree turn to the left, after crossing that gently sloping bridge which carried people into a more gardenesque segment—flower beds around open spaces and each lined with trees. Two further parallel *viali* would then take visitors either along the lagoon edge or through the centre of the garden. Those who walked through the centre of the gardens found their path aligned on the Motta, for the summit of which in 1813 Selva designed and installed a modest wooden pavilion, again a borrowed item from the repertoire of European picturesque *fabriques*. This fi-

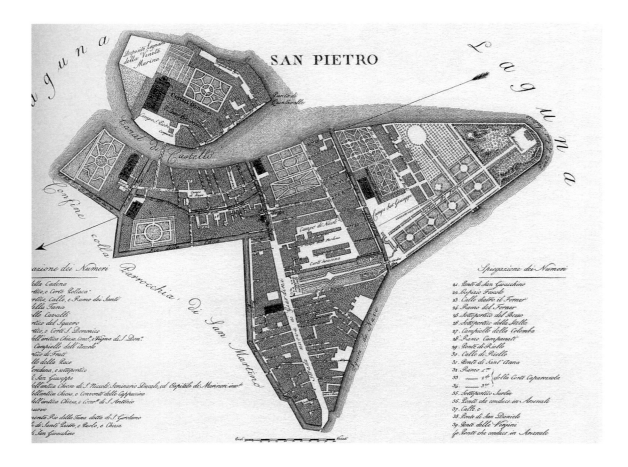

VII.14 Map by Paganuzzi, 1821, of the area that includes the Public Gardens.

nal section of the gardens that surrounded the mount on all sides was laid out as a swirling set of narrow paths meandering through shrubbery, once again a typical French device for augmenting the previous regularity with an emphatically "picturesque" layout. Most interestingly, the wind mills on the eastern end of the site, something of a symbol of the "old Venice" and certainly not incompatible with contemporary picturesque taste, were demolished, though not without some hesitations[22]. In the end they went the way of all the other properties, private and monastic, that were removed to install the Giardini Pubblici (they are marked by Selva on Figures VII 11&13, but they have been eliminated in Figure VII.12)[23]. The extent of these clearances can be seen on two site plans that Selva had drawn up earlier to show the existing urban forms, on one of which the outline of the new gardens was marked in black ink; both show the convents and their gardens and orchards that would be comman-

deered and cleared Figure VII.13, including the church of Sant'Antonio, from which a fragment, an arch attributed to Sanmicheli, was re-erected in the gardens in 1822 by Giuseppe Salvadori[24]. Trees and shrubs existing on some of the long-established sites now cleared for the public gardens were apparently re-used by Silva and his botanical colleague, Pier Antonio Zorzi[25].

A LABORATORY FOR THE MODERN CITY

During the remainder of the 19th century the gardens saw other proposals for re-working their layout, all of which followed the Selva mix of "Italianate" regularity with "English" romanticism. These change their forms slightly between Selva's own proposal and the renderings in both Paganuzzi's map of 1821 and the Combatti map of 1847 Figures VII.14 & 15; for instance, the two *viali* that extended down the second, regular sector have different layouts in the two mappings. But

VII.15 Map by Combatti, 1847, with detail of the Public Gardens.

all show essentially the same spaces. What is interesting is how the various renderings play with different syntax for regularity–straight axial lines and visibly organized planting on the one hand–and the new "naturalistic" mode–winding paths, denser shrubbery with natural clearings on the other. And in the two original "revisions" see Figures VII 9 & 12 even some combination of the two by an insertion of regular geometrical forms inside the irregular meanderings.

The topic of public gardens was necessarily a vital one at this time, and it clearly preoccupied many people in Venice at a moment when the former Republic was being integrated, whether it liked it or not, into Europe. At issue was what was apt for the city, which Selva had specifically noted was not on the mainland, thereby implying that some special, indigenous character needed preserving or inventing. But there was also the need to provide something that was distinctly and deliberately modern, drawing upon current design thinking about landscape architecture that could be relevant for the new Public Gardens. The issue of modernity was therefore prime: the fall of an exhausted and much damaged Republic, the establishment of a new power centre based beyond the Veneto in Milan, the intervention of post-Revolutionary France (among the most conspicuously "modern" of European states at that time), along with the claims of neo-classicism to be a purifying, contemporary vision, posed a challenge that was not susceptible of any easy solution.

This was at issue from the beginning, in the earliest commentary on the "romantic" segment of the Public Gardens by Antonio Diedo in 1815–20: about the question of a suitable style, he wrote that it needed "neither the poetry of English gardening, nor the enchanted palaces (*palagi*) of Ariosto" [26]; in other words, neither foreign modernity nor indigenous but antiquated Italian romance. The remark surely alludes to current debates, that Selva himself would

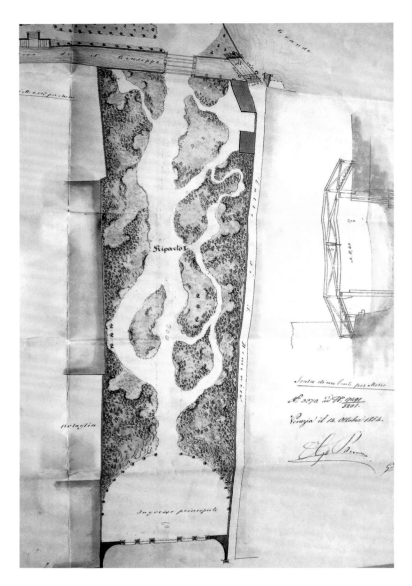

VII.16 G.Bianco, proposed picturesque redesign for the first segment of the Giardini Pubblici, dated October 1854.

have known, concerning the appropriate character to give a truly Italian mode of natural or modern gardening (ever since Horace Walpole's influential essay, these terms were deemed synonymous). In Ercole Silva's *Dell'arte de' giardini* of 1801, Luigi Mabil's *Sopra l'indole dei giardini moderni* of 1796, and Ippolito Pindemonte's "Dissertazione" of 1792 arguments are advanced for designs that address the new Italian gardening in northern Italy under Austrian and French rule and accordingly argue for drawing upon indigenous sources like Tasso, Ariosto, the *Hypnerotomachia* and early gardenist skills (fountains) and plantings rather than relying upon a homogenized "English" or

"modern" style[27]. The rejection by Diedo of Ariosto and the world of romance might suggest some attempt to avoid any eclectic Italian tradition or atavistic nostalgia, but contrariwise by offering nothing in its place he neglected specifically Venetian resources. The vehemently anti-French writer, Gaetano Pinali, also raised issues of form and meaning between the options of "so-called English" designs and the "antica italiana moda ed industria felice che coll'apparenza di infingere la più semplice natura maneggia" (the antique Italian mode and happy industry that seems to invent the simplest forms of nature). But his anger was mainly directed at the wholesale destruction of a cultural segment of the city ("quasi un museo di belle arti" [almost a museum of fine arts]); he lamented the lost opportunity to make of this unique site within the city what amounts to a picturesque sculpture park, where Venice herself could have displayed the same "erudition and good taste" as other nations for collecting and displaying "antichi monumenti, e figurati ruderi ancora a decorazione de' più splendidi e vaghi giardini" (ancient monuments, and ruined sculptures to decorate the most splendid and delightful gardens)[28]. This does seem to be a plea for creating something specifically local rather than the banalities for which he blamed Selva and the French authorities. What was generally appreciated as a specifically local character was the opportunity for wonderful views over the lagoon that the site of the gardens provided; however, this kind of commendation seems to have studiously avoided saying anything about the garden themselves. Zanotto's *Descrizione della Città* (1847), for instance, was much more impressed with the views outwards from the far end of the Gardens, whereas the overall design was suited, he thought, only to a "giardin di passeggio, che demanda larghi e diritti viali, e proscrive ciò tutto che tien del difficile e complicato"[29] (a garden for strolling, that requires wide, straight avenues, while proscribing anything that involves the difficult and complicated). Later visitors and residents would echo this kind of distinction: W.D.Howells, who was the American consul in Venice during the 1860s, noted its "glorious lookout over the lagoon", but otherwise was condescending: "The Gardens were made by Napoleon.... are pleasant enough, and not gardens at all, but a park of formally-planted trees—sycamores, chiefly. I do not remember to have seen here any Venetians of the better class..."[30].

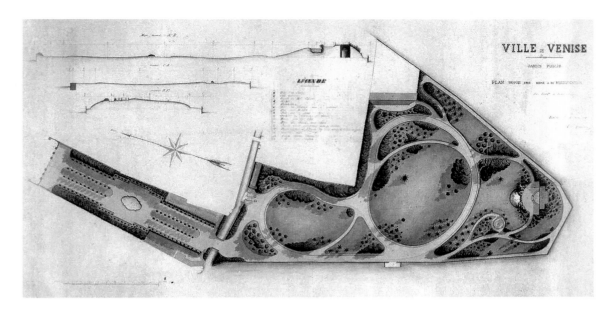

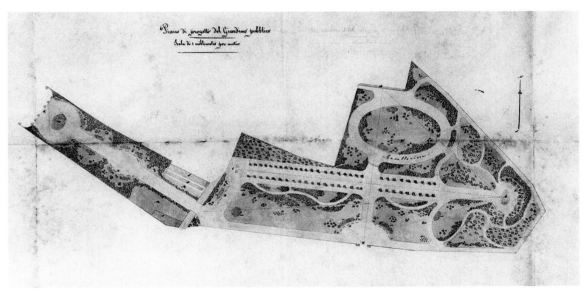

VII.17 Marco Guignon, proposal for the redesign of the Giardini Pubblici, March 1867.

VII.18 Nicola Grimaldi, proposal for the redesign of the Giardini Pubblici, 1867.

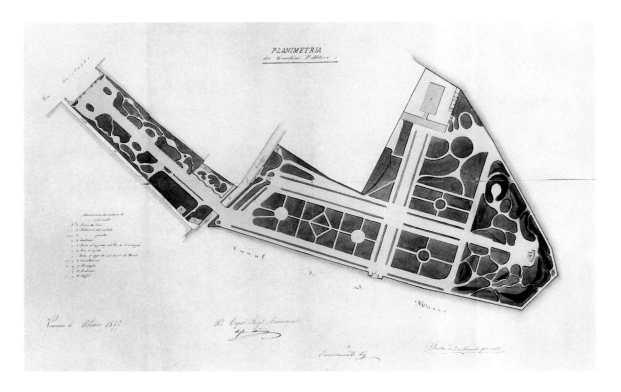

PLANIMETRIA
dei Giardini Pubblici

VII.19 Proposal by the Municipal Engineer A. Forcellini for the redesign of the Giardini Pubblici, October 1877.

What may appear to be Selva's main debt to Silva, who had himself derived his ideas from the German garden and park theorist, Christian Hirschfeld, is an emphasis upon finding appropriate designs for public gardens generally (though not specifically in Venice), a topic that had surfaced in the theoretical literature by the end of the 18th century and that Selva himself addressed in reflections on his Napoleonic work in Venice [31]. Some design solutions for the Public Gardens, however, were simply not a success: Pietro Selvatico considered the whole site utterly monotonous: "gretti e monotoni viali ... ed aggiungervi monticelli sgarbati con male distribuite macchie di verde" (stingy/narrow-minded and monotonous allées,... and unpleasing little hills added, with badly distributed debris/ruins of greenery). He saw its total failure to achieve any "poetry" of gardening as an inability to learn creatively from the current advances in European gardening that mingled regular and irregular spaces in exciting and above all surprising ways [32]. This demand, bred of a more romantic and less strictly neo-classical taste than Selva's would, in fact, become the favoured mode of several private Venetian gardens during the rest of the 19th century.

It was certainly the last part of the Public Gardens that afforded the best opportunity to experiment with picturesque designs, while leaving the very stiff and regular segments alone. Subsequent designs, perhaps drawn up to address the wear and tear in Selva's original layout, are also interesting, each of them adjudicating the spaces differently and several bringing the picturesque irregularity back into the very first segment [33]. None of them seem to have been implemented. First of all, in 1854, G. Bianco proposed turning the whole of the first, regular avenue into a picturesque adventure Figure VII.16: after the exedral entry plaza the central pathway wandered towards the end of this sector, but branched off into side excursions within a dense shrubbery; this surrender of the original axial segment to less regular handling seems to have been an influence on subsequent designs. A plan Figure VII. 17 devised by Marco Guignon, a French architect based in Turin, who would later intervene at the Giardino Papadopoli, does in fact propose bringing the irregular swirls of lawn, studded with clumps of trees, right up to the end of the main avenue, which also gets somewhat reduced in severity with flower beds inserted down its centre, but is by no means as radical as in the previous scheme [34]. The loops and curves of his design exactly replicate designs for smaller bourgeois properties that were offered by a series of French design manuals during the 19th century [35].

Yet another version tackles the regular/picturesque mixture **Figure VII.18** with better skill: first it eliminates the rigidity of the first *viale*, blurring its edges with flower beds and shrubbery in a series of exedral openings, then affirming the central axis of the next section leading eastwards from the triumphal arch and making the ground between it and the lagoon more relaxed with a meandering path, scattered flower beds and a formal opening towards the water; elsewhere it invokes the curving ovals of the first plan yet sets them out with what seems a far more sensitive response to the spaces that have to be filled. Another plan from 1877 **Figure VII.19** attempts to soften the hard lines of the main avenue by lining its sides with irregular and winding paths within shrubbery that break from time to time into the main *viale*; yet it also seems undecided about how to cope with the climax of the third sector, dabbling with unconvincing and amorphous shrubberies around the coffee house that had been established there by the time of Combatti's map.

All in all, then, the area designated by Napoleon for the public gardens served as something of a laboratory for making Venice into a modern and neoclassical city with a strong appeal to the "natural" [36]. The terms of that appeal have clearly to be understood within contemporary appeals to neo-classical simplicity mixed with a romantic taste for the absence of conspicuous artifice in landscape representations; in this respect, rather ironically, it echoes similar appeals – but to very different modes of the natural – made by early Venetian mythographers and historians, celebrating in their case the natural situation of Venice safely centred in her lagoon (see above Chapters Three and Six). But the new modes of the natural to which Selva, the main architect of the public garden schemes, seems to have appealed were those observed during his extensive travels through Europe, visiting gardens and urban sites at a time when new, modern and picturesque values were being expressed [37]. The journal of his visits suggests the extent to which he was exposed to considerable and varied European experiments with the "picturesque" taste in landscape. Furthermore, he

was good friends with Pindemonte, one of the more thoughtful theorists of the new national styles of gardening; and he knew Giacomo Quarenghi, a fluent and accomplished draughtsman whose landscape designs and *capricci* meld a pastoral fascination with rural imagery to produce an inventive repertoire of classical structures and ruins [38]. Selva also knew Canova, who often accompanied him on visits to French sites. But Selva's travel notes also make clear that he was less than enthusiastic about modern English gardening (he visited Blenheim, Stowe, the Leasowes, and Hagley) and that he preferred French work, which goes someway to explain his thinking and proposals for Venice under French control [39].

The scattering of neo-classical buildings that Selva proposed for the gardens constituted an austere repertoire of architectural possibilities, but formulated along the lines of many pattern books that provided picturesque designers with all sorts of imagery and structures to decorate and service gardens without any particular regard to their coherence or even location. In this context, it is important to realize that the stiff neoclassical architecture that Selva favoured was not somehow in conflict with picturesque taste, where all stylistic modes, in fact, could be called upon to promote associations and different experiences, as was suggested by the eclectic imagery purveyed in innumerable pattern books of this period [40]. This complex appeal is made quite clear by Selva's unexecuted proposal for the small temple to be set amid the irregularly planted and (what Selva himself deemed) "sentimental" greenery on the extreme point of the Gardens. Its design is an austere, upstanding neoclassical rotunda, suitable for this "natural" part of the site. Under the dome was a sculpture of two full-length classical figures, its circular platform punctuated by lions crouching on eight plinths that jut out into the surrounding scenery; its eight columns were to have re-used some antique ones from the demolished church of Sant'Antonio, which (along with the lions) might be taken as a formal gesture towards Venice's cultural legacy; the whole was – wrote Selva – to have been a monument to the Venetians' recognition of the "Augusto Sovrano" (i.e. Napoleon!) [41].

And this is how we might also see the subsequent insertion in 1822 of the triumphal arch, which marked the point where the first axial *viale* or *passeggiata* leg of the Public Gardens turned towards the extremity of

VII.20 The lagoon edge of the Public Gardens.

the site and where the second avenue, now aligned down the central stretch of the next sector, was on axis with the far mount. The insertion of the arch acknowledged neo-classical taste, being after all a Roman type re-imagined by a renaissance architect, while at the same time it contributed another picturesque item to the overall ensemble of imagery and associations. As picturesque insertion, furthermore, it was literally a fragment of an earlier, demolished church, and might have been thought appropriate because of its historical association with a now lost piece of the older city. As triumphal arch, it constituted a permanent version of the temporary ones that had often been devised to welcome visiting dignitaries, including and most recently Napoleon when he visited Venice in 1807 [42]. It is unclear whether this insertion was designed as yet another deliberate challenge to Venetian traditions and myths that viewed any imported Romanitas with little enthusiasm and were inclined to boast the city's independence of

classical Rome, to which the free-standing arch nevertheless now gestures [43].

When in 1887 the Public Gardens were taken over in part for the Esposizione Nazionale Artistica, which subsequently morphed into the Biennale, a variety of pavilions for the exhibits took the place and may be seen as perpetuating the role of picturesque fabriques that Selva had originally proposed for the public gardens. The Biennale site, its different pavilions and the stages of its development are outside the scope of this chapter. They are also forlornly out of reach to modern users of the Public Gardens when the Biennale itself is not being held, and only then by payment of a fee. And yet they could easily be re-admitted into the overall parkland at this end of Venice, and the whole site given perhaps for the first time a genuinely Venetian significance as a garden of the arts. As it is, visitors in search of a newer picturesque and its fabriques have often to make do with glimpses of their sometimes exotic architecture from outside the Biennale parkland. (Fig VII.20)

Old ruined gardens and new modern gardens

Chapter Eight

What a garden could be made of the abandoned orchard, what scope for planting, what an escape from constant idleness, what a relief from ... the lagoon"

F. Eden

Murano, wrote Ruskin, "was once the garden of Venice", and some years later in 1866 Vincenzo Zanetti's guide to Murano noted that gardens of the Palazzo Trevisan were no longer recognizable and lamented the Venetian failure to stop such ruination[1]. This refrain of "ruin", "desolation", or "decrepitude" runs continuously throughout 19th- and indeed the early 20th- century commentaries on Venice's urban fabric. Alvise Zorzi's patient chronicle of the lost buildings and sites of Venice – *Venezia Scomparsa* (1972) – would seem indeed to confirm this depressing emphasis; though he is not primarily focused on gardens, fragile entities in any case and liable to be lost or damaged more easily than buildings, Zorzi frequently notes that it was precisely during the 19th century that splendid or ample gardens and plant collections disappeared along with the palaces to which they were attached. Yet he also notes in passing how certain of these spaces, once occupied by these lost palaces, were re-formulated as gardens: along the Grand Canal it is possible to identify several such new gardens – the early 20th-century neo-gothic Palazzo Stern by Giuseppe Berti has a small garden protected by a little "gothic" arcade at the corner of the Rio Malpaga Figure VIII.1, while the Casa Ravà by Giovanni Sardi from 1906 has its own garden Figure VIII.2; in each case these are positioned between the palace façades and the Grand Canal itself rather than, as was traditionally the case, behind the building. These are, then, two rival perspectives – that Venice was (in Ruskin's melodramatic phrase) a "ruined garden" and, contrariwise, that new gardens were also being created. But even these new gardens did not always choose to avoid some play with ruin; this may be explained, at least in part, by the dominance during the 19th century of picturesque design which valued, among other aspects, a taste for ruination.

"RUIN" AND REALITY

This diversity of attitudes towards garden styles and of actual built sites in Venice at this time may all be considered as part of the response by Venice to the loss of the Republic, along with her need to determine how she might envisage and conduct a future under new European auspices. In this respect the garden is but one element of a much larger cultural re-assessment[2]. While Napoleon's forceful move to establish public gardens, with one implemented and another (on the Giudecca) unrealized, provoked some (like his architect Selva) to invent garden forms that were new for Venice, the results irked others either because they lamented, even decried, the loss of old spaces or because they could find no virtue in new designs that had a distinctly "foreign" complexion. Marooned, as it were between these extremes, were those sites that preserved the old unchanged even if degraded, at best perhaps subject to improvised and piecemeal renewal ("ruins, or fragments disguised by restoration"[3]). But ruin, as Georg Simmel reminds us, also holds a positive value in that, even while something decays, something else ("forms of nature") may grow in its fissures[4].

VIII.1 Palazzo Stern on the Grand Canal. Both here and in the following figure a modern garden has been created fronting the Grand Canal as opposed to the rear of the property.

VIII.1a The meandering path in the picturesque Patarol Garden, Cannaregio.

VIII.2 Palazzo Ravà on the Grand Canal.

The "ruined garden" theme (as both metaphor and literal description) became a commonplace in writings on Venice, even sometimes against the grain of its context. Robert Hénard's account of what is evidently the turn-of-the century garden of Frederic Eden on the Giudecca celebrates with enthusiasm its leafy, green retreat, where nature has found a new grace, and where its gardeners seem an "integral part" of the natural scenery (thus presumably minimizing its artifice and maintenance). Yet the acknowledgement of the statuary remnants – "restes d'un luxe ancien" – and the admiring references to the decrepitude of its two buildings are implicit with the familiar re-

frain of decay; the two desultory photographs that accompany the French text **Figure VIII.3** also convey an impression of overgrown bowers and a somewhat somber, dark pool[5]. This "old garden", in short, is both admired for its longevity and the consequent depredations of time, while in fact its upkeep and (if it is indeed the Eden garden) its recent make-over are both acknowledged.

The theme of a ruined Venice partakes of a pan-European, Romantic fascination with ruin in general. In particular, at least for English speakers, it was fuelled by Byron's celebration of the city in *Childe Harold's Pilgrimage*: at the very start of the hero's European travels the poet sets him "To meditate amongst decay, and stand/A ruin amidst ruins"; a later phrase, "The weeds of nations in their last decay", hints at what would become a more focused theme. For if Venice seemed an apt location for this general romantic relish for ruins, as the century wore on the trope was discovered to have very literal meanings and to be reified throughout the city; even earlier, in 1780, Beckford noted "many a grass-grown court, and silent pathway", a phrase that Ruskin repeats in his *Stones of Venice*[6]. By the second half of the 19th century Ruskin had lent his considerable authority to the theme of Venetian ruin by highlighting the Renaissance decadence, as he saw it, of the Byzantine-gothic city. But his predilection for ruin was not driven solely by the architectural narrative he chose to tell. In many other respects the place was ruined for him from the very beginning of his long relationship with it. Even before he reaches the city, certainly tutored by his reading of Byron, his narrative of arrival registers how the villas along the Brenta were "sinking fast into utter ruin, black, and rent... with what were once small gardens". Once arrived, he wrote to his father that Venice was "simply a heap of ruins"[7].

The litany grows in volume and in the number of voices joining its chorus. The botanist Ruchinger's survey of urban plants endlessly notes the "rovinezza" or ruination of the city that he scoured for specimens. Rowing up the Grand Canal, Samuel Rogers observed "many a half ruined painting, Giorgione's perhaps" on palace façades. Chateaubriand's Venice is "dying amid all the graces and smiles of nature", and he takes especial delight in contemplating the skulls at San Cristoforo or seeking out the sites of death, like the new cemetery on San Michele and the abandoned Jewish cemetery on the Lido. Browning's lament for Galuppi's music is for an unrecoverable past ("dust and ashes, dead and done with"). M.Valery's *Venise et ses environs* began by noting the "ruine actuelle", the "désolation actuelle" of the city, sadder than any ordinary ruins[8]. Vernon Lee in her *Studies of the Eighteenth Century in Italy* (1880) writes it off as a "crumbling city". James Thomson's *City of Dreadful Night* recalls "the ranged mansions" of Venice being "still as tombs". Henri de Régnier could find decay and desolation, perhaps as poetic extensions of his own personal circumstances, when he writes of the Palazzo Vendramin at the Carmini that it was "morcelé, divisé, décrépit" and its "pauvre jardin", a dump for all sorts of rubbish and lines of washing. Henry James, too, writes that the Venetian "habitations are decayed", that the city has become "the most beautiful of tombs", "a mausoleum with a turnstile", and that it exhibits a "decadence and decay ... more brilliant than any prosperity". And he relies upon this particular emphasis in *The Aspern Papers*, where the first sight of the decayed house of the Bordereau women is of its patchy walls. And elsewhere, still harping on ruin, James observes that "behind the walls of the houses ["and their beautiful blighted rooms"] the history of occupation was thick and Baedeker might give these places multiple stars", yet he does not himself expatiate upon this socio-historical "thickness" in order to counterbalance the suggestions of ruin[9]. The chorus gains so much in volume and authority that Venice seems inextricably linked with decay and decadence–James's Milly Thrale dies in the city in *The Wings of the Dove*, and the theme emerges in the very titles of *Amori et Dolori Sacrum: La Mort de Venise* (1903) by Maurice Barrès, or Thomas Mann's *Death in Venice* (1913). In September 1913 Frederick Rolfe, self-styled Baron Corvo, published "An Ossuary of the North Lagoon" in *Blackwoods*, in which he narrated his discovery of an abandoned graveyard, where were dumped the corpses of Austrian soldiers, and where he saw serpents wriggling through the eye sockets of their skulls.

The ruin theme is pervasive and undeniable. But it is, in fact, one bred and nurtured largely by outsiders'

VIII.3 A scene in the Garden of Eden, from Hénard's *Sous le ciel Vénitien* (1911). This famous garden on the Giudecca (see Figures VIII.17-20) was much appreciated by its many visitors.

writings about the city [10]: "Venise n'est ruiné que dans la littérature" (Venice is only ruined in literature), was an early observation of J. Lecomte, writing in 1844 even before he could have read many of the writers cited above, or before he could perhaps also have acknowledged some painterly versions of the same phenomena. J.M.W.Turner, for example, found Venice not only an ideal location for his luminous studies of light and seascape, but a civilization on which to project his pessimism, explored in the verses of his "Fallacies of Hope" and in such paintings as *Venice. The Sun of Venice Going to Sea*. At first glance but a richly evoked study of a fishing boat putting to sea (its name emblazoned on the sail), yet the verses attached to the painting in the 1843 Royal Academy exhibition catalogue made clear Turner's sense of doom and destruction, albeit unexplained (perhaps because by then already a cultural commonplace about the city):

Fair shines the morn, and soft the zephyrs blow,
Venezia's fisher spreads his painted sail so gay
Nor heeds the demon that in grim repose
Expects his evening prey.

But perhaps the most eloquent, because muted, pictorial commentary upon the decay and ruinated urban scene comes in Whistler's etchings, where the very work of the etching tool recalls the wisps and fragments of decay in stone and woodwork. One in particular from his second set of Venetian etchings of 1886 is dedicated to "The Garden" Figure VIII.4: it takes the viewer's eye through a framework of patchy stucco and exposed brick into a garden courtyard where rampant bushes and a spindly tree provide the setting for a family. It is an image that matches an affectionate regard for human circumstance (the cat is a nice touch) with the artist's instinct for the harmonies

VIII.4 Whistler's *The Garden*, etching. Garden incidents, like this, seem to have been of particular fascination to foreign artists who sought out less frequented spots throughout the city in order to represent aspects that earlier, grander perspectives by artists like Canaletto and Guardi had seemed to neglect.

VIII.5 Another glimpse of hidden gardens and a pergola-shaded terrace by F. Hopkinson Smith, *Venice of Today* (1902).

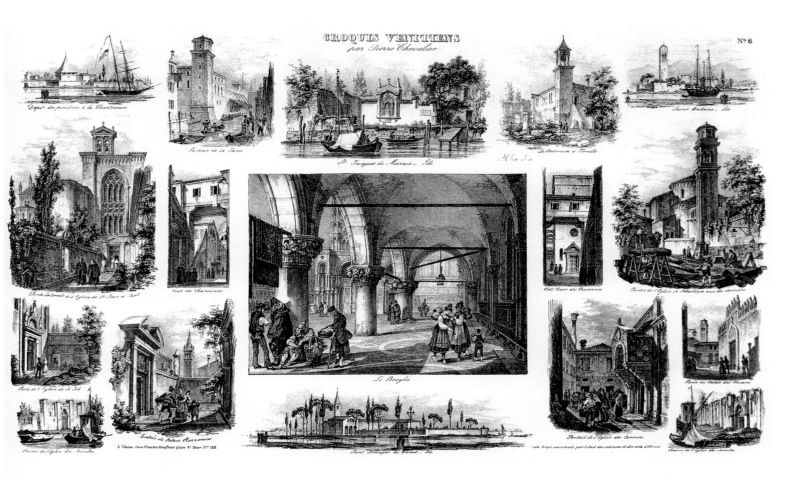

VIII.6 Pierre Chevalier, page of picturesque Venetian scenes, many of which are characterized by hints of gardens and leafy courtyards. First half of the 19th century.

that emerge from dissonance and decay. In other etchings and drawings Whistler, who clearly explored and knew the city intimately, observes courtyards with well heads and vine-covered pergolas, *traghetto* stations also with their garden episodes, and those peculiarly Venetian moments when through doorways on *calle* or canal are glimpsed some inner, maybe derelict, retreat. Otherwise, the painterly attention to garden decadence is far less obsessive than is the literary, unless you count many pictorial versions of canals where the trailing creepers and canopy of trees emerge from behind high walls and generally evince scenery of rampant and uncontrolled growth; such are the images that Hopkinson Smith provides and that several late 19th-century photographs also record Figure VIII.5 [11].

The reality on the ground, however, does not entirely corroborate the gloom and despondency of writers and artists. For sure, gardens, *corti* and *campi* require a certain amount of maintenance, and after the fall of the Republic there was much inertia in face of French and then Austrian occupation. Picturesque vignettes of the city also enjoyed depicting scenes where spontaneous, apparently volunteer planting added a hint of decrepitude Figure VIII.6. But despite the specific emphasis of Ruskin's "ruined garden", echoed no doubt by those who resented the urban deprecations under the foreigners, the actual gardens of Venice were not by any means all ruined. Indeed, there was something of a fresh energy and attention to design in many of them, something of a renewal of garden culture and the idea of the garden Figure VIII.7. Vernon Lee's characters in "Lady Tal", in her collection *Daughters of Decadence*, are clearly not alone in finding time and opportunity to walk in a garden on the Zattere with its intimations of fertility and growth [12]. One might suspect, in fact, that the presence of French and (for

VIII.7 V.Chilone, *Venetian scene*, painting, 19th century.

THE ADVENT OF PICTURESQUE DESIGNS

The picturesque vogue in design allowed the relatively small spaces of Venice to be diversified in new ways. Where the traditional, long rectangular sites remained, as at the Patarol garden in Cannaregio, the substitution by new owners of a winding pathway through shrubbery for the straight, axial vista across different sectors, as depicted by de' Barbari, produced a very different experience. The length of pedestrian walks was increased, and the psychological effect of a denser more complicated and therefore larger space was also achieved. Space had always been relative in Venice: small risers gave steps a "terrace" effect; an axis or sequence of "rooms" seemed to lengthen a garden; borrowed views enlarged its restricted enclosures. But now, as the Patarol garden still shows, a much more busy garden experience is achieved by the meandering pathway, Figure VIII.1a, the denser planting that effectively occludes long vistas – until you reach the *casino* at the lagoon's edge – and by the addition of a cluster of typical picturesque items. The *montagnola* or little mountain, crowned with a neo-gothic turret, extends this Venetian garden upwards in new ways, while the cave or grotto in its base adds a moment of descent Figure VIII.8.

A picturesque garden tended to augment and complicate any given territory, especially when it was of limited size: so the flat Venetian sites are almost invariably lifted up and down by artificially creating hillocks and little valleys. That in its turn provides the occasion for small bridges (a number of which still exist, for example at the Palazzo Querini Papozze); these span the declivities, the sides of which can be piled with rocks to imply a "natural" geological eruption of stone from the ground beneath. Even in the Zenobio garden, shorter than the Patarol, this slight heaving of the site, the exposed rocks and the little bridge Figure VIII.9, all seem to lengthen the ground between palace and *casino* by making it busier; in addition, a photograph published by Damerini in 1931 shows that the path between *palazzo* and *casino* has been led in a deliberate meander, winding its way around lawn, flower beds and a rocky pool with a jet of water[13]. However, such treatment rather diminishes the calm and *gravitas* of that intervening space as evinced by both earlier 18th-century interventions and its state today. Ruchinger junior records that even

a longer period) Austrians in the city certainly meant that theories and practice of European garden design would percolate into Venice, and the new practices and principles of picturesque gardening given widespread currency in publications throughout France and the German-speaking states would also have some effect here. Indeed, a French edition of one such publication, Johann Gottfried Grohmann's and Friedrich Gotthelf Baumgärtner's bilingual (German and French) *Ideenmagazin für Liebhaber von Gärten* was even issued in Venice as well as in Paris and Strasbourg between 1796 and 1806; its focus upon providing owners of modest means and restricted grounds who could not afford professional services with ideas for both scenery and *fabriques* certainly would have found a warm Venetian response in the century that followed. Furthermore, for those who indeed wished for a more modern profile for the city, the picturesque provided exactly such a medium.

VIII.8 a & b The grotto and mountain in the former Patarol garden. Picturesque re-formulations of earlier Venetian garden spaces often tried to vary the flat, level land of sites as well as create meandering routes that extended their limited and rectangular spaces.

VIII.9 The hillocks and bridge in the garden of Palazzo Zenobio.

VIII.10 Dionisio Moretti, view of the site of the later Papadopoli Gardens, with glimpses of somewhat old-fashioned garden forms, 1828–29.

VIII.11 Map by Combatti, detail showing the Papadopoli Gardens, a large private garden complex developed on the former grounds of a religious institution; a small part of this would eventually form the existing public gardens near Piazzale Roma.

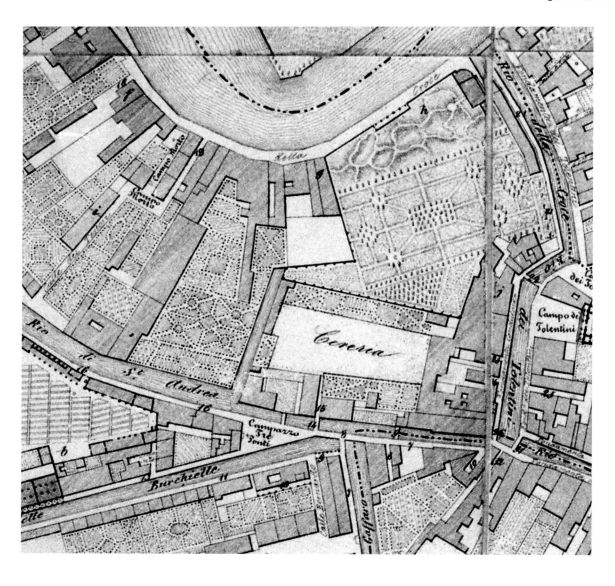

in the quadrilinear *orto botanico* at San Giobbe, various picturesque forms were introduced: a tunnel, a wooden bridge and a small mount constructed from monastic debris with a tiny platform or "piazzaletto" on its summit, reached by tortuous paths ("tortuosi vialetti")[14]. But where a site was in itself extensive and irregularly shaped, then the 19th-century Venetian garden could exploit the fresh style with energy and impunity. And among the most impressive examples of this new manipulation of space was the large garden created after 1834 for the Count Papadopoli.

To judge the original Papadopoli gardens by their present state – truncated by the creation of the modern Rio Nuovo, bombed in the Second World War, eroded by the building of the Palace Hotel (today the Sofitel), and generally abused by neglect and for a while by vagrant inhabitation – is to miss what must have been an extraordinary creation. Designed in the first instance by the prolific scene designer, Francesco Bagnara, it would have been a logical extension of Venice's theatrical culture, crafted now – as were many of his stage designs – to please a determinedly picturesque taste. The ground which the Count Papadopoli purchased included a former orchard of the ex-convent of Santa Croce ai Tolentini, already demolished, along with a garden somewhat developed by the Quadri family – a glimpse of its very old-fashioned green cabinet peeping over the garden wall is caught in Dionisio Moretti's panorama of the Grand Canal from the late 1820s Figure VIII.10. Combatti's map shows the re-design of the whole site Figure VIII.11: the northwestern segment was elaborated into a crazy weave of paths, while the remainder was more regularly set out with clusters of trees or *boschetti* where the allées intersected; a less regular grove occupied the southernmost sector. By 1847 the garden was "riche en toutes sortes de fleurs"[15].

Another generation of Papadopoli decided upon some re-designs in 1863 and called upon the French architect Marco Guignon, who was also involved in new proposals for segments of the Public Gardens. This new formulation of the Papadopoli produced an infinitely more extensive and coherent design, though no less scenographic, dominated throughout the site by a profuse planting of Asiatic species. First, Henry Harvard in 1876 and then Cecchetti the following year celebrated the rhododendra-lined pathways, the prize-winning species, the three bridges, the Chinese

pagoda, a little lake, nymphaea, the exotic birds in the soaring iron aviary, the rabbits in their *capanna*, and the raised terrace along the glasshouses that allowed views out over the adjacent canals. There was also a riding track. The whole, effused Cecchetti, was the result of art and good taste. All in all, it was an extraordinary addition to the Venetian townscape; its neo-gothic imagery perhaps even signalling some significant continuity with the now lost past – Gera thought so at any rate. Although only opened to the public in the 1920s when the site was acquired by the city, it had obviously been a garden where visitations were possible, given its inclusion by Antonio Quadri in 1847 in his list of notable places in which to walk[17]. The complex survived into the next century, much engraved and photographed, particularly the neo-gothic exterior walls (adapted from the former convent) and

VIII.12 Mid-19th-century photograph of the neo-gothic corner of the Papadopoli Gardens.

the wonderful corner hothouse with its pairs of ogive windows Figure VIII.12. The greenhouses along the inside of the wall beside the Rio dei Tolentini were adapted to other purposes in the 1920s, including open-air classrooms that still exist Figure VIII.13.

The botanical profusion in the Papadopoli and other 19th-century gardens, like that of Luigi Borghi and Virginia Tabaglio in their famed garden on the Fondamenta di San Trovaso[18], was not anything new in itself. Venice had always prized botanical collections – part of their enterprising commercial outreach – and had cherished all opportunities to grow and display both rare and local plants. And to this day, attentive visitors can appreciate elaborate window boxes, roof gardens on the *altane*, improvised flowers gardens created from maritime leftovers, or vernacular confections of windmills and "sails" Figure VIII.14 and see Figure IX.6. But the range and density of pictur-

VIII.13 The ruined greenhouses in the Papadopoli Gardens, 1929.

esque planting – exotics from Japan and the Americas, alongside local species – were encouraged both by the much more expansive sites now dedicated to the new gardening style and by the need in such designs to fill out a denser plant cover than had hitherto seemed apt for the lagoon situation. The novelty was often acknowledged: the Galvagna garden at the Palazzo Savorgnan in the Cannaregio was hailed by Quadri as a "très elégant....nouvelle création" [19]. And Gera records how the Baron Galvagna, who was his own gardener, wished "to imitate nature in her most ample and purest forms", her curves and lines, the irregularities of soil and site, along with a similar repertoire of architectural forms (pagoda, classical temple, and Etruscan house) [20].

Another large garden, still appreciated today by its local community, if no less diminished from a turn-

of-the century richness, is the public Groggia park, entered from the Calle del Capitelo in the Cannaregio Figures VIII.15 & 16. Once a large and densely planted bourgeois garden attached to a villa, it survived its owner Giuseppe Groggia's bid to sell the site for popular housing in 1910 [21]. Fragments of the villa, its *fabriques*, greenhouses and adjacent buildings survive and serve nowadays, along with the open spaces of the garden, as a community centre. But even as recently as the 1980s it retained some semblance of its original horticultural scope. It invoked some genuine gothic remnants that survived from the rear of the Palazzo Donà, largely demolished in 1823, and annexed these to a small exedra with classical heads on top of pilasters; there was a classical temple in the form of a tower or turret that seems to have marked the entrance onto a stone path spiralling up a small "mountain", fragments of which are still visible. Quite when the whole site, also comprising fountains, rockwork, a collection of statues and busts, and sundry seats and fountain basins, was put together is unclear: as late as Luigi Querci's map of 1887 (that largely follows Perissini's of 1866) the site is shown simply as divided between a rectangular garden crossed with diagonal paths meeting a circular bed in the middle and, alongside the lagoon, an orchard. Presumably the somewhat overwrought picturesque re-working comes therefore towards the end of the 19th century, the project perhaps of Giuseppe Groggia himself. The site is now cleared of much of the busy plants and objects that were still there when the place was photographed for me in the early 1980s, including handsome magnolia trees. The current neatness speaks of limited maintenance and resources as well as an ongoing commitment to its park-like amenities.

The climax of picturesque gardening in Venice, even as it was also its least extravagant manifestation, was Frederic Eden's eponymous property on the eastern end of the Giudecca. His own account of its creation, published by *Country Life* in London in 1903 Figure VIII.17, makes clear how he steered a careful line between respect for the "genius of the place" (the surviving rectilinear grid of paths from the former fruit and vegetable garden, for example), the perspectives of the current picturesque vogue (he bought the garden in 1884 and started work immediately) and – one supposes – the inspiration derived from his sister-in-law, the gardener Gertrude Jekyll [22]. From her perhaps

VIII.14 An anthology of today's window boxes, *altane*, and occasional or improvised gardens. Venetians are hugely inventive with alternative "gardens" created in elements of their lagoon furniture as well as their window-box displays.

VIII.15 & 16 Two views of the Parco Groggia (2007), a public park on the site of an earlier private villa in the Cannaregio.

came a certain commitment to local craft traditions – pollarded willow poles to make the pergolas – and to local materials – crushed seashells from the Lido instead of gravel for paths. A real well was sunk deep beneath the lagoon, though the resulting water was not good. He also re-enacted something of the early garden-making of the Venetian city, when he bought (or rather felt he was obliged to purchase) the municipal refuse dump just outside his seawall on the south, which he thereafter made into a further segment of his property (Damerini has a photograph of the *viale* along this edge [23]). He refused to pander to the picturesque delight in meandering paths as being locally uncharacteristic ("the universal measure that rules at Venice is the square, and the square is never square" [24]). The exigencies of the ground meant that only lateral-rooted trees would thrive (p.43) and earthworms expired upon reaching the salinated soil; Ruchinger, too, at the San Giobbe garden had lamented the "poco profondità. Un metro dalla superficie si trova l'acqua salmastra" (the shallow depth. One metre below ground and you reach salt water) [25]. But Eden, like other Venetian gardenists before him, triumphed over such setbacks, thus amply disproving

the rather odd, and somewhat un-Venetian remark of his own gondolier – "Venezia, tomba dei fiori" (p.13) – by establishing a rich and fecund retreat. By the time the four-acre garden was photographed for his book nearly twenty years after its acquisition **Figures VIII.18 & 19**, it was well-established: shady vines over the pergolas, masses of flowers besides the walks, dense clumps of lilies and roses (at about the same time Henry James wrote how the "roses of Venice are splendid" [26]). A small herd of cows provided members of the English community with fresh milk. And the invalid Eden recovered his health.

In 1884 Eden had purchased what he termed a "scene of neglect" (p.17). But he knew well that the best "picturesque" gardening is not a question of even benign let alone outright neglect, but requires as intensive a maintenance as any so-called formality and, furthermore, he recognized that gardens grow. Those who succeeded him at the Garden of Eden – Princess Aspasia of Greece and the American scholar, Elizabeth Gardner – knew this as well and the latter, especially after the disastrous floods of November 1966, strove to remake the gardens in ways that Eden might have appreciated. This was not, unhappily, the view of the

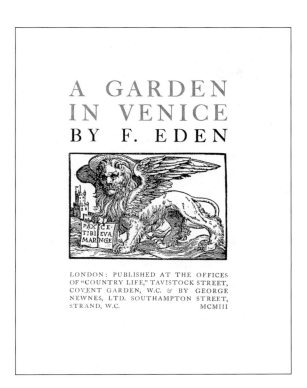

VIII.17 Title-page and frontispiece from Frederic Eden, *A Garden in Venice* (London, 1903).

VIII.18 &19 Two photographs from Frederic Eden, *A Garden in Venice* (London, 1903).

next (and through his foundation, current) ownership: the Austrian painter Hundertwasser believed in
letting nature grow into wilderness, permitting spontaneous vegetation in a mindless misunderstanding of
ecological purity, not to say, since he let no one in,
an odd re-enactment of God's total exclusion policy
from the original Eden! Fortunately, he did change his
mind (which God did not), to the extent that he then
wished to restore the garden to something approach-
ing its original state (whatever that would mean for a
garden, the impact of which lay far less in its structure
of paths and terraces and walls than in its rich plantings and their continuous growth and upkeep; gardens are not like paintings capable of being restored
carefully to *a priori* or "perfect" conditions). But mean-
while much harm had been done. But above all, the
virtual prohibition of access to the Garden of Eden has
meant that its fate is to survive Figure VIII. 20 & 21 – as
no garden in fact can ever exist – without occupation
(apparently there is not even a caretaker on site). John
Hall's account of a rare visit in February 2003 described
broken statuary, desolate bare trellises, trees cut and
logged, empty basins, a messy because totally un-
documented chronicle of destroyed or altered buildings, including the disappearance of a "Moorish" kiosk; rather perplexedly he concluded that the garden
was yet "in good heart". A handful of photographs
supplied to this author by another lucky visitor in 2005
offer no more promise of any suitable or sensible
maintenance; contrasted with the photographs that
Eden himself published and some additional ones in
Damerini's *Giardini di Venezia* of 1931, this once large
and hospitable zone is desolate and again returning
to the state in which Eden himself found it[27].

That sad narrative does suggest an important but
– during the 19th century, if not later – largely neglected
truth: that Venetian gardens prospered best when
they observed forms and structures consistent with
their local circumstances; delightful as Eden's creation must have been in its prime, or as exotic and
flamboyant as that of Papadopoli family, the "English"
or "picturesque" garden travels abroad and endures
foreign parts as awkwardly and impatiently as some
of its own citizens. The English Eden's thoughtful understanding of what was involved in the making of
his Giudecca garden suggests that the often frantic
cult of the picturesque as a design palette for Venetian gardens during the 19th century did not entirely

VIII.20 The entry to the Garden of Eden. Effectively closed now to any visitation, this access to the Eden garden seems, aptly perhaps, as forbidding as
the biblical site guarded since the Fall by an angel with a fiery sword to
prevent its re-occupation by humans.

satisfy or indeed work: this is especially true when we
review the condition and state of such sites today; a
hundred years later they have worn far less well in
comparison with the spaces of many older gardens.
This is due, inevitably, to three important factors: the
older gardens were usually smaller than some of the
larger picturesque examples (Groggia, Papadopoli,
Eden) and therefore susceptible to better and more
conservative maintenance; they were also mainly architectural, and less vulnerable to plant decay and
outgrowth; thirdly, several of the larger and "English"
gardens were open to the public, with inevitable repercussions on their wear and tear. But taste is also
fickle, Venetians are of a conservative nature, and a
long established type of Venetian garden continued
to enjoy some vitality, despite the blandishments of
the picturesque. And, furthermore, the more regular
spaces of older Venetian gardens furnished a more
satisfying contrast with the surrounding city than did
the busy meanderings of the picturesque.

Venice was not alone in experimenting with a range
of garden design styles and effects during the 19th
century, but her particular history and situation, confronted with the need after the fall of the Republic in
1797 to review her situation both internally and vis-à-
vis the larger world, were very different from those of
other emergent nations. Foreign occupation enforced
changes, not least in the urban fabric and city govern-
ance and therefore also in the social fabric of the city.

VIII.21 Inside the Garden of Eden.

VIII.22 Inside the garden of the Palazzo Albrizzi. A very private oasis, created in the 19ᵗʰ century on the site of a destroyed theatre.

Gardens may have been a minor element in this fresh appraisal, but they were by no means irrelevant, given their earlier role in Venice's self-fashioning. Whereas gardens had been private realms as far as concerned ownership, occupation and use, with Napoleon's creation of the Public Gardens, even for those for whom the results were less than pleasing, there was now the opportunity to have "places to walk", in Antonio Quadri's phrase. And once people took advantage of the new spaces of the Giardini Pubblici, the Giardini Reali and the Orto Botanico for that new recreation, the expectation was advanced that other notable private enclaves would nonetheless permit some availability. Quite how and on what terms access was granted to gardens like those of the Papadopoli, the Gradenigo, Zenobio or Galvagana is not clear[28]: but gardens throughout the Italian peninsula had always been relatively open to suitable visitors, and one suspects that social networking and personal contacts (Venice being a tight-knit community) played a significant part in obtaining entry for certain citizens and visitors into the city's private gardens. And so the previous balance and negotiation between public and private in the city were opened to scrutiny and revision, both among inhabitants and even more among the increasingly numerous foreigners, many of whom came for extended periods and doubtless brought with them expectations of public promenade as well as of private luxury.

A REPERTOIRE FOR FUTURE GARDENS

It remains then to see what if anything might be learnt from two centuries of garden culture since the fall of the Republic, now projected upon Venice's future. Many private gardens have been lost to various urban projects during that time, as well as to simple decay or lack of funds for upkeep. But equally many new private as well as public gardens were established during the 19ᵗʰ and early 20ᵗʰ centuries on sites that had been cleared of ruinous or unwanted buildings: bits and pieces of a new and revised Venice arose upon the clearings of the old. Eden was unusual in that he took over a large space hitherto dedicated to fruit and vegetable production, and the Groggia seems to have inherited an already gardened site. But just as both the Public and the Royal Gardens, along with the new *Orto Botanico*, rose on sites cleared of earlier convents, churches, housing, courtyards, windmills, granaries, *magazzini, depositi*, or other unwanted commercial structures, so after 1833 the Patarol garden replaced a famous and functioning botanical collection; that of the Papadopoli took over ex-conventual grounds; that of the Palazzo Balbi Valier Sammartini at San Vio was created on ground where an earlier palace was demolished and that of the Palazzo Cavalli Franchetti, San Vidal, when the 15ᵗʰ-century building was reconstructed in the 19ᵗʰ. The Albrizzi garden took over the site of a demolished theatre, making the most of the restricted space with winding paths and dense planting, even maintaining a small rise where the stage had originally been Figure VIII.21; the garden of the Palazzo Querini Papozze expanded to fill a structure destroyed by fire.

All in all, this post-republican chapter of Venice's garden history highlights two basic and related themes: what place does an expanding and modernizing city have for gardens and open green spaces? And what kind of garden–what sort of design, what range of uses–would be apt in this particular historical city as it turned efficiently and relentlessly modern even while maintaining its peculiar identity? In short, what grounds of being are needed, desired and feasible here in the 21ˢᵗ century? Some answers can be provided, some maybe provocative suggestions advanced, in a final chapter.

IX.1a Carlo Scarpa's garden for the Fondazione Querini Stampalia.

Possible gardens: grounds for change

In Venice, even today, we feel ourselves to be partakers of a dramatic version of a wider history than our own under the aegis of so many good objects seen about us....

Adrian Stokes[1]

Chapter Nine

That the Venetian garden cannot readily be subsumed into the modern narrative of the *giardino italiano* was clear to the magazine, *Rivista di Venezia*, in 1931. Reviewing the big nationalistic garden exhibition held at the Palazzo Vecchio in Florence[2], its author rejected the umbrella term "Italian" and remarked that it would be easy to put together an exhibition room which demonstrated how, from the 15th century "at least until the gardens of Romanticism", the Venice garden had established its own identity and forms. The previous chapters have had to perform the role of that display (as well as to suggest that the "romantic phase" itself did not lack particularly Venetian interests). But the last chapter here needs to attempt something further.

The Florence exhibition was mounted in large part as a means of promoting a renaissance of garden art in Italy along nationalistic lines[3]; without succumbing to the invidious political agenda of that endeavour, it is perhaps useful to suggest some ways in which Venice might draw upon its own particular garden traditions for the 21st century, when the future of the city and its physical structure and habitation are seriously challenged. Such an invocation of the past for present or even future purposes has an ancient Venetian precedent, since a 15th-century historian of its lagoon ecology, Marco Corner, urged a knowledge of the past as a means of understanding the future[4].

The potentialities of a future Venice are indeed endlessly raised, though not many of them have devoted much thought to a role for gardens in any visions of a future city. A book published by Electa in 1985 on historical projections for Venetian urban development and experimentation, edited by two distinguished art historians, Lionello Puppi and Giandomenico Romanelli, was entitled *Le Venezie Possibili da Palladio a Le Corbusier*. The city has always existed—and even relished its existence—between the impossible and the possible, as with Sansovino's admiring celebration of the very paradoxical founding of Venice "nello impossibile" and its many subsequent and altogether possible achievements, "le Venezie possibili"[5]. In 1666 Michelangelo Mariani's *Le Meraviglie della città di Venetia* gushed over a city "entirely fabricated of

marvels" (fabrication and the marvelous being the two poles of possible and impossible): there was its plentiful fresh water amid the salt sea, its abundant fertility amongst so much unpropitious "sterility", and its own solidity in a "più instabile Elemento" (A3 verso). Napoleon's promotion of public gardens against the grain and certainly over the ruins of much existing urban structure was yet another example of the impossible or at least the unthinkable made possible. And the city continues to come up with an astonishing range of proposals for its plausible continuance amidst conditions that seem on the face of things wholly impossible. The control of flooding in the lagoon, the debates about the Moses project, and the endless interventions to counter *acque alte* are but one obvious instance, not to mention more recent plans to dig twelve holes around the city's edge and pump seawater underneath to raise the whole city by one foot, or to create a metro system under the lagoon to bring tourists to the Fondamenta Nuove in the north of the city and relieve congestion on the west[6].

Venice has always seemed to attract visionary, and sometimes very immodest, proposals. They have generally run foul of those admirers and historians alike for whom Venice is unchangeable, those who endorse and encourage the "trope of 'Venice-as-past'"[7]. The "intoccabilità di Venezia", the untouchable essence of Venice as far as new architectural and urban interventions go, has often been a major cry of those who wish to preserve what they see as its historical "authenticity". Palladio's Romanizing architecture was mistrusted by his contemporaries, while Ruskin hated Renaissance intrusions into an essentially Byzantino-gothic city. Frank Lloyd Wright's design for a tiny *palazzo* was turned down by authorities nervous about its appropriateness next door to the enormous Palazzo Balbi. Napoleon's public gardens have been much denigrated, not least for their destruction of former green spaces. Even Calatrava's exhilarating new bridge across the Grand Canal linking the Piazzale Roma with the railway station has its detractors today, who cannot accept that its lazy curvature is an elegant rebuke to the nearby stiff climb of the Scalzi bridge. In short, the city can manifest a determinedly conservative streak in face of modern suggestions: Gino Damerini once noted that every time improvements were proposed for the greater "viability" of existence on either land or sea in Venice, there was a sudden outcry, protests arose, strong emotions were called into play, and (at the very least) debates were initiated[8]. Sometimes, anything new was dismissed outright: when the Frenchman Sergent-Marceau proposed a plan for the streetlighting of Venice in 1807, he reported that the local response was that citizens had always been able to see clearly at Venice for centuries, so there was nothing to gain from his proposal[9]. Not too long afterwards, however, gas lighting was introduced, and the building of gasworks at San Francesco della Vigna entailed the loss of yet more gardens.

It is as if the city's very untouchableness makes it an especially inciting challenge for those who wish most to enhance its scope, facilities and amenities. From Cornaro in the 16th century, to Bettini in the 18th, down to Frank Lloyd Wright, Le Corbusier, Carlo Scarpa, Eisenman, and now Kathryn Gustafson and Neil Porter as well as Calatrava, Venice has attracted or called upon a cluster of designers with visions of the possible future city. And what is also most interesting is how many of these projects, realized or not, have invoked gardens, including the competition sponsored by 2G, the architectural review published by Editorial Gustavo Gili: indeed, for Mariani in 1666, among the impossible miracles of the city, among its extraordinary and astonishing amenities like bridges and cloisters, was to be counted, above all, "l'amenità di tanti Giardini" (A4 recto). Napoleon considered he was doing the conquered city a favour by introducing new forms of public park and promenade, and some have agreed with him.

Cornaro's 16th-century proposals for the Bacino di San Marco, as we saw in Chapter Three, were deemed inappropriate, including as they did a permanent island theatre, another island landscaped in the latest irregular style of layout, and the whole city surrounded by a ring of walls topped with public gardens. In the mid-18th century Francesco Bettini, one of the most inventive and experimental of European garden designers and technological inventors, drafted a scheme for the cleansing of the canals by the ebb and flow of the tides that also seems to have incorporated

IX.1 Frank Lloyd Wright, Project for the Masieri Memorial, 1953. Balconies draped with foliage take up the habitual Venetian love of windowboxes and roof terraces in this unexecuted proposal.

–perhaps with reminiscences of Cornaro's proposal and anticipating Napoleon's work by fifty years–a series of tree-lined promenades. One of these would have stretched from the Fondamenta Nuove across the lagoon to Murano; then from Murano another promenade jutted in a series of elbow bends, touching another island, probably San Secondo or maybe Campalto, before finally rejoining the western end of the city near San Giobbe[10]. In the early 19th century Luigi Casarini thought the ruin of Venice could be arrested by joining it to the mainland with a wide road and sidewalks, planted with trees[11]. Then in the 20th century Le Corbusier's project for a new hospital, also at San Giobbe, drew upon traditions of Venetian corti, calli and roof gardens, and certainly indicated that trees would be planted in the first, while Wright's design for Cà Masieri on the Grand Canal, also unbuilt, would have had "gardens" or green balconies and Murano glass on its angle pilasters Figure IX.1 [12]. Louis Kahn also produced plans and a model of a congress hall intended for the gardens of the Biennale [13]. Scarpa, more luckily (a native Venetian, after all), actually created a new garden at the Palazzo Querini Stampalia, drawing (as we shall see) upon an eclectic repertoire of Venetian garden ideas.

At issue in almost all those urban "possibilities" has been the degree to which the "authentic" and old city of Venice could or should be modernized. But at least with gardens, modernization had been creeping in all along. We think now of the picturesque gar-

work in the south of France [14]. And yet Bac makes fun generally of those who perceived the need to modernize Venice: one of the fictional anecdotes of his *Le mystère Vénitien* of 1909 begins as "M de Guerande, rendu à sa solitude, se dirigea vers le palais sanseverino, restauré somptueusement par la princess, née Jonathen de Philadelphie...(M de Guerande ... made his way towards the palace at San Severo, sumptuously restored by the princess, née Jonathen from Philadelphia)". This American lady waxes eloquently on various modern amenities that would do the city a world of good, including motor cars, and a landing strip for aeroplanes at St. Mark's! Bac is fairly unsubtle

IX.2 Two photographs of gardens destroyed by the excavation of the Rio Nuovo, 1933. Urban work, largely to bring Venice into the 20th century and accommodate its ever-increasing visitors, frequently necessitated the elimination of considerable open and cultivated spaces in the centre.

den as a historical, old-fashioned style; but for Selva and contemporary garden theorists like Pindemonte or Mabil it was essentially modern, and to be separated (if possible) from any connection with a purely English-derived or English-endorsed landscape taste. Hence the Public Gardens imposed by the Emperor Napoleon were in one fundamental way an experiment with new urban forms and modern amenities, pleasing some and alienating others for precisely the same reason.

The Public Gardens were later dismissed by the exotic French garden designer, Ferdinand Bac, largely one suspects because his own designs show he had other, more symbolist and therefore more modern notions of garden scenery, though his interventions and work for the Johnsons at the famous Contarini dal Zaffo garden were not as extravagant as some of his other

in his ironies about "une santé nouvelle infusé à ces ruines", a modernizing rehabilitation of a ruined and unhealthy Venice to be financed with foreign monies derived from trade (where else did Venice's original money come from but from trade, though admittedly its own?); nonetheless, his satire identifies as one peculiarly Venetian dilemma the proper choice of suitably modern facilities and forms [15].

Yet, notwithstanding that American lady's vision of a landing strip on the Riva degli Schiavoni, the city had already entertained or would soon bravely enter the new world of modernity. The train had been crossing the lagoon since 1845; cars and buses would follow alongside it on the Ponte della Libertà in 1931–33. A pedestrian reorganization of the city and its transformation into a more land-based, urban zone involved bridges over the Grand Canal in front of the new railway station (1854) and at the Accademia (1853), along with many more, industrially fabricated iron bridges over smaller canals; *calli* were enlarged, many *rii* filled in [16]; *campi* were enlarged – that of Sant'Angelo by the demolition of its church in 1831 – or created anew by the levelling of Santa Maria Nova; gasworks came to San Francesco della Vigna by the end of the 1870s; a vaporetto service started in 1881, but already in 1872 Ruskin was appalled by the "accursed whistling of the dirty steam engine of the omnibus for Lido"[17]; industry continued to spread around the northern edges of the city; the Rio Nuovo was cut through the southern part in the 1930s to allow a quicker access from the Grand Canal to the area of the railway station, destroying many gardens and *orti* in the process Figure IX.2; modern housing clusters would be established around the edges of the city, sometimes with open areas and tree-lined *allées* between them, but often enough set down as unappetizing blocks with minimal and characterless open spaces between them.

Venice has therefore had a long experience of being poised between the possible and impossible, between "safe" authenticity and "dangerous" innovation. In which situation, therefore, we might enquire what Venice might conceivably do with her gardens. Such a question about the future possibility of Venetian gardens need not be idle, though it has seldom been asked and at any rate never properly answered. In 1952 the distinguished garden designer, Pietro Porcinai, addressed the IV. National Congress of Urban Planners in Venice, and he denounced the reduction of green spaces and their relegation to the edges of the city; he criticized projects lacking character or spiritual value, lamented the failure by urban designers to command adequate botanical knowledge or to respond creatively to the ecological systems (he castigated, in particular, the nervous re-direction of water back into the sea in concrete channels)[18]. And a contemporary Venetian landscape architect who has best studied the topic is right to note that the 20th century has not been a "happy phase" for the "patrimonio di verde storico della città"[19]. When in 1905 the Comune published its catalogue of monuments, and historical and artistic fragments throughout the city, organized by *sestiere* and then by parish, gardens are virtually lost sight of, unless they happen to be the site of sculpture. Otherwise, while well heads, inscrip-

tions, carved shields and escutcheons are faithfully recorded, gardens have no place in this artistic schedule[20]. Yet former gardens or their erstwhile spaces still survive throughout the city; they are reminders, if sometimes only fossils, of the long and rich tradition of gardens that have been called upon to enhance Venice's political self-fashioning. Are they to be left largely uncared for and redundant?

The Giudecca was once, with Murano, the garden suburb *par excellence* of the city, almost a country retreat for many of the nobility. Many of its famous sites have disappeared, recalled now only in surviving doorways or by toponyms (see the Gazetteer, Chapter Four). Yet even a casual tourist cannot help but notice that a not inconsiderable patchwork of gardens, mostly in private hands, still survives. Walking the length of the *fondamenta* beside the Giudecca Canal the alert visitor may glimpse gardens, some clearly stretching all the way through to the lagoon on the southern side of the island. In addition, as aerial views make clear, there are substantial areas of cultivated gardens, whether the lawns of the Cipriani Hotel, the inaccessible thickets of the Eden Garden see Figure VIII.17-19, or the productive gardens of the Redentore monks who occasionally permit visits. Penetrating down some of the *calli* away from the Giudecca Canal, visitors might further observe how frequently the inhabitants of the considerable modern public housing have installed garden plots in the open spaces between buildings (a more emphatic green supplement than the rather desultory trees that also line parts of the projects)[21]. Equally there are gardens deliberately hiding behind

IX.3 A former orchard (?) beside the Pio Loco delle Penitenti, which has been projected as a revived green space.

IX.4 View of the site of the original garden of the Palazzo Gradenigo. Fragments like this of earlier and larger gardens can still be seen throughout the city.

closed-up *claires-voies* or boarded-up gateways.

The same pattern, though much more infiltrated by industrial enclaves, can be observed throughout the Cannaregio. Indeed, to wander in this northern *sestiere* is to observe many places where, though a garden culture has been lost, its plausible spaces have not been entirely eliminated. Alongside the ruined (but about to be reconstituted) Pio Loco delle Penitenti is what looks as if it was a small orchard, now overgrown and its fruit trees neglected. **Fig. IX.3** From the nearby Ponte Moro there is an extensive view of a large open area with many trees entered from the Fondamenta Coletti (no.2991), and further down on the Fondamenta delle Capucine there are abundant green spaces behind the high walls of the ex-convent of San Gerolamo. Further, now on the Fondamenta de la Misericordia, more high walls do not entirely hide the existence of one of the few surviving productive gardens in the city, belonging to the Servite nuns, into which their lucky neighbours can have views **see Figure V.13**.

Thus it is still possible to recognize how much of Venice is dedicated to gardens in even the densest urban areas. To go on foot from the Piazzale Roma or the Ferrovia towards the Rialto (the necessary route for many tourists) is to encounter, if the eye chooses,

IX.5 Three Burano gardens today, typical of the eagerness and affection with which inhabitants of the lagoon, otherwise unpropitious to gardens, nonetheless make them wherever possible.

many vestiges of gardens even in this densest of urban areas. At the end of the very first *calle*, before taking a left turn, a glass doorway allows glimpses into the courtyard and remaining court and garden of the Palazzo Gradenigo, now a condominium (a short detour to the right at the next bridge allows a better view into what remains of that garden) **Figure IX.3**. Further along the route there are gardens and garden courtyards on all sides, even walled enclosures where private gardens still survive in spaces that were once ecclesiastical territory. The Campo di San Simeone Grande has two trees beside the Grand Canal and a hotel garden on its left-hand side, while behind the church itself another garden shows. Along the Lista Vecchia dei Bari a left-hand turning into the Corte Pugliese ends at an open-grille with extensive gardens beyond. Further gardens declare themselves with overhanging branches down both sides of the Salizada di Cà Zusto (to the right) and of the next Rio Terà (on the left). As you cross the Rio di San Zan Degolà into the Campo San Zan Degolà there are gardens overhanging on your left and a distant glimpse of gardens on the far side of the Grand Canal. The small Corte Corner sports four trees, and around the Rio di Cà Tron (itself with the remains of a fine garden: see Gazetteer, Chapter Four) are considerable open spaces into which *claires-voies* give occasional views; a fig tree flourishes in a small side garden by its canal. As the visitor approaches the more commercial areas of the Rialto, hints of gardens diminish steadily. It is a miscellaneous repertoire: not all are maintained or even obviously cherished as gardens, but they are clearly there, an ineluctable element of the urban fabric.

There is something of a paradox in all this. On the one hand, everywhere around the edges of the modern city there are tracts of open land left derelict or barely tended, given over at best to basketball courts or to industrial enterprises that do not, on the face of things, look very thriving (let alone, of course, very inviting). On the other hand, it is obvious that Venetians do enjoy gardens in a variety of forms, and cleave to their sometimes random occurrence within the urban fabric. Among the striking "garden" moments in the city, indeed, are the many window boxes, the decoration of the roof terraces or *altane* (a very Venetian phenomenon, visible ever since the earliest city views of Carpaccio and later Canaletto [22]), the floral embellishment of landing stages (especially gondolier stations, where vines are trained on pergolas [23]) and the inventive re-use of various abandoned utensils, including old boats, in which to make gardens (see the group of "gardens" in **Figure VIII.14**). Julia Cartwright was quite right when she observed that "Few Italians take greater pleasure in flowers and gardens than the people of Venice" (p.102). And where space is less pressured, as on Burano, the incidence of garden plots is remarkable **Figure IX.5**. Sometimes this is done with a zest and invention, as well as wit: some years ago behind the Scuola di San Rocco (but unhappily removed in the meantime) was a fantastic display of window decorations, coloured windmills, flags and

IX. 6 Window "garden" display on Castelforte, San Rocco, 1970s. Instead of the usual flower displays this "windowbox" invokes imagery of the lagoon, sails and windmills, to make its own "gardenist" contribution to the cityscape. Unhappily no longer there.

miniature sails – an "alternative garden" strung along the rio façade of the Castelforte block of apartments, where the mills whirled in response to the changes of the winds and, unlike conventional window boxes, did not need to be refurbished with seasonal plants Figure IX.6. It was a private, yet very publicly visible, and extremely inventive "garden".

In asking what a revived garden culture might possibly hold for a Venetian future, it is important to make two major points. First, that this question is not driven by a conventional and sentimental craving for "green space" in the midst of a labyrinthine and watery city; rather it is because gardens, courtyards and grassed squares were and still are an ineluctable part of Venice, and, more particularly, part of individual urban complexes the ensembles of which need to be considered [24]. Second, that the quality of these spaces is peculiar to Venice and not susceptible to appropriation linguistically or physically: the American landscape architect, Lawrence Halprin, got it absolutely right when he noted that if spaces between buildings – as on the Lido – get too big then they "fill with green and suburbia creeps in" [25]. It is the scale and focus of Venetian gardens that make them special.

Carlo Scarpa knew this instinctively. He also displayed the inventiveness, ingenuity and flair of ordinary Venetians in their pursuit of garden effects. Two of his gardens survive in Venice. That in the entry to the University Architecture School at the Tolentini was created after his death, but retains something of his vision Figure IX.7 & 8. The flatness, the horizontality of Vene-

tian ground, is emphasized (more authentically than by contrasting it with a piled-up, picturesque montagnola) by the classical doorframe laid on its side and filled (sometimes) with water; Scarpa-esque concrete frames that echo and enclose it allow a sly element of terracing (they can also be used to sit on). Both those rectangles and the walled entry, with its very modern gate, insist upon the garden's enclosure, a small segment that anticipates the large cloister within; for all the comings and goings that cut through the garden and into the University building, it somehow maintains its quietude. And, above all, even while it renegotiates an old Venetian space, it does nothing to conceal or repress its careful modernist vision.

The same is even more true of Scarpa's designs for the Fondazione Querini Stampalia [26]. The wonderful modern bridge from the small campiello first takes the visitor into a hallway where the pedestrian floor is raised in places above channels that, as the high tides enter the buildings, fill with water. At the far end of this modernized androne or aula (hall) is the garden. Glass doors across the whole opening reveal first the pillars of its portico, then the raised lawn Figures IX.1a & 9–12. This is the first sign of Scarpa's play with small-scale adjustments of level, a familiar device in earlier gardens where the flat topography of Venice allowed no strong vertical movements so common in gardens elsewhere in Italy. The small size of the garden makes more prominent Scarpa's resourceful manipulation of levels, like raised plinths for the well or the bronze pool and for the miniature labyrinth; the spiral pool, in

contrast, *descends*. Water also is allowed to fall from tiny chutes, while the miniature "canal" passes across the whole garden in front of the palace, the first element encountered on the raised lawn. The garden gathers this eclectic anthology of Venetian items, but denies them their expected roles: the little lion of St. Mark's crouches to dominate the length of the "canal"; the wellhead is genuine but "dry", with no cistern beneath. Textures crowd upon the visitor – different materials, the patina of humidity, the abrupt contrasts of plants with stone and metalwork. All of these details fill the visitor's attention, owing in part to the relatively small space; yet their rich plenitude also seems to make the garden bigger than it can actually be. The main garden, small as it is, even has a further courtyard segment, glimpsed and then reached behind the free-standing wall that is decorated with a line of mosaic by Mario DeLuigi and from which we can look back into the main garden that is suddenly perceived as "larger". It could be nowhere but in Venice, yet it avoids any hint of pastiche.

A third, Scarpa-like garden-courtyard has been inserted among modern ENEL office buildings off the Fondamenta Malcanton, behind the Campo di Santa Margherita. An antique wellhead stands in the middle, with stone drainage covers at the four corners of the brick courtyard **Figure IX.13**. Stone ledges surround it on four sides (the fourth is taken by the wall of a building), with very slight risers nonetheless executing a movement upwards to another square plot, this time planted, while beyond a third area is grassed.

IX.9 – 12 Garden of the Fondazione Querini Stampalia. This wonderful creation is wholly modern in spirit, yet invokes an anthology of Venetian references and local garden elements.

Once perfectly visible through iron railings along the *calle*, the hedge is now overgrown, the view occluded and the whole looking somewhat desolate. Whether it was ever used or was designed simply as a space-filler, albeit in the Venetian mode, to be looked at from the rows of office windows is unclear: it now seems to be enterable through a University institute on the *rio*.

There is a rather different, modern Venetian garden at the Guggenheim Collection, designed by Giorgio Bellavitis in 1983. It responded both to different spaces and to different uses, but in no sense did it lose sight of its locality, not least that it was appended to an unfinished *palazzo* and could itself play with different ways in which a 20th-century Venetian garden could be "finished". Essentially a rectangle laid (in this instance) parallel to the Palazzo, it functions as both a foyer to the Museum and a place for the display of sculpture Figure IX.15. In more recent years it has been augmented by the Museum's lease and purchase of buildings along the Rio delle Torreselle and the subsequent connection of their small back garden-courtyards to the original Bellavitis space Figure IX.14. In fact, this enlargement has produced what is wonderfully apt for a museum – a succession of small exposition spaces – while maintaining a typically Venetian collocation of discrete garden rooms. The original rectangular garden loses its rigidity and potential constriction in a geometrical pattern of various stonework that seems a witty reversal of pavement patterns elsewhere in the city: There white Istrian stone traces out forms that recall the outlines of *parterre de broderie* or real flower beds Figure IX.16, of the sort illustrated by Serlio, who said his designs could also be used for ceiling decoration or other things ("usus ad alia")[27]. Here at the Guggenheim the much more cubist forms draw out the space in unfamiliar shapes, which are then interrupted by low planting beds and the marble-pillared gazebo Figure IX.17; ivy on the walls mutes, too, the sense of built enclosure.

Four such modern gardens in Venice, three open to visitation and the fourth potentially visible to passers-

IX.12 A wall hides a small courtyard in the Fondazione Querini Stampalia garden.

IX.13 Courtyard in modern office building at Dorsoduro 3449 (1980s). This modern space recalls, without slavish imitation, some traditions of the Venetian courtyard and garden.

IX.14 Garden of the Peggy Guggenheim Collection, designed by Giorgio Bellavitis, one of the leading architects of Venice; it responds to the particular site and its use as a museum, while also re-imagining modern configurations of the Venetian tradition of palace gardens. The sculptures are by Barry Flanagan (on the left) and Giuseppe Spagnulo (right).

IX.15 Garden of the Peggy Guggenheim Collection.
The sculpture in the left foreground is by Isamu Noguchi.

by, are hints of what a garden agenda might do for the city at its best. None of them contribute to what Dennis Cosgrove calls the "Disneyfication of Venice", nor yet to what Henry James called "a battered peep-show and bazaar" [28]. They are not in the same league by any means as endless emporia selling *papier maché* and Murano glass and carnival costumes throughout the year. Nor is it (though thank heavens nobody has

IX.16 A Venetian pavement pattern of "flower beds". This patterning of the pavements in open spaces and colonnades throughout the city seems to replicate the layout of flowerbeds.

IX.17 Another view in the Guggenheim garden: the view is of the grave of Peggy Guggenheim and her dogs. The gazebo is a survivor from her early garden of the 1950s

suggested this) as if they had recreated a zoological garden in imitation of the collection of lions and leop-ards kept by Lorenzo Celsi at the Doge's Palace in the late 14th century [29]. They do contribute, it must be ad-mitted (two of them literally), to the sense of the city as a "vast museum", which Henry James identified as early as 1882. But then he was shrewdly prophetic in his understanding of Venice as a "city of exhibi-tion", not necessarily referring only to carnavalesque theatricality, so much as to Venice's larger skills of self-display, as when only five years after he wrote the Public Gardens were transformed into the site of the Esposizione Nazionale Artistica. This was itself translated into the Biennale of Visual Arts in 1895, to which music and theatre were added in 1930 and 1934

Nourishment
[Abundance]

Remember
[The Store Room]

Enlightenment
[Contemplation]

0   10m 20m   40m

IX. 18 The site of Kathryn Gustafson's and Neil Porter's garden, "Towards Paradise", 2008.

respectively, and in 1932 the Esposizione Internazionale d'Arte Cinematografica (known as a "Mostra" from 1934), which continues in summer film shows in the Campo San Polo. Venice has made itself so successfully into a stage for festivals that an exhibition or festival of gardens does not seem such an impossibility.

And this is precisely what the Architecture Biennale initiated by asking the distinguished landscape architects, Kathryn Gustafson and Neil Porter, to exhibit in 2008. Their firm's temporary creation was installed on the much overgrown site of the former Convento delle Vergini see Fig. V.9 at the furthest extreme of the Arsenal beside one of the towers that marks the entry to the Darsena Nuovissima and faces across its canal the cathedral church of San Pietro di Castello Fig.

IX. 18. Rather than clearing the site completely, three insertions were made into its dense thickets: a "Store Room", a recollection of older cabinets of curiosity, now with the Latin names of flora and fauna inscribed behind its shelves Fig. IX. 20; a luxuriant vegetable garden Fig. IX. 19; finally an open, oval clearing Fig. IX. 21, grassed and where helium-filled weather balloons held up cloud-like veils of white fabric (though these were apparently only there for the opening). The poetry of this design, entitled "Towards Paradise" was undeniable, even if its gestures towards locality were somewhat slight. In a recent lecture Gustafson herself explained how she was inspired by a painting of paradise seen in the Accademia, a connection that was necessarily lost on site; the "clouds" above the

IX. 19 The vegetable and fruit garden in the Gustafson Porter Garden at the Biennale.

open grass mounds she also compared to Tiepolo-like cloudscapes in 18th-century Venetian painting, while the vegetable garden, as she told her lecture audience in an aside, was created where the original convent *orto* had been. Its wonderful profusion of this space, with plants grown in advance to replicate the former institution's self-sufficient *broglio* was a stroke of genius, the more palpable for coming upon it after negotiating one's way through the empty and desolate spaces of the old Arsenal[30].

Le Corbusier saw Venice as "aujourd'hui encore un admoniteur"[31]. He was presumably thinking of how the city might still admonish and even lead some creative thinking in urban development. Yet if his own contribution may be gauged from the unexecuted proposals for a hospital at San Giobbe (cut off by his death in 1965), it must be confessed that they respond only partly to the Venetian context, though they obviously fascinate those who are excited by his architecture and by the possibilities of modernist urbanism in the city (Peter Eisenman saw it as "one of the last anguishes of heroic modernism")[32]. Its planted courtyards would have been perhaps an acknowledgement

of Venetian prototypes[33], but the blind, windowless blocks that turned their backs on the city as well as denying patients any outside views seem misguided, and the scale of the footprint much too large. Its advocates laud its superimposition of a grid upon the irregular fabric of the city, a modernist re-formulation that was also advanced more generally over the western Cannaregio area. But the problem with Venice is that the urban palimpsest cannot be ignored, and though Eisenman explicitly rejects them, his playful graphic explorations of Venice's own unique spatial and labyrinthine elements are much more attentive to this local experience. Despite acknowledging the gardens of that area and their surrender to modern industry and infrastructure (slaughterhouses, dye works, mills, factories), he plays only with built elements.

Other proposals, that also came to naught, have failed even more grossly to grasp the particular scale and scope of Venetian gardens. In a move that seemed ironically to replicate Napoelon's dismemberment of the city and the installation of large swaths of public gardens (though this parallel was never apparently remarked upon at the time), the communist city council in the mid-1970s proposed to confiscate all the gardens along a considerable stretch of the Dorsoduro to establish what would have amounted to a green ribbon of public open space; other parts of the city would also have been annexed for "Verde Pubblico". Given that most areas in question were privately owned, the outcry was not surprisingly huge, and dozens of residents lodged their formal protests, in

protest elicited, is a fund of ideas and suggestions for a much more sensitive and nuanced celebration of Venice's green spaces.

Napoleon, Le Corbusier and the communist city council have not been alone in failing to produce any convincing proposals for the use of urban gardens.[35] In a variety of projects, some official, others exploratory and emerging from University design studios, the is-

IX.20 "The Store Room" or Cabinet displaying the names of extinct flora and fauna, in the Gustafson Porter garden at the Biennale, 2008.

IX.21 The Clearing for "Enlightenment & Contemplation", the third element of the Gustafson Porter garden at the Biennale, 2008.

texts of which are many glimpses of the city's already established garden culture[34]. Peggy Guggenheim reminded officials of the public access to the gardens of her own collection and its eventual donation to the city; Sir Ashley Clarke, former British ambassador to Italy, noted how his own 18th-century property had recovered the "classic form" of a Venetian palace garden, with "grass, shrubs, flowering plants and trees"; others who formally lodged objections included Alberto Gianquinto, Herbert Hériott, many academics, architects and artists, several religious orders (including the Opera Pia Zuane Contarini) and even the Società Canottieri Querini (a rowing club). While each protest inevitably had its own agenda, a leitmotif of them all was the plan's utter disregard of the historical, piecemeal patchwork of traditional courtyards, gardens and their close links to different built structures throughout the city. The reaction was effective enough to stop the project in its tracks (indeed, how it could ever have been implemented without another Napoleon is a mystery). However, the documentation of this network of urban open spaces, along with their historical character and contemporary uses, which the

sue of open green space plays a small role in what is often, admittedly, a much larger programme of confronting environmental decay and urgent housing needs. But the "lack of gardens" is isolated by Elena Bassi in *Venice for Modern Man*, and (on the basis of historical evidence) their replacement urged; a study of popular housing in San Giuseppe (Castello) in the same volume eliminates overcrowding by removing built insertions in 16th-century blocks and substituting "green areas" between units. Several proposals seem to urge a proper historical regard for a specifically Venetian situation, without necessarily showing how it might be exploited: Stefinlongo's book *Il "Giardino" del Doge. I Giardini del Popolo. Studi sul restauro urbano ...*, as its title indicates, is an exception, yet even his review of the various forms of garden throughout the city is transposed in the assembled student projects only to the outlying lagoon areas where islands afford more scope for new design. Their projection of the lagoon itself as an accessible and popular "garden" (p.59) envisions a recuperation of both historical structures and the lagoon environment for consumption by more than the daily tourist. As their choice of sites im-

Mención
Mention

FJ749
(The Batrachian and the Wader)
Gauthier Le Romancer,
Guillaume Derrien

Francia France

The lagoon of Venice combines both extremely refined architecture originating from its position between oriental and western civilisations, and primary landscape born when life was only amphibian. A gigantic contrast that gives this territory an extra-ordinary dimension.

It is J.M.W.Turner painting Venice through the mist of the lagoon.

Our proposal leads you to imagine the site of Sacca San Mattia as the extension of a natural and wild landscape. Thus, as you cross the boundaries of the city, you will be able to experience a world which, until then, lay too far out in the lagoon, off tourist tracks.

The park of Sacca San Mattia will as much as possible be designed by nature itself.
To facilitate reconquest, the old wasteland will be reshaped, less high, closer to the water and allowing it to flow through. The contours will be less precise, more blurred.
To achieve this, the bank will be punctuated with a network of wooden poles that will retain sediments, propitious to the formation of an amphibian ecosystem.
In time, the network will disappear under the marshes. But, here and there, some of the poles will still stick out like the *bricolles* that delimit the canals in the lagoon. We will use them as moorings for our lagoon prototypes.

Altanas float on the roofs of Venice.
Altanas are small wooden terraces fixed on the roofs of buildings. These light structures allow a breath of fresh air on hot summer evenings, but mostly provide distance to admire the city.
The lagoon prototype repeats this Venitian archetype.
The altanas will now float above the lagoon.

And like urban altanas they will top a home, a gite, partly buried in the ground, hidden, almost invisible. Our lagoon prototype aims at making us sense the intimacy of the lagoon in all its dimensions.
It offers two points of view: from inside, in this ambiguous part-water, part-earth place, and from above, in the haze and the sea breeze: the batrachian and the wader.

THE BATRACHIAN & THE WADER

IX. 22 One of the proposals for the Park on the Sacca di Mattia, Murano, 2007.

plies, the appeal to contemporary designers of "edge conditions" finds considerable opportunities around the outskirts of a city that often seems restricted simply to a historical core packaged for tourisms. Yet what emerges is largely new architecture rather than landscape design (see, in particular, *Venezia Novissima*); where the latter is invoked, it seems to draw its inspiration from non-Venetian sources (Beverly Pepper and American land art in *Lavorare sui bordi*). A sponsored investigation of new urban designs for the Giudecca in 2003 was almost by necessity obliged to recall its gardenist history, yet the student projects display mainly just a dutiful response to that precedence, scattering trees, inserting picturesque mounding and meandering forms as "visual buffer". Many of the proposals seem thoughtful, yet apt and useful for any location, without sufficient regard to the Venetian context, with the exception of the interface of public and private in new housing and the renewal of traditional modes of collecting rainwater and run-off.

A more sustained and determined effort to see how landscape architecture might contribute to new designs and urban forms in the Venetian lagoon was the large international competition sponsored in 2007 by the magazine *2G* for the 31-hectare area on the northern edge of Murano, the Sacca San Mattia[36]. The project invited designs for both a "lagoon park" (with a programme of jetties for lagoon transportation, boat rentals, sports facilities, performance space, and a visitor centre) and what were somewhat oddly listed as "lagoon prototypes" (a refuge, an observatory, a landing stage, "energy way stations" and a "signposting system" for weather and tourist information). And while many of these items were indeed provided, what strikes a reader of the subsequent publication is rather the entrants' exuberant manipulation of digital imagery rather than any demonstration of what the designs, if implemented, would look like and how they would enhance a modern visitor's response to the city. Furthermore, despite much lip-service paid by both jury and competitors to the unique physical, cultural and historical situation of Venice, few of the entries displayed any ability to localize their responses. The ecological demands of the lagoon were the constant focus, to be sure, but for most entrants the solutions were scarcely site-orientated. Interestingly, little attention – playing fields apart – was paid to the permanent inhabitants of either Murano or the lagoon

generally. That the subsequent publication included three more historically informed essays makes even more conspicuous by its absence in the competition an informed knowledge of Venetian urban and garden history (to call the Piazza di San Marco an "urban void", for instance, simply beggars belief!). The first prize awarded to what one juror called a "post-apocalyptic" proposal to cover the whole site with a green canopy of industrial, seaweed-derived tubing over picnic grounds was an indication that, in the final result, attention to the specific site and its meaning for visitors and residents alike held less interest for designers than their own creative adventures. At its best, the competition will have perhaps provided, as another juror argued, a "field of possibilities" for a future Venice, hints for a subsequent but as yet undefined self-fashioning.

Indeed, much about this competition was initially persuasive and suggestive: the choice of site – a *sacca* was the place where Venice had long since managed to extend its land surfaces by dumping urban debris; and Murano itself, traditionally the site of large-scale Venetian gardens and estates and where some vernacular gardening still persisted on open ground (see pp.102), surely invited some reconsideration of its former gardenist profile, if only to set against the island's current emphasis upon glass manufactory, the debris from which has filled this particular wasteland. Some of the entries also reveal both acute understanding of the Venetian situation and, its corollary, a determination to reveal the lagoon to visitors with a very limited sense of Venicity (a limitation professed also by some of the jurors). Thus one entry returns the *sacca* to its watery marshland, with hides from which to watch the wildlife (utilizing, nicely, the Venetian *altana* Fig. IX.22). Another proposes a series of floating archipelagos (gardens, fields, boathouses, stages, stadia), while yet another invites different pedestrian excursions across a variety of inventive pathways and bridges (all in the interests of curbing boat traffic Fig. IX.23. Many of these entries also struggle to bring the short-stay tourist out of the city and into a richer lagoon experience. In the final resort, the size of the site presented a very un-Venetian challenge (Napoleon's public gardens being the only possible precedent); so Murano gets itself a park, in some versions of which its unique lagoon situation is celebrated, but in too many cases it simply receives features that characterize park-

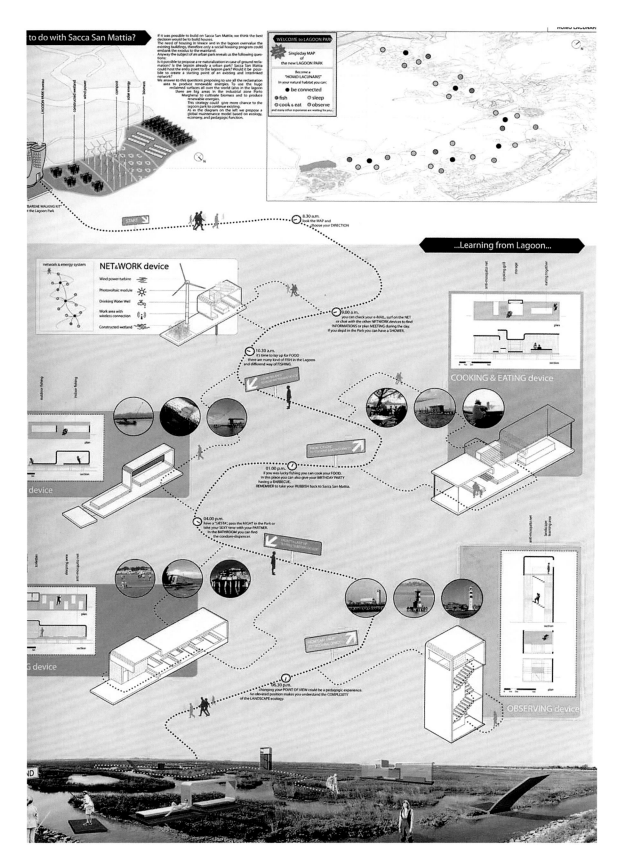

IX.23 Another project in the 2007 *2G* competition.

lands anywhere and would not be much of a draw for visitors anticipating something particularly Venetian. All of these explorations of a possible Venice have come as responses to the clamorous demands for "Trasformazioni urbane" in the last 15 years, and many reach away from the historical core simply because there, in the outer sections on abused industrial land and in abandoned environments, the opportunities for incisive and striking interventions are more apparent and tempting. As the protests from the 1970s, however, made, clear, it is the small-scale, more modest and inevitably more subtle opportunities of the city itself that are its unique contribution, too often neglected until they are under threat.

So it still remains to be asked to what extent, and how, a historical perspective of the Venetian city garden can instruct and admonish (to echo Le Corbusier) those in whose hands lies the future of the city's fabric and topography. Gardens are often, if emptily, touted in the various proposals that have punctuated the city's self-scrutiny as long ago as the 1920s: during that and the following decade some efforts were made to "green" the city with trees—they were planted in Campo San Giacomo dall'Orio and along the Zattere in double formation; a Festival of Trees was held on Murano in November 1928[37]. In virtually all cases the planners ignored both the special typology of Venetian gardens, with its freightage of myth and symbolism, and the various uses to which these have been put. They also ignored the role that the different kinds of open space—*giardino* (or to use a local dialect word, *broglio*), *orto*, *campo*, *corte*—have variously played in both the real life of the city and its various fictions, many self-constructed. At issue today, above and beyond the key technical problems, much debated, of flood or tide control, is how to envisage a life for Venice in the 21st century. What role might gardens play in the necessary and anyhow inevitable self-fashioning that Venice must undertake?

As this book was in press, came news of a new garden to be created on the island of San Servolo; it is to be a "Chinese" garden designed and built by Ye Fang from Suzhou, the south China city twinned with Venice[37a]. It will be an epitome of traditional Chinese gardens—wandering streams, a pond, waterfalls, pavilions, pathways, seats, and even "mountains", recalling the gardens that Marco Polo would have encountered in his Asian peregrinations, and it is indeed a "gift" offered to Marco Polo, or at least to his city. This small Chinese garden will be, it is claimed, "in harmony" with the original ambience of the island. Plants will be those that grow in the Veneto, but "annotated with the traditional Chinese cultural senses", and indeed the whole is animated by an elaborate, symbolical and mythological apparatus of associations and philosophical references. There will, however, be gestures towards the symbiosis of Venetian and Chinese cultures—a traditional Suzhou archway made of Murano glass, a transparent peach tree also of glass, and other sectors decorated with fluorescent coloured mosaics (shades here of the glass garden in the *Hypnerotomachia Poliphili*). But there will also be electronic displays inside a grotto—a symbol, we are informed, of the "looking-glass in the depths of our heart". Shelves of writings on Marco Polo's travels and on Italian and Chinese garden art will be installed in one of the pavilions. All of which could be welcomed, perhaps, in the spirit of Italo Calvino's *Invisible Cities*, except that now we will have a real place, implausibly and materially anchored in the lagoon, rather than the virtual impressions of many cities, "discontinuous in space and time". Maybe this new garden on San Servolo will turn out, after all (but we didn't know it), to have been included in the Great Khan's atlas that contained "the maps of the promised lands visited in thought but not yet discovered or founded".

The larger issues are all too evident and the alarms clearly raised: the authors of *Venice the Tourist Maze* even claim that it's not meaningful to talk about Venice as a city anymore, because the city is basically already a lost cause[38]. Plausible economic revitalizations don't work—factories cannot be built. Houses prices and the cost of restorations drive more and more residents to the mainland, even though some new middle-class housing is being built around the edges (Castello, Santa Marta, Cannaregio). Bakeries and butchers close down; their places are taken by shops that seek to cater to the ever increasing visitors who look to take away a tangible souvenir of an authentic Venice. The *vaporetto* service is so over-charged that the ACTV briefly instituted a service down the Grand Canal only for residents[39].

Assuming—optimistically, in the view of many—that the city survives its salt-water location for another hundred years, habitation and existence will depend upon fresh negotiations between the private and the public, between those who continue to be able to live here and those who come in as visitors. Public and private have always been contested in urban centres, but are even more pressing in a city that finds itself less and less a place of habitation and livelihood and increasingly a stage of tourism. In all of this the garden seems a very minor player. Yet, even if W.H.Auden was right that "art makes nothing happen", garden art has contrariwise often performed an enabling social role, especially when it has taken its public responsibilities seriously (which is not to say *only* in making public parklands). Seemingly, Venice's default position on open space is to fall back on the provision of *campi sportivi*; important as those are, as a mantra for open space it is not nearly sufficient, though perhaps a tendency upon which to build. Spaces, of which there are many in Venice and not all of them laid out in basketball courts, cry out to be used ("Lo spazio chiama l'azione"[40]), above all in a city where space is at a premium and where the scale of things, relative at the best of times, is here endlessly revised. Spaces in Venice have been used with extraordinary skill and imagination, and the challenge is to re-invent those possibilities. So here are, finally, a few suggestions – from a "foreigner" (always suspect and repudiated by true Venetians), but from somebody whose study of the city's gardens and open spaces over the last 35 years encourages him to entertain some "impossible" possibilities for this untouchable city. I offer them in a series of theses:

1. The ecological history as well as the ecological health of the lagoon can be promoted and interpreted for a public that is increasingly alert to the importance of these issues. There are projects for an Eco-Museum near the Arsenal and for the reclamation of the island of San Giorgio in Alga as the home of the Forum for the Lagoon run by the University of Minnesota, which has been active in debating possible interventions where preservation is not valued "for its own sake", nor as establishing a "sterile museum" but as a means of adding value and promoting the territory. All of which is important in itself – if Venice is to disappear, we might as well have a museum of the site into which it has vanished. But the larger ecological context should also help to focus attention at the much smaller scale of gardens, which have always been part of the whole picture.

2. The existing public garden spaces need to be restored and introduced into the public consciousness of tourist and resident alike. The wonderful, but decaying greenhouses in the midst of the Public Gardens need to be conserved and put to some use – either as a municipal nursery or, better still, as an interpretation centre for the history of the Public Gardens (restoration of their structures had belatedly started in the spring of 2008). Similarly, the 19th-century iron pergola that runs down the length of the Royal Gardens should be restored, and this actually very pleasant retreat on hot summer days resuscitated. The former botanical gardens at San Giobbe, to all intents and purposes idle as the ENEL social club, could be dedicated to a new botanical garden, in which the plants and botanical scholarship of Venice can be displayed. It is in fact astonishing that the city's resonant traditions of botany for medicinal, productive and pleasurable ends are not celebrated; the Museum of Natural History seems uninterested in such an role, which should anyway be carried out in practice, with the actual plants and their histories made available, for which the present Museum has no space. (Such a use for the San Giobbe site need not necessarily exclude the use of part of the site as some social centre).

3. Next, the recovery and provision of open green space – not just for athletic purposes – is vital and, given the amount of derelict land, relatively easy. The island of Sant'Angelo delle Polveri is already destined to be a "verde pubblico" (*Isole Abbondonate della Laguna*, p.103), and a rather undistinguished park has been newly established at San Giuliano on the nearby mainland. But there should be other opportunities within the city itself. The rehabilitation of the Pio Loco delle Penitenti, already mentioned, has usefully accepted to refurbish the adjacent *orto*. Many more opportunities like that exist at all scales. That some might well encroach upon private property is likely; but Venice, that has always invoked private space as part of its public persona, that has always featured green spaces on its maps, could well accept that one of its genuine public riches in the 21st century is its private gardens.

4. But that proposal could be carried much further in various ways. A very simple method would be to make private gardens and open spaces accessible to the sight of passers-by. The innumerable wall openings or *claires-voies* through the city are a very old element of gardens

and many of them do indeed give onto such spaces; but they are usually blocked by iron sheets, just as open lattice-work doors are covered to ensure privacy Figure IX.24. If they were opened up, the untended gardens behind might be exposed to view, and that, too, might be an incentive to gardeners to work their ground more effectively (see Thesis 6).

5. Doubtless a more contentious issue – it smacks of the failed communistic "take-over" of Dorsoduro gardens in the 1970s – would be to open up private gardens for limited periods. There are already some garden tours organized by the Wigwam Club[41], and a guidebook by Mariapia Cunico includes four city gardens in its itineraries, though two of them can be accessed so infrequently that the opportunity is in fact meagre. But a start has nonetheless been made, and given the incidence of gardens throughout the city some considerable extension of the possibility could be made. The well-established and familiar annual publication of the UK "Yellow Book" of private gardens, opened for brief periods yet announced in advance, offers one model. This thesis builds upon

IX.24 A selection of *claires-voies* and blocked garden doorways in Venice (2008). The modern visitor is confronted endlessly with gates and fences that yield views into the open spaces behind, some of which are cultivated; many such private enclaves, however, are blocked off from prying and curious eyes.

IX. 25–28 Four views in the recently restored gardens of Palazzo Soranzo Capello: the loggia at the garden's end, the *brolio* flanking the palace, and two views in the main garden.

the suggestion by Giorgio Bellavitis in 1971 that more buildings and urban complexes be open to public use and visitation[42].

6. But if we are being visionary, then let us also take a leaf out of that masterpiece of European civic projection, Sir Thomas More's *Utopia*, and propose that Venice hold annual garden competitions among the *sestieri*. These could be conducted in various categories or classes: competitions for window boxes, *altane*, ad hoc and improvised locations, commercial properties, private gardens occasionally open to the public, private gardens only viewable from the outside, abandoned spaces recovered for a variety of garden uses, and so on. If Venetians do love flowers as much as everybody claims, then this might well be a means of cultivating that taste and yet opening its private pleasures to public view.

7. There is also the proposal, articulated by Leonardo Ruffo, to restore some historical sites. This has already been done, magnificently, for the garden of the Palazzo Soranzo Cappello (see p.80). However, apart from a distant glimpse of its refurbished spaces through glass doors and down the long hallway of an office building, it is not open to visitors. It is intimidating to try and gain access to it, even to look into it, although it is also understandable that visitors cannot be coped with and kept under the eye of a single

porter at all times. (Ironically, though, the building houses the offices of the Soprintendenza per i Beni Architettonici, per il Paesaggio e per il Patrimonio Storico, Artistico e Etnoantropologico di Venezia e Laguna!) Fig. IX.25–28.

Ruffo's proposal was to identify a series of historical prototypes and, selecting a Venetian site that corresponds to each, recreate that garden. It obviously takes its cue from the Piano Regolatore Generale of 1992 that provided, as a prelude to any planning or new interventions, for the classification of every one of the city's buildings on the basis of historical typology, but unfortunately ignoring the palimpsestial character of Venice, which is also recognizable in many of its gardens. I am in two minds about Ruffo's project that, on the one hand, might enlarge the understanding of gardens in the Venetian culture by opening a string of what would amount to garden-museums, but, on the other hand, tilts uncomfortably towards yet again presenting Venice in a frozen series of theatrical peep-shows. A better version of his proposal, already put into practice at Palazzo Soranzo Cappello by the Soprintendenza, would be to identify a series of significant gardens that could be researched and restored and then perhaps opened for limited visits with some provision for their interpretation. There might even, a last wishful thought, be sponsors to take on this saving of an essential part of the Venetian cultural scene. Such restorations should include some or all of the pub-

IX. 27

IX. 28

lic gardens, the Garden of Eden, and some open spaces where private gardens were nonetheless once opened to public visitation, like the Palazzi Vendramin and Foscarini at the Carmini; it should also, since there are so many of these really secret gardens, include at least one ecclesiastical *orto*.

But once resurrected, these gardens must be open to at least occasional visitation: gardens without users are empty in more than the obvious way. Tourists might then be able in reality to follow in the footsteps of fictional characters who have access to gardens in the Venetian city, like Commissario Guido Brunetti in Donna Leon's *The Death of Faith* (1997), who in its eight chapter enters the courtyard of the Fathers of the Sacred Cross ("near the Church of San Francesco della Vigna" [43]) and finds it crammed with many species of lilac.

8. Finally, since what is strenuously to be avoided is pastiche or kitsch, the creation of a few important landscape architectural competitions would contribute to rethink the Venetian garden in the spirit (but, again, not in the manner) of Carlo Scarpa and Giorgio Bellavitis, two distinguished modern architects of this city. Their imaginative and intellectual investment in the urban history of Venice, matched with their individual design vision, was exemplary. It also posits a challenge for others to revisit and re-imagine Venetian gardens once

again. Too much of the landscape architectural thinking, as sketched above, is bland, pragmatic and, above all, homogeneous: it could be used anywhere, anytime, in any town. One would hope that the newly established Department of Landscape Architecture at the University of Venice would not only prepare professionals for the larger world beyond the city but also foster historical sensitivity towards their own local conditions to which an exemplary creativity could be directed.

Much is written about Venice's self-mythology, and recent historical scholarship has turned its attention to a careful scrutiny of just what that meant and how it has been challenged or sustained [44]. But it is by no means a topic of only historical interest [45]. The projections for a future Venice by modern-day planners are every bit as dedicated to a received or probably re-invented mythology as were, say, Tintoretto's or Sansovino's. And since gardens have been, in as different contexts as de' Barbari's woodcut and Napoleon's urban reforms, key elements in those mythical constructions, they have clearly a role to play in them once again. The issue will be whether Venice can utilize both its many surviving garden spaces and the possibility of new landscape creations as serviceable "fictions or half-truths" on which to ground its existence in the decades to come.

Notes

Chapter One   A new approach to the Venetian city garden

1   Respectively, *Gondola Days*, p.58, and *Collected Shorter Poems*, p.59.

2   I refer here to the invaluable book on "minor" architecture edited by Giorgio Gianighian and Paola Pavanini, which actually acknowledges gardens on its very first page of text (p.7) and provides some visual evidence of their open spaces. There is also Trincanato's book on what she terms *Venezia Minore*, though its focus is largely on traditions of non-élite housing units.

3   Charles Burroughs, *From Signs to Design. Environmental process and reform in early Renaissance Rome* (Cambridge, MA, 1990), p.1 (italics added).

4   See *Tristes Tropiques*, translated John and Doreen Weightman (New York, 1974), pp.114-5. For a parallel set of examples see Jay Griffiths, *Wild. An elemental journey* (London, 2007), which chronicles various modern dominations and "conversions" of targeted populations by the manipulation of their physical environment and their stories about it.

5   Many publications used the word "theatre" in their titles to suggest a completeness: see my chapter "Garden and Theatre" in *Garden and Grove*.

6   *Social Formation and Symbolic Landscape*, p.1.

7   Charles Tomlinson, *Some Americans. A personal record* (Berkeley, CA, 1981), p.112: he was writing of Sicilian writers whose poems were "an entropic history that can only consume, a history turning itself into fable...".

8   *The Aspern Papers* (1888), chapter 3.

9   Robert Bargrave, "Travels", Bodlean Library MS Rawl. c.799, folio160 verso, italics added.

10   Evidence perhaps to support the contention of the Venetian diarist, Girolamo Priuli, that "foreigners", by which he meant all those not "born in the city", couldn't be trusted, even if they were elevated to the nobility! (cited Zorzi, *Venice*, p.167, see below note 19).

11   *The Diary of John Evelyn*, ed. E.S. de Beer, 5 vols (Oxford, 1956), II, p.461. By "rare" he would have meant "infrequent" as much as "precious". Doody also thinks "gardens are rare" (*Tropic of Venice*, p.174), despite the modern coffee-table books devoted to them which seem to be her authority for the few pages that she dedicates to them.

12   Lassels, *The Voyage of Italy* (London, 1670), p.417, though he adds that he was more impressed by the Procuratore himself, "the greatest ornament of the Venetian State". He also visited San Giorgio Maggiore, but makes no comment on its gardens (p.416).

13   Misson, *A New Voyage to Italy*, 2 vols (London, 1699), I, p.165. I have not been able to determine which guidebook Misson could have referred to; however, there are guidebooks, cited elsewhere in this study, as well as other documents that confirm the "promotion" of the garden as a significant Venetian feature for visitors and inhabitants alike. Misson later notes that Vicenza is known as "the garden of Venice" (I, p.335), as much for its supply of fruit and vegetables as for it being the site of country retreats.

14   *Some Observations made in Travelling Through France, Italy, Etc In the Years* 1720, 1721 and 1722, 2 vols (London, 1730), I, p.62.

15   *A New Journey over Europe* (London, 1717), p.103.

16   This seems a useful translation of the Italian term, "Venezianità", especially as the English word Venicity now includes the notion of "city"! For the Italian usage, see Salvatore Battaglia, *Grande dizionario della lingua italiana,* 21 vols (Turin, 1961-2002), XXI, p.737, column 1.

17   3 vols (1957), II, pp.280-95, citing Casola, Aretino, Ortensio and the garden list of Sansovino, and drawing upon Damerini's 1931 book. At the conclusion of this "breve digressione" Miozzi resumes his more detailed discussion of interior décor and furnishings.

18   *The Italian Gardens of the Renaissance and other studies* (London, 1914), pp.102-134. This is also the case with almost all of the essays collected in *Il giardino Veneto*, ed. Margherita Azzi Visentini (Milan, 1988); though of course the adjective "Veneto" may be allowed to cover both *terra firma* and the lagoon city, even if sometimes the authors suggest that what transpires on the mainland has equal validity in the city.

19   *Una città, Una Repubblica, Un Impero. Venezia 697–1797* (Milan, 1980); revised English edition, 2001 translated by Judyth Schaubhut Smith, cited as Zorzi, *Venice*.

20   Brown 2004, pp.48-50 and 67-8 for the garden discussions and illustrations. Her earlier essay, "Behind the walls. The material culture of Venetian élites", in *Venice Reconsidered*, also contains a page on gardens (pp.311-2), this time quoting Giovanni Maria Memmo on gardens in 1563 and illustrating a 19th-century courtyard with a rampant pergola vine.

21   This is reprinted in Stefinlongo 2000. Bettoni also published *Lettere sui Giardini Pubblici di Venezia* (Milan, 1820), which was critiqued by A.A.Michieli, "I Giardini di Venezia e un curioso libretto di Niccolò Bettoni", *Rivista Mensile della Città di Venezia* (October, 1929), pp.593-6.

22   Damerini's books were the first I consulted at the very start of this work; thirty years later, returning to the 1931 volume in search of a reference, I realized how much his keen focus on both Venetian gardens and how to discuss them has influenced my own approach. There is also an interesting essay by Enrico Motta, "I Giardini di Venezia", published in *Le Tre Venezie* (August 1925), pp.23-32.

23   His *Amor di Venezia* (Bologna, 1920). See Alberto Zajotti's review of Damerini's early work, "Gino Damerini e *I Giardini sulla Laguna*", in *Le Tre Venezie* (August 1927), pp.31-5.

24   *Giardini sulla Laguna*, p.57.

25   A smaller format edition had been published in 1899 with the title, *Gondola Days*, with the same text as the later folio but with different illustrations. References are, however, given to the larger, elaborate edition, the "Prefatory" note to which is date-lined "New York, December, 1895" and the book's copyright 1894.

26 See Lee Bacon, "Venice Gardens", *Century. A Popular Quarterly*, LXII (August 1901), pp.532-42, and the poem, "A Venetian Garden" by H.G.Dwight, ibid, p.562. Another, later example might be William Mathewson Milliken's chapter, entitled "My garden is beyond the wall", in *Unfamiliar Venice* (Cleveland, OH, 1967).

27 This is an issue stretching beyond the Venetian garden; see James Elkins, "On the conceptual analyisis of gardens", *Journal of Garden History*, 13 (1993), pp.189-98, republished in his book, *Our Beautiful, Dry and Distant Texts: Art History as Writing* (University Park, PA, 1997).

28 I have relied upon them specifically in Chapter Four's gazetteer of gardens. Typical, however, of garden history scholarship in the 1980s is the fact that Cunico's extensive and suggestive notes give no page references for the many sources she cites, which somewhat impedes their usefulness for other scholars.

29 http://www.geniuslocivenezia.blogspot.com/. Cunico 1996 has also produced a guide book to Veneto gardens, in which four (out of thirty-two) are to be found within the city. My final chapter will be the place best suited to considering this intriguing development of gardenist activity in the Venetian city.

30 Gianluca Aldegani and Fabrizio Diodati, *Le Corti. Spazi pubblici e privati nella città de Venezia*, con saggi di Egle Renata Trincanato (Venice, 1991).

31 I am thinking of the imagery so admirably analyzed by Patricia Fortini Brown in her *Venetian Narrative Painting in the age of Carpaccio*.

32 (Chapel Hill, NC, 2001), p.2. On the mythopoeic strategies of Venice there is a huge literature: but see, among others, the catalogue, *Venezia Da stato a Mito*.

33 As seen and described by Lady Mary Wortley Montagu in 1740 (see below Chapter Six).

34 See below Chapter Three.

35 "il recupero....non solo della storia dello stesso, ma anche del contesto urbano nel quale esso si iscrive" (the recovery not just of their history but also of the urban mix into which they are inscribed), in the words of Professor Pier Luigi Cervellati, the *relatore* for the *laurea* thesis of Leonardo Ruffo, p.7.

36 An odd distinction at the best of times, especially if one thinks of "Capability" Brown's naturalistic play with the forms of earth, trees, and bodies of water – a formal play by a notoriously informal designer.

37 I am therefore skeptical of the typological diagrams of garden styles (16th-century, baroque, romantic) offered by Leonardo Ruffo in his *laurea* thesis of 1997/98 and reproduced in its abridgement: *Il giardino storico Veneziano: una metodologia d'intervento* (Venice: DAEST, no. 6, n.d.).

38 *Rivista de Venezia*, X (1931), p.21: "Venezia meritava, ripetiamo, un trattamento più vasto, più preciso e più significativo, e non sarebbe stato difficile mettere insieme una sala dimostrativa che, partendo dal secolo XV° arrivasse con l'iconografia anche sintetica almeno ai Giardini del romanticismo". It is worth stressing, too, that the Venetian city garden is something distinct from the Veneto mainland garden, which itself has been rightly claimed to be individual and distinct from other Italian regions: see Lionello Puppi, "The Villa Gardens of the Veneto", *The Italian Garden*, ed. David R.Coffin (Washington, D.C., 1972), pp.83-114.

39 Florence-Antella, 1997, second edition.

Grounds for being: garden-making and the lagoon ecology

1 Giorgio Bellavitis, "Il sistema lagunare", in *Difesa di Venezia*, p.39. The bibliography of this topic is huge and, as argued in the main text, does not concern in detail the historical analysis of gardens: but in particular see *La Laguna di Venezia*, a many-volumed study coordinated by Giovanni Magrini (1933 ff.), with essays on lagoon morphology, on natural history, the fishing industry, etc., and the works cited in the next note. A usefully succinct explanation of the lagoon structure, history and current issues is that by Fletcher and Da Mosto.

2 Her essay, "Towards an Ecological Understanding of the myth of Venice", in *Venice Reconsidered*, is a useful and concise introduction to her work and contains an extensive set of further references; but her other fundamental researches, upon which I have relied extensively, are contained in four books listed in the bibliography. On the early formation and building of the city, the two volumes of Wladimiro Dorigo 2003 have been consulted. See also the essay by Pavanini on 16th-century urban developments and regulatory action.

3 James, *The Aspern Papers* (1888), chapter 3; Pound, *Collected Early Poems*, p.248.

4 Eden, pp.131-4.

5 Crouzet-Pavan 1992, II, section of maps. See also the urban development plotted by the historical atlas, *Venise au fil du temps*, from which I have borrowed my example.

6 James Lees-Milne, *Venetian Evenings* (London, 1988), p.20. The decline of this productive horticulture and agriculture is the subject of Crouzet-Pavan 1995, especially Chapter 5 ("Les Horizons d'un ancien monde: entre prairies, vignes et bois").

7 Sanudo, p.20.

8 Cassiodorus, *Opera*, book XII, no 24.

9 Cecchetti 1871, p.67-8; and for the others items, pp.97, 99-101 & 104. Also see Cecchetti "La Vita", XVII, p.13.

10 Tassini, *Curiosità*, p.465; in the modern street directory there are still four such street names in the Cannaregio, Castello, and Giudecca.

11 Schulz 1991, p.421.

12 A similar point is made about the emergence of a campo at Santa Giustina in the middle of the 13th century: see Crouzet-Pavan 1992, I, p.389.

13 Schulz 1991, p.422, provides two examples of this official control: "four and a half acres of fill were licensed in 1303 at the eastern fringe of the archipelago; eighteen acres were licensed between 1318 and 1332 at the southern fringe".

14 Ibid, p.432. See also Franca Cosmai and Stefano Sorteni, "Venezia e il fango", in *Storia Urbana*, 115 (2007), pp.37-56.

15 Crouzet-Pavan 1992, I, p.68.

16 Ibid I, p.133, for examples on the Giudecca in the early 16th century.

17 Ibid I, p.133 (citing ASV, S.E.A., reg 219, f.7verso), though in this instance a garden was not in question.

18 Ibid I, p.99, citing ASV, C.R.S., S Gregorio, B.2, f.18v.

19 Ibid I, p.302.

20 Ibid I, p.121, citing ASV, Grazie, reg.3, f.55 verso.

21 Ibid I., p126, citing ASV, C.R.S., S Andrea de Zirada, B.18.

22 In the latter case, we know this because of a permission granted to build a palissade: see ibid I.129, citing ASV, S.E.A., B.460, f.2verso.

23 Ibid p.75, citing ASV Grazie reg. 23, f.39recto (1432) & 76 citing ibid reg.3, f.55recto and 82 (note 121).

24 See Schulz 1984, p.33, and S Borsari, "Una famiglia veneziana del Medioevo: gli Ziani", in *Arte Veneta*, 5th series, 10 (1978), pp.331-7.

25 Schulz 1993.

26 Crouzet-Pavan 1992, I, p.523. Marbles in courtyards are represented in the Michiel herbal books later in the 16th century: see Chapter Three, Figure III.33.

27 See Crouzet-Pavan 1992, I, p.470 and tables of land sales.

28 Ibid, I, pp.488, 524 & 712.

29 Ibid I, pp.487-8, citing ASV, Proprio, Lezze, F.9, f.17r & v. See also Schulz 1993, p.412, for another record of a dispute over blocked light in 1501.

30 Ibid I, p.487, citing ASV, Proprio, Estraordinarii, Lezze, F.10, f. 81verso-83recto

31 Ibid, I, p.795, citing ASV, Dieci Savi, Condizioni, 1514, B.71, no.71.

32 Ibid I, p.471 note 9, drawing upon ASV, Esaminador, Investizioni, F.1 (1374–1380).

33 Ibid I, pp.477-8.

34 Vittorio Rossi, "Jacopo d'Albizzotto Guidi e il suo inedito poema su Venezia", in *Nuovo Archivio Veneto*, V (1893), pp.397-451.

35 See the relevant plans in *Venise au fil du temps* which locate major *palazzi*. Gardens in and after the year 1500 are discussed in Chapter Three.

36 Juergen Schulz's study of mediaeval palaces constantly notes and documents this feature: see Schulz 2004, pp.7, 40-41.

37 All the surviving *corti* in modern Venice are usefully listed and reviewed in the book by Gianluca Aldegani. Old photographs also record this essential feature of the Venetian city: see the images reproduced in Grieve's *Whistler's Venice*, pp.43 (showing planting), 129, 150.

38 Cecchetti 1871, pp.100 & 103 (italics added). For the reference to livestock in courtyards, p.72.

39 Giorgio Gianighian 2001 has rightly insisted upon the importance of this feature. See also M.Costantini, *L'acqua di Venezia* (Venice, 1984) and Cunico 47 and notes.

40 See Jean-Claude Hocquet, "Technologie du marais salant et travail du saunier dans la lagune de Venise au moyen age", in *Studi Veneziani*, IX (1985), pp.15-41.

41 See Gino Voltolina, *Le antiche vere da pozzo veneziane* (Venice, 1981).

42 *Filarete's Treatise on Architecture*, translated and with an introduction by John R. Spenser, 2 vols (New Haven, 1965), I, p.290. A detailed modern account of this water-collecting system is given by Giorgio Gianighian, "Building a Renaissance double house in Venice", *ARQ. Architectural research quarterly*, 8/3 & 4 (2994/5), p.301.

43 Bassano, 1787, third edition, p.97. He also notes the need for planting delicate plants in moveable pots and sheltering them from winds.

44 *Iconografia delle trenta Parrocchie di Venezia*, second page of letterpress. On the *campi*, see the two volumes by Marina Crivellari Bizio and the work by Janson and Bürklin. The former is largely descriptive; the latter has less a specifically local and historical focus than a phenenological approach to the architectural experience of squares, for which Venice provides case studies.

45 Schulz 1991, p.433.

46 On both these plans a "Broglio" is marked along the Ducal Palace: see Brusatin, figs 177 and 20 respectively.

47 *The Forestiero Illuminato [i.e. Enlightened Foreigner]* of 1772 has an entry on the *broglio* which is described as the open space where nobles went to conduct their "Uffizi" (p.46), presumably referring at this date to the area alongside the Ducal Palace.

48 Zorzi, *Venice*, 62.

49 Sanudo, 14. Bernardo Trevisan also discussed what he calls the "bruollo ora broglio" at San Marco, p.65.

50 Trincanato, p.37.

51 *Guida de' Forestieri* (Venice, 1724), pp. 229 (for Servites) and 239 (for other *orti*).

52 *I cinque libri dell'architettura de M. Vitruvio tradotti e commentati* (Venice, 1567), pp.270-1.

53 *Della Laguna di Venezia*, p.113.

54 The literature and commentary are extensive: for a brief overview see David Rosand, *Myths of Venice. The figuration of a state* (Chapel Hill, NC, 2001). I draw upon this book in what follows.

55 Rosand, pp.2 & 7 (for Petrarch). Also Schultz 2004, p.74, n.4, citing Petrarch's letter of 1367/8 to Urban V.

56 See John Prest, *The Garden of Eden: the Botanical Garden and the Recreation of Paradise* (London, 1981); also my *The Afterlife of Gardens* (London, 2004), pp.25-8. Miozzi meditates briefly on Venetian nostalgia for early gardens (II, pp.281-2).

57 All examples borrowed from Rosand, pp.117 & 138.

58 Some discussion of the terminology of "garden" is deferred to Chapter Five below, pp.102.

59 See Giorgio Bellavitis, *Palazzo Giustinian Pesaro*.

60 An edition of his treatise, *De natura deorum*, was published in Venice in 1508.

61 *Venice Reconsidered*, p.41.

1 The considerable literature not specifically cited in subsequent notes includes: G.Cassini, *Piante e Vedute Prospettiche di Venezia* (Venice, 1982); Deborah Howard, "Venice as a dolphin: further investigations into Jacopo de' Barbari's view", in *Artibus et Historiae*, XXXV (1997), pp.101-11; Lucia Nuti, *Ritratti di citta: visione e memoria tra Medioevo e Settecento* (Venice, 1996), pp.154-5 & 202; Terisio Pignatti, "La pianta di Venezia di Jacopo de' Barbari", *Bolletino dei Musei Civici Veneziani*, IX (1964), pp.9-49; G.Romanelli and S.Baldone, *Venezia Piante e Vedute*, supplement to *Bolletino dei Musei* Civici Veneziani (Venice, 1982); Balistreri-Trincanato and Zanverdiani.

2 See Martin Kemp's entry on the panorama in the exhibition catalogue, Circa 1492: *Art in the Age of Exploration*, ed. Jay A. Levenson, National Gallery of Art (Washington, D.C., 1992).

3 Kolb's petition is printed in Schulz 1978; also in *Venice a Documentary History* p.373.

4 Schulz 2004, p.100, where he notes (as also on p.205) ways in which the woodblocks became distorted during production.

5 See Schulz 1970.

6 Ignazio Danti's painting hangs in the Gallerie delle Carte Geografiche in the Vatican. There is also the painted perspective of Venice by Fialetti in the collection of Eton College: see M.A.Visentini, "Ancora un'inedita pianta prospettica di Venezia in un dipinto di Odoardo Fialetti per Sir Henry Wotton", *Bolletino dei Civici Musei Veneziani*, ns. XXV/1 (1980), pp.19-25. Also Christopher Lloyd, "An unpublished view of Venice dating from the 17th century", *Arte Veneta*, XXVII (1973), pp.276-83, where *orti* on the Giudecca are roughly indicated (see especially his fig. 397).

7 As stated in the catalogue, *An Exhibition of Views of Venice in the Graphic Arts...*(Dickson Art Center, UCLA, 1969), n.p.

8 ASV Filza 526 (*Licenze per condur terreni...*).

9 Schulz 1982, p. 108, note 18, citing a Correr MS (Donà dalle Rose, no.457, item 31) on the profits that the government realized from fees generated by this dumping enterprise.

10 Puppi 1978, also drawing on de' Barbari, establishes a typology of Venetian gardens, but does not see any territorial symbolism in them.

11 Balistreri-Trincanato and Zanverdiani usefully isolate many details of different elements of the urban fabric including orchards and gardens (pp.231ff. and165ff. respectively), but careful perusal of the woodcut reveals further examples, some of which are offered here.

12 This surely contradicts emphatically the assertion of A.Wirobisz that the urban centre of Venice had completely eliminated all open spaces including gardens: "L'attività edilizia a Venezia nel XIV e nel XV secolo [sic]", *Studi Veneziani*, VII (1965), pp.307ff.

13 This detail is confirmed by Marc Antonio Sabellico, in his *Del Sito di Venezia Città*, p.14, where he notes a grassy place ("luogo erboso") and fields for dyers and cloth-makers near San Rocco.

14 For an exploration of this trope and for extensive further reading, see Monika Schmitter, "Odoni's façade. The house as portrait in Renaissance Venice", *Journal of the Society of Architectural Historians*, 66/3 (2007), pp.294-315.

15 *Il libro dell'arte de mercatura*, ed. Ugo Tucci (1990), pp.235-6.

16 *On the Art of Building in Ten Books*, translated by Joseph Rykwert et al (Cambridge, MA, 1988), esp. Bk 1, and the index under "locality" and "area".

17 I have explored this perspective on garden-making in some detail in chapter three of my *Greater Perfections. The practice of garden theory* (London and Philadelphia, 2001). See also Tom Beck, "Gardens as a 'third nature': the ancient roots of a Renaissance idea", *Studies in the History of Gardens and Designed Landscapes*, XXII (2002), pp.327-34.

18 Zorzi, *Venice*, p.34.

19 Casola, p.142.

20 Damerini recapitulated the original list in *Giardini di Venezia*, pp.30 ff. I have here freely rendered Sansovino's original listing (the Italian text taken from the Gregg reprint of the 1663 edition).

21 Sansovino, ed. cit., p.369; on pp.369-370 his list of gardens is extensively augmented with Giustiniano Martinioni's later additions.

22 Texts are taken from the critical edition by Giovanni Pozzi and Lucia A.Ciapponi (Padua, 1980), vol. I, p.116, and the modern English version by Joscelyn Godwin (London, 1999), p.124. Further references will be to these two versions, but my figure captions refer to the folios of the original edition which are preserved in the modern editions. On glass gardens manufactured in Murano, see Chapter Six and Figure VI.7.

23 Respectively, Zorzi, *Venice*, p.44, and Lillian Armstrong, "The illustration of Pliny's *Historia Naturalis* in Venetian manuscripts and early printed books", in *Manuscripts in the Fifty Years after the Invention of Printing*, ed. J.B.Trapp (London, 1983), pp.97-106.

24 This debate is briefly addressed in the second volume (pp.3ff.) of the critical edition (note 22); see also the special double issue, "Garden and architectural dreamscapes in the *Hypnerotomachia Poliphi*", ed. Michael Leslie and John Dixon Hunt, *Word & Image*, 14:1&2 (1998).

25 Vol. I, pp.116-7, and the modern English translation, pp.124-5 (further references are to these two texts). A partial Elizabethan version of 1592 plays the scene with more astonishment than the dry modern version: "a Garden of a large compasse, made in the form of an intricate Labyrinth allyes and wayes, not to bee trodden, but sayled about, for in steade of allyes to treade upon, there were ryuers of water... The waters being environed upon either sides, with roses, trees, and fruits" (*The Strife of Love in a Dreame*, reprint, New York, 1973, pp.142-3).

26 I, p.305; p.311.

27 I, p.308; p.314.

28 See the detailed analysis of this horticultural plenitude in Ada Segre's "Untangling the knot: garden design in Francesco Colonna's *Hypnerotomachia Poliphili*", in *Word & Image* (note 24).

29 I, pp.286-7; p.293.

30 I, p.288; p.294.

31 For further illustrations from Venetian printed books that throw additional light upon local garden culture, see Carlo Enrico Rava, *Arte Dell'Illustrazione nel libro Italiano del Rinascimento* (Milan, 1945), Lillian Armstrong, "Il maestro di Pico: un miniatore veneziano del tardo quattrocento", *Saggi e Memorie di Storia del'arte*, 17 (1990), pp.7-39 & 215-253, and her *Renaissance Miniature Painters and Classical Imagery: the Master of the Putti and his Venetian workshop* (London, 1981); also G.Mariani Canova, *La Miniatura Veneta del Rinascimento* (Florence, 1969). I am indebted to Lillian Armstrong for valuable direction in this exceptionally well-studied field of early illustration.

32 Ettore de Toni published three times on the herbal: "Un codice-erbario anonimo", *Memoria della Pontificia Accademia Romana dei Nuovi Lincei*, XXII (Rome, 1904); a biography of Michiel in *Ateneo Veneto* (July-September 1908), pp.69-103, and his *I Cinqui Libri di Piante* (1940).

33 Cunico's 1989 book invokes the herbal's imagery in her discussion of planting. Those images were published after I first consulted these important volumes some years ago towards the start of my research; on a more recent visit to the Marciana Library I was categorically refused permission to consult the volumes because of their rarity and state of preservation.

34 *An Account of a Journey, in A Collection of Voyages and Travels*, ed. Churchill, vol VI (1732), p.501. Pots were clearly valued and sought after: in 1534 the Duchess of Urbino selected some fine vases to send for a "bellissimo Giardino" in Venice that belonged to the Emperor (Archivio Storico Firenze, Ducato di Urbino, Cl.I, Div.G, Filza 235, c.334) – a reference kindly communicated by Sabine Eiche.

35 See, for example, images on folios a7recto and q2recto. This is probably coincidence; yet the illustrated book could have been available to Domenico Delle Greche and fuelled his invention for the herbal; in which case the evidence for any actual Venetian landscape is short-circuited – images breed images rather than look to actual sites. The Michiel image is illustrated in Cunico, pp.57.

36 *Art and Illusion* (1960), pp.87-8. Charlotte Pauly in her 1916 book on Venetian pleasure gardens also relies largely upon paintings and engravings for her discussion (pp.5-17), though devoting much of her book to mainland gardens and on pp.39-44 to the place of gardens in Venetian culture.

37 The painting was offered for sale at Christie's, New York, on 10th January 1990. Given the impossibility of reproducing the whole corpus of relevant Venetian paintings that yield information on gardens ideas, references to their reproduction elsewhere will be given.

38 David Rosand and Michelangelo Muraro, *Titian and the Venetian Woodcut* (Washington, D.C., 1976), p.89, fig. 1-12.

39 The painting in Berlin dates from 1521; another Lotto, now of *Susannah* (Florence, Uffizi, 1517), shows much more clearly this familiar trelliswork fencing surrounding enclosures, though the garden and courtyard depicted nestle in a hilly landscape.

40 *Tintoretto, Le Opere*, Rodolfo Pallucchini and Paola Rossi, 2 vols (Milan, 1982), references are in the text to this study, catalogue followed by figure numbers.

41 In other *Susannahs*, (Madrid 182/240, Munich 191/251, Washington 377/487), in an *Annunciation* (Bucharest 380/491, also showing patterned flower beds and a casino), a *Muses* concert (Rome, private collection 190/252), and an attributed picture in Amiens (A3/632).

42 Cartwright, p.109, nonetheless compares its "stately columns and marble halls" with the villa of Sante Cattaneo on the Giudecca.

43 Illustrated in the exhibition catalogue, *Venice and the Islamic World 828-1797* (New Haven, 2007), p.85.

44 I rely here upon Schulz 1982, p.73-82, who himself relies upon accounts from 1833 and 1834 and who quotes the Priscianese description on p.62. The house still exists, though now, with land fill, is distanced from the lagoon and its immediate surroundings have changed; the 19th-century print of the house and garden was published in the *Rivista di Venezia*, X (1931), p.212.

45 Schulz 1982, pp.82ff., building upon Giuseppe Tassini, "Della abitazioni in Venezia di Pietro Aretino", in *Archivio Veneto*, 31 (1886), pp.205-8.

46 *Lettere*, ed. Gian Mario Anselmi (Rome, 2000), pp.110-2. His final remark may be something of a rhetorical topos of foreigners' response to Venice: Casola writes of the fruits and vegetables in San Marco that "it seemed as if all the gardens of the world must be there" (p.131).

47 *Sei giornate*, ed. G.Aquilecchia (Bari, 1969), p.352.

48 *Lettere sull'arte di Pietro Aretino*, ed. Ettore Camesasca, commentary by Fidenzio Pertile, 4 vols (Milano, 1957), I, pp.47-8.

49 See Amedeo Quondam, "Nel giardino del Marcolini. Un editore veneziano tra Aretino e Doni", in *Giornale Storico della Letteratura Italiana*, CLVII (1980), pp.75-112, who is interested almost entirely in the emblematic resonances of the garden in Aretino's text. I quote from the 1914 edition of Aretino's text.

50 Quoted Monika Schmitter, op. cit. (note 14 above), p.308. This is a familiar topos: cf. Italian sculpture collections "speak Roman history more palpably than any author" (John Raymond, *Il Mercurio Italico. An Itinerary contayning a Voyage made through Italy in the yeare 1646, and 1647*, 1648, p.78) or Lord Arundel's sculpture gardens in London that did "transplante old Greece into England… [so] as to persuade a man that he now seeth two thousand years ago" (Henry Peacham, *The Compleat Gentleman*, 1634, pp.104-6). For an inventory of Odoni's property in 1555, cited by Schmitter, ASV, Cancelleria inferiore, Miscellanea notai diversi, busta 39, carta 58.

51 *The Travels of Peter Mundy*, ed. Sir Richard Carnac Temple, Bt., 5 vols (London, 1907-25; reprint 1972), I, p.91; he stayed, he writes, in "a very fine house".

52 See Z. Morosini, *Murano, le sue officine e I suoi orti* (1500: 1882); F. Pellegrini, *Gli Orti di Murano. Cenni storici* (Venice, 1877); Puppi 1978, pp.281-4; and Crouzet-Pavan 1992, pp.699-714, for a discussion of the special case of Murano.

53 *Vita de Trifone Gabriele…* (Bologna, 1543), n.p.

54 Published with an Italian version *en face* by Jacopo Bernardi (1868).

55 *Diario di Murano di Francesco Luna 1625–1631*, edited and illustrated by Vincenzo Zanetti (1873), p.60 note. Further notices of the repertoire of Murano gardens were compiled by Ortensio Landi in 1552. Some examples are cited by Cermenati, p.184 note, from what he says is a rare publication, *Sette libri de Cathaloghi a varie cose*.

56 *Idea dell'architettura universale* (Venice, 1615), I, bk 3, chapter 14, p.280.

57 The main materials on this garden are to be found in Navagero's own *Opera Omnia* (Padua, 1718), E.A.Cicogna, *Della vita e delle opera di Andrea Navagero* (Venice, 1855), and M.Cermanati, "Un diplomatico naturalista de rinascimento", in *Nuovo Archivio Veneto*, new series XXIV (1913), pp.164-205; the site of the garden no longer survives except as a public park with playground. See Gazetteer, Chapter Four.

58 Cartwright, pp.116-7 gives a very loose translation of the original Latin, which it quoted by Cermenati (op. cit.) from Longueil's *Epistolarum libri IIII* (Basel, 1558); I have augmented Cartwright's version from this text.

59 Giacomo Filiasi, p.261.

60 These projects are discussed and the verbal proposals graphically interpreted by Manfredi Tafuri, *Venezia e il Rinascimento* (Turin, 1985; English edition, Cambridge, MA, 1989), pp. 139-60 in the English edition; but he does not address at all the significance of the state's rejection of Cornaro's projects of the kind of gardens proposed. See also Roberto Cessi, "Alvise Cornaro e la bonifica veneziana nel secolo XVI", *Rendiconti della R. Accademia Nazionale dei Lincei: classe di scienze morali, storiche e filologiche*, series 6, vol12 (1936), pp.301-23.

61 Sanudo reiterated (p.20) this concept when he wrote that Venice had no walls, needed no gates that closed at night or guards that other cities had for fear of their enemies. On an early mistrust of "foreign" architects (including those from the mainland) see Schultz, p.44. The following inscription is cited by Brusatin 1980, p.6.

62 See R.Cessi and A.Alberti, *Rialto; l'isola, il ponte, il mercato* (Bologna, 1934), pp.105-21. A similar rejection by patricians greeted Palladio's suggestion to completely rebuild the Doge's Palace after fires in the 1570s: see Tracy E. Cooper, *Palladio's Venice. Architecture and society in a Renaissance republic* (New Haven, CT, 2006), pp.197, 209-211.

63 The "extremely strong conservatism" of Venetian art and architecture is frequently remarked upon: see Schulz 2004, pp.14 and 23; for further remarks and examples of this conservatism, see pp.51, 61, 69 & 72.

64 Schulz 2004, p.76.

1 Bassi calls them "molto lacunose" (p.360).

2 See *Indicatore Anagrafico di Venezia*, edited Jonathen Del Mar (Venice, 1996); I have also used the Venetian "A–Z" by G.P.Nadali and R.Vianello, *Calli, Campielli e Canali* (Spinea VE, 2003 edition), which indicates in green considerable amounts of open space throughout the city, including sites invisible behind high walls. Where it is useful, reference is also made to the modern aerial survey of the city, *An Atlas of Venice*; however, since the photography for that volume was done in the height of summer, tree cover may indicate the presence of gardens but hides most details of them.

1 See the tables of property descriptions and holdings following the individual maps of urban sectors in Dorigo 2003, vol. 2. The maps themselves shade in green any spaces that are identified as not being built upon, such as courtyards; however his special index of "Cose Notevoli" includes only one entry (though with many citations) under "terra vacua" for the terms he had culled from archival sources.

2 For instance, p.233 (two small houses in Castello 318-320, dating from 1700, joined by gardens), or pp.341-2 (small palace on Rio Terà). San Vio at Dorsoduro 490 with gardens on each side, the western one belonging to it).

3 I am drawn to this book, too, by the passion of its prefatory essay by Agnoldomenico Pica and its adoption of the metaphor that I have also invoked – when she insists that the architectural study of "Venezia minore" is a study of the "fertile humus" (p.16) on which the city was grown, what I have called its grounds of being. My in-text quotations are also from this introduction (pp.14 & 16).

4 *The Diary of John Evelyn*, ed. E.S.de Beer, 5 vols (Oxford, 1956), II, p.434. At least one modern toponym recalls the site of a herbalist/pharmacist: Ruga dei Spezieri at the Rialto. See also G. Meneghini, *La farmacia attraverso I secoli e gli speziali di Venezia e Padova* (Padua, 1946). Zanetti's guide to Murano (pp.285-6) notes the early botanical-cum-medicinal gardeners on that island.

5 Respectively pp.10, 24, 21, 20 & 13.

6 ASV Misc. Mappe 23, reproduced in Hunt 1981, p.62, fig. 13.

7 ASV Misc. Mappe 619. DS.55/18.

8 ASV S.E.A.Laguna 25 1616 P.13 and Misc. Mappe 39 respectively.

9 Quoted Luis Ramón-Laca, "Alcoba and Cuadra...", *Studies in the History of Gardens and Designed Landscapes*, 29 (2009), p. 272.

10 See F. du-Pre, *Elogio Storico di Girolamo Zanichelli* (Venice, 1816).

11 *Coryate's Crudities*, 2 vols. ([1611], Glasgow, 1905), I, pp.395-6.

12 Lillian Armstrong, "The illustration of Pliny's *Historia Naturalis* in Venetian manuscripts and early printed books", in *Manuscripts in the Fifty Years After the Invention of Printing*, ed. J.B.Trapp (London, 1983).

13 Eden, pp.27-36.

14 *Giardini di Venezia*, pp.45 ff.

15 *The Life and Letters of Sir Henry Wotton*, p.220 (writing in December 1621).

16 Quoted Howard, p.246, note 4.

17 Doody 165 forgets plants brought back from the east when she talks of Venice as an engine of commerce. Equally, there is no mention at all of botanical imports in Howard, nor in the 2007 exhibition and catalogue, *Venice and the Islamic World*.

18 See Ferguson, pp.261, 274 & 165 respectively.

19 "La Flora Urbica", p.126.

20 Lucia Tongiorgi Tomasi, *An Oak Spring Flora* (Upperville, VA, 1997), pp.35-8. Another album of plant drawings by Marco Ricci, probably indicates his contacts in Venice in the last years of the 17th century, though it has been argued that the drawings were done in the Veneto – see W.G.Constable, "An unusual early work of Marco Ricci", *Arte Veneta*, XV (1961), pp.256-7.

21 *See Venezia e Istanbul*, pp.90, 200-1, 237 & 151 respectively for these glimpses of Venetian knowledge and interest in eastern gardens and horticulture. Yet it is a topic that requires much more research.

22 Cermenati, p.27. The claim for the Murano gardens as early botanical collections is also made by Zanetti, pp.284-5.

23 His "Priolani Ruris ad Murianum Delitiae" was published with an Italian translation by Jacopo Bernardi in 1868: it lists a range of plants in the "bel giardino" (p.19). Castaldo must have know Navagero since he wrote an epigram on his death. Cicogna gives many pages to Navagero throughout his *Iscrizioni* .

24 In his book on the Lido Malagola accepts that, though it was not among the most productive islands, there were in the early 16th century still enough gardeners to form a confraternity in 1536 (p.25).

25 The literature is vast and scattered: but see the section in Cunico, especially pp.11-8, for an overview and the following notes here for detailed references.

26 Ugo Stefanutti, "Maestro Gualtieri chirurgo", *Quattro figure significative nella medicina del passato* (Venice, 1959), and *Documentazione cronologiche per la storia della medicina, chirurgia e farmacia in Venezia dal* 1258 – 1332 (1961).

27 "Curiosa memoria d'un orto dei semplici a Venezia del 1334" (P.D. 506/21). I am grateful to Lucia Tongiorgi Tomasi for this reference.

28 See I.Tiozzo, *I Nostri. Note biografiche intorno a Chioggiotti degni di ricordo* (Chioggia, 1928), pp.148-9. On the range of later botanical collections throughout the Veneto region see Krzysztof Pomian, *Collectors and Curiosities. Paris and Venice, 1500–1800*, translated by Elizabeth Wiles-Portier (Cambridge, 1990), pp.223-6.

29 See M A Visentini, 1984; also Dennis E. Rhodes, "The Botanical Garden of Padua: the first 100 years", *Journal of Garden History*, 4 (1984), pp.327-31.

30 The copy in the Marciana (Rari V 632) is annotated by Giovanni Marinelli, skeptical of some of the information – "falsa omnia" (p.142)!

31 See the series of brief notes by Michelangelo Minio, "I Botanici veneziani", *Annuario dell'Istituto Magistrale di Venezia* (1925/6), and the exhibition catalogue, *La botanica nel libro Veneto* (Padua, 1965). On the history of early botanical studies in the lagoon, see *La Laguna di Venezia*, ed. Giovanni Magrini, vol. III, Pt V, tomo ix, fasc.1 (1938) and fasc.II (1941); and P. Giulini, "Il giardino e la botanica", in Visentini 1988 (2).

32 MS.Lat.VI.LIX (2548). See de Toni 1919-25. This manuscript has been re-attributed to Nicolo Roccabonella by Minio 1952-53.

33 See works by Ettore de Toni, including the biography published in *Ateneo Veneto*, pp.85 & 86 for details used here.

34 De Toni 1940 transcribes all the entries including the notes on location ("Luogho") that cover all parts of Italy, Germany, Greece, Macedonia, Crete, Spain, among other places.

35 Cicogna, *Iscrizioni*, vol. 5.

36 A detailed narrative of the Patarol-Rizzo family and their garden at the Madonna dell'Orto is given in Cicogna, *Iscrizioni Veneziane*, pp.110-22.

37 Giannina Piamonte, *Venezia vista dall'acqua* (1968), p.139.

38 P.A.Saccardo, *Della Storia e Letteratura della Flora Veneta* (Milan, 1869), pp.106-7, for the Ruchingers. See also below for a discussion of the garden's history as a botanical site.

39 I am particularly indebted to Count Marcello for giving me a copy of his out-of-print monograph.

40 See below in Chapter Nine. What follows draws variously upon Vianello and Giormani (with substantial further references), Cecchetti 1887 (1), Cecchetti "La Vita", Berlese 1843, and Ruffo, pp.91-6.

41 See *Gazzetta di Venezia*, 16 March 1885, n.71.

42 For the churches, less relevant here, see the useful chronological survey of Venetian churches by Umberto Franzoi and Dina Di Stefano, *Le Chiese di Venezia* (Milan, 1976), the bibliography of which volume contains references to guidebooks where churches are described.

43 *The History of Philip de Commines* (London, 1596), p.305.

44 Casola, p.142.

45 Much reproduced: see the 2003 exhibition catalogue of Lagoon mappings at the Correr Museum, *La Laguna di Venezia nella cartografia storica a stampa*, ed. G.Baso, M.Scarso and C.Tonini, fig. 1.

46 In what follows I draw upon the 1978 exhibition catalogue, *Isole Abbandonate della Laguna. Com'erano e come sono*, by Giorgio and Maurizio Crovato (Padua, 1978). There are various reproductions of Coronelli's engravings, only a few of which can be shown here: see *Le Isole della Laguna di Venezia dalle incisioni del '700*, with an introduction by Ugo Fugagnollo (Venice: Fantoni – Libri Arte, n.d).

47 "An ossuary of the north lagoon", in *Three Tales of Venice* (London, n.d.)

48 I have drawn upon a variety of sources, which are referred to briefly in the text: two exhibition catalogues of the State Archives: in 1987 on *Boschi della Serenissima* (abbreviated as B) and in 1989 on *Ambiente e risorse nella politica veneziana* (cited as A) and *Isole Abbandonate* (cited as IA – see note 46 above).

49 Cecchetti "La Vita", vol. 29, p.38 note and vol. 27, p.11.

50 ASV Misc Mappe 318.

51 Toursaint de Limojoin, p.12.

Chapter Six   Garden, theatre, and city

1 See in particular J.C.Davis, *The Decline of the Venetian Nobility as a Ruling Class* (Baltimore, MD, 1962) and Oliver Logan, *Culture and Society in Venice, 1470 – 1790* (London, 1972), and Georgelin.

2 See for instance, the exhibition catalogue, *The Mask of Venice*, with its subtitle, *Masking, Theatre & Identity in the Art of Tiepolo & his Time*. Doody (p.59) even writes (in many ways, incorrectly) that "Venice never left the eighteenth century", and she seems to have enjoyed staying there herself.

3 See *Venezia dell'Ottocento*, and a large proportion of the anthology, *Venise entre les Lignes*.

4 As reported in 1805 by A.-F.Sergent-Marceau, *Coup-d'oeil sentimental, critique et historique sur Venise*, ed. N.Zuffi (Geneva, 1981), p.54. The Frenchman, De Brosse, wrote that he found it difficult to describe private life in Venice as visitors were not easily admitted in Venetian society: *Selections from the Letters of De Brosse*, trans. R.S.Gower (London, 1897), pp.34-5.

5 Not an altogether reliable book anyway, but symptomatic nonetheless: p.30. On p.143 it also notes that wives take off and disappear "under arcades and into gardens", but nothing more is vouchsafed.

6 For Antonio and Francesco Guardi, see the two-volume monograph *I Dipinti* by Antonio Morassi (Venice: Alfieri, 1984), and the one-volume *I Disegni* (1984 [1973]); for Canaletto, W. G. Constable's work in the 2nd edition revised by J.G.Links (Oxford, 1976).

7 A detail that shows the garden more distinctly is in Pallucchini, *La pittura nel Veneto*, I, fig. 605.

8 Canaletto's views of San Michele and San Cristoforo, notably that in the Dallas Museum of Art, and his capriccio in the Pierpont Morgan (cats. 653 and 799) reveal the presence of gardens, albeit behind high walls. The persistence of gardens in such imaginary or invented views need not be taken as utterly erroneous: as André Corboz argues convincingly in his *Canaletto. Una Venezia imaginaria*, 2 vols. (Milan, 1985), the intention of this topothesia is to make the actual Venetian scenery more palpable. As Feste puts it in Shakespeare's *Twelfth Night*, "The truest poetry is the most feigning".

9 Guardi, *Dipinti*, II, figs 606-624 all depict islands, most with their gardens.

10 William Beckford, *Dreams, Waking Thoughts and Incidents*, ed. Robert J.Gemmett (Cranbury, NJ, 1971), p.110. References to other remarks by Beckford will be included in the text.

11 Ibid, p.128. He refers to the history of Venice, when people from Altino took refuge from invading hordes on the islands of the lagoon.

12 The drawing held at the Boymans-van Beuningen Museum, Rotterdam is reproduced less distinctly in the volume of *Disegni*... See below for an extended analysis of this Guardi garden. For these "villa" paintings see *Depinti*, I, figs 635-642.

13 See *Mask of Venice*, p.19. This provides a useful, brief survey of the issues of masking and theatricality.

14 In *Toeput a Treviso*, ed. Stefania Mason and Domenico Luciani (Asolo, 1988) there are useful discussions of villa scenes by Pozzoserrato [Toeput's name] and his representations of Susannah in her bath (pp.71-78 and 89-96 respectively).

15 See, for example, Goldoni's *La Cameriera brillante* (1753). See Decroisette, pp.96-104.

16 Illustrated in Brusatin 1980, plates 72 (Museo Correr) and 90 (Museo Civico, Bassano dell Grappa) respectively.

17 *The Mask of Venice* catalogue, with no mention at all of the setting depicted.

18 The painting was stolen and recovered in 2007, as announced and illustrated on the website for *La Repubblica* for Tuesday 5th June that year.

19 See Lionello Puppi, "Il melodramma nel giardino", *Venezia e il Melodramma nel seicento*, ed. Maria Teresa Muraro (Florence, 1976), pp.327-47. Another suggestive Pozzoserrato *Villa and garden by a river* is in the Collez. D'Arco, Milan. For other images of these mainland sites see Rodolfo Pallucchini, *La Pittura nel Veneto*, 2 vols (Milan, 1995), II, figs 544, 630, 644, 887.

20 See, for instance, Zorzi, *Venice*, pp.231 ff.

21 Quoted Brusatin 1980, p.38.

22 Decroisette, p.88.

23 In his *Octaves vénitiennes* of 1760, cited by ibid, p.109.

24 A temporary stage in the Campo San Luca is illustrated in Mazzarotto, *Feste*, p.141.

25 See Morassi figs 269, 277-280, 287-8 and 305-8. Brusatin 1980, figs 21-5 and 39 illustrates various rear-rangements in and decorative settings in the Piazza for these events, and he discusses the Festa della Sensa, pp. 214-5. A few Guardi drawings of the Festa are reproduced in *Disegni*, figs 279-278.

26 These and over three dozen other views by Gabriel Bella are held in the Fondazione Querini Stampalia, which also produces a booklet (*Views of Venice by Gabriel Bella*) that reproduces them all.

27 One might compare the erection of these platforms in front of the Scuola di San Marco on that occasion with the hillside garden of the monastery of Santa Chiara at Brescia, a 1762 engraving of which is illustrated by Brusatin, fig. 246.

28 Sotheby's catalogue, 20 May 1993, which noted the several other paintings by Carlevarijs and Canaletto of this same event.

29 Op. cit., pp.72-73. On the scope, occasions, types and sites of various festivals and outdoor spectacles see Tassini [1891] 1961 and Mazzarotto, *Feste*.

30 Pp.39-40.

31 The two volumes of *I Teatri del Veneto* devoted to Venice reproduce several examples: see I, pp.177, 253 & 397 (all for Goldoni plays) and II, p.75. See also, for earlier illustrated examples, the tradition of pastoral stage sets which continued through the 18th century, Simon Towneley Worsthorne, *Venetian opera in the seventeenth century* (Oxford, 1954). Also *I Teatri Pubblici di Venezia, exhibition catalogue*, ed. L.Zorzi et al. (Venice, 1971) has other illustrations of gardens as stage scenery; also *Rivista di Venezia* X/1 (1931) for a 1753 stage set for the San Samuele theatre.

32 For Torelli see Per Bjürstrom, *Giacomo Torelli and Baroque Stage Design* (Stockholm, 1961); for the later designers, see Gino Damerini, *Scenografi*.

33 See in particular L. Zorzi, *Il teatro e la città* (Turin, 1977), pp.237-91, including extensive bibliography; Lionello Puppi, "Il melodramma nel giardino", *Venezia e il Melodramma nel seicento*, ed. Maria Teresa Muraro (Florence, 1976), pp.327-47; Franco Mancini, Maria Teresa Muraro, Elena Povoledo, *I Teatri del Veneto* (Venice, 1995), the first two volumes of which are dedicated to improvised and built theatres in the city; Brusatin 1980, pp.24-42 discusses the theatres, providing a useful bibliography (pp.40-2) and a map of the location of theatres and churches. See also Georgelin, pp.447-9, and Andrieux, pp.182-200.

34 The text of his proposal for this theatre in the Bacino is transcribed in *I Teatri del Veneto*, I, xxviii-xxix. See also Tafuri 1986.

35 *The Complete Letters of Lady Mary Wortley Montagu,* ed. Robert Halsband, 3 vols (Oxford, 1965-67), II, pp.190-2.

36 This drawing is in Bettini's "Caos e Farragine", vol. III, folios 198-9, Archivio Doria-Pamphili, Rome. For a note on Bettini see below, Chapter Nine. For other designs of exotic, floral gondolas by Tiepolo among others, and paintings of them, see *The Glory of Venice. Art in the Eighteenth Century*, ed. Jane Martineau and Andrew Robison (New Haven, CT, 1995), p.383. For other images of extravagantly decorated gondolas, see Mazzarotto, *Feste*, pp.54, 68 and fig. 5. See also in this context Urban 1980.

37 *Disegni*, figs 304-311.

38 *La Regata di Venezia*, second edition amplified by E.A.Cicogna, in modern facsimile edition, 1974.

39 Ibid, pp.114 & 113; see also Alberto Cosulich, *Venezia nell'800* , p.230.

40 See Charles Malagola, *Le Lido de Venise à travers l'histoire*, pp.74-6; also Urban 1992, pp.68-9.

41 See A Dorigato, *Catalogo dei vetri di Murano del '700* (1981).

42 I draw here upon illustrations of glass gardens and the small commentary in Paola Bussadori, *Il giardino e la scena*, pp.115-8. She reproduces a glass garden from 1920, and I gather they are still occasionally made (personal communication from Carlo Moretti, the distinguished glass designer of Murano).

43 Brusatin 1980, pp.34-5 writes briefly of these private theatrics and he also notes (p.17) various women architects using their own gardens for such entertainments.

44 See Bassi, *Palazzi*, p.49 and *I Teatri del Veneto*, I 422-5, which also illustrates garden settings created in the courtyard of the Ca' Foscari in 1709 for the visit of the King of Denmark (I, 78).

45 *Giardini di Venezia* (1931), p.74.

46 This according to Fontana 1865, p.419.

47 Manlio Brusatin, "Qualche donna e l'architettura funzionale a Venezia nel '700", in *Per Maria Cionini Visani* (1977), pp.126-9; Brusatin, p.138, note 74.

48 E.g. the Villa Widmann at Bagnoli, carved by Antonio Bonazza: see Giuseppe Fiocco, "Statuaria Veneta da Giardino", *L'Illustrazione del Medico*, 63, anno XXVI (1959), pp.13-7.

49 Selva, *English diary*, p.229.

50 Fergusson, p.284. See also Tassini, *Curiosità* under "casin", also for some of the accusations of illicit behaviour in them.

51 Georgelin, pp.733-4; for reference to the Tsar, p.963, note 239.

52 *The Italian Journal of Samuel Rogers*, ed. J. R.Hale (London, 1956), p.179.

53 *The Story of My Life*, translated Stephen Sartarelli and Sophie Hawkes (Penguin Books, 2000), pp.203, 212 (with detailed account of the casino's layout and amenities – including a small library), 222, and 224. No gardens are mentioned, but peep holes from room to room were concealed in carved flowers on the wall, p.228).

54 Tassini [1891] 1961, p.138.

55 Andrieux, p.132 without references.

56 *Sull'architettura...*, p.469.

57 Fontana 1865, p.366. "Scena" or scene continued to have a theatrical connotation.

58 Sixty-six years after de' Barbari, so near the time of Merlo's map, Sansovino noted the property as having "lodges, courtyards and loggias", p.369.

59 *A Tour Through Italy* (London, 1791), 417.

60 Basaldella reports on a variety of casinos on the Giudecca: see pp.53-58.

61 See above in Chapter Three, and P.Morachiello, "Alvise Cornaro e Cristoforo Sabbadino: un dialogo sulle techniche e sulla natura", in *Alvise Cornaro e il suo tempo*, pp.133-5; Tafuri 1985, and Tafuri 1986.

62 For details of the map's publication see Cassini, pp. 138-140.

63 *Venezia*, caption to fig. 117, also for the following remark.

64 In the Correr Museum is an 18th-century engraved sheet by F.Bordiga (F54 [Sullan coll 1949], tav II) showing a glossary of different signs for indicating, among other topographical features, meadows, orchards and gardens, or woodland in maps and charts: that for "orti e Giardini" sets out five shapes of the sort Ughi also uses.

65 *See Palazzo Soranzo-Cappello*, ed. Tiziana Favaro, p.17, a publication that gives a full analysis and narrative of the conservation of this site.

66 See Antonio Morassi, "Settecento inedito (11)", *Arte Veneta*, IV (1950), p.50.

67 See note 5 above.

68 This is illustrated without much clarity in Morassi, *Disegni*. See also the Gazetteer entry above.

69 Correr MSS P.D. c 2434/1.

70 Clarici, *Istoria...*, p.102. The reference to amphitheatre is doubtless to the mode of ranking plants in graduated tiers, tall ones at the rear.

71 Correr MSS P.D. 2434/4 and for the printed one, containing some small differences, Correr MSS P.D. 2434/13.

72 I quote from a 1749 updating of the sale agreement: Correr MSS P.D. c.2502 / II. See also Chiappini di Sorio, in Pool, p.38.

73 The Italian heading at this point ("Nella Baceila di Gazon di montagnola, scalini, cansonali & messarie") is obscure, but refers to the little mountain, steps, and something apparently suspended or in mid-air.

Chapter Seven   The invention of public gardens for the modern city

1 The full extent of the French and Austrian rethinking and reformulation of the conquered city does not concern us; they have been discussed by a variety of authors, some of which attend to the garden elements: these are Giandomenico Romanelli in *Venezia Ottocento* (to which I am particularly indebted), Alvise Zorzi in both *Venezia austriaca* and *Venezia Scomparsa*, E. Trincanato in *Venezia nella storia urbana*, R.Chirivi's "Eventi urbanistici dal 1846 al 1962", *Urbanistica*, 52 (1968), and Plant, *Venice Fragile City*.

2 See the very suggestive article by Martha Feldman, "Opera, Festivity and Spectacle in 'Revolutionary' Venice", in *Venice Reconsidered*.

3 This visit is chronicled by Ugo Fugagnollo, *I dieci giorni di Napoleone I a Venezia*, of which there is modern edition (Venice, 1982).

4 *Paradise of Cities. Venice in the 19th Century*, pp.46 & 39.

5 Romanelli 1988, p.54, answering those who have objected to the destructions of buildings to make way for the gardens.

6 The full list is given by Romanelli 1988, p.118, note 39 and again in *Le Venezie Possibili*, p.158. See also the dissertation of Chiara Mezzalira, "Definire un margine. Il bordo sud-orientale di Venezia tra il fine della Repubblica e l'annessione all'Italia", University di Venezia (IUAV), 2005, pp.43ff; I am grateful to its author for discussions on this major piece of urban restructuring and for generously sharing her research with me.

7 See Kerstin Appelshauser, *Die öffentliche Grünanlange im Städtebau Napoleons in Italien als politische Aussage*, for which reference I thank Sonja Dümpelmann.

8 Romanelli 1988, pp.19-27.

9 *Les Tristes Tropiques*, translated by John and Doreen Weightman (New York, 1974), pp.114-5.

10 Zorzi, *Venice*, p.112.

11 There were many illustrations of this, including an anonymous oil painting reproduced by Romanelli 1988, fig.2, all of which highlight how inapposite such an arboreal and French addition to the city could be.

12 Two large folders in the Municipal Archives document this slow and eventually abandoned project: AMV 1807 Giardino pubblico alla Giudecca 1807–1808.

13 The original drawing of Fig. 2 could not be found for me at the Museo Correr in November 2007; I have therefore had to rely on the photograph of it, where the legend, for example, is not legible. Of Fig. 3 there are two versions, one (not illustrated here) explores the geometry of the proposed intervention and marks small squares in pencil across the whole site, but does not set out the allées and open squares.

14 Quoted Romanelli 1988, pp.62 and 123 (note 64).

15 See Visentini 1988 (1), p.68. Façade-ism, a strongly scenographic approach, has been invoked in more modern times to accommodate new structures and uses while preserving original façades; it smacks of nervous compromise in urban renovation.

16 On this urban phenomenon see Richard Clary, "Making Breathing Room. Public gardens and city planning in 18th-century France", in *Tradition and Innovation in French Garden Art*, ed. John Dixon Hunt and Michel Conan (University of Pennsylvania Press, 2002), pp.68-81. This understanding of the consequences of such a formal promenade is noted by Zanotto (see below in this chapter, p.148).

17 The scope of Selva's involvement is set out in his letter of 5 May 1808, cited in full in Romanelli, pp.118-120, note 40. On the Public Gardens see also G.Romanelli, "Per G.A.Selva urbanista: inediti sui giardini di Castello", *Arte Veneta*, XXVI (1972), 263-71. The doctoral dissertation of Chiara Mezzalira (note 6), particularly pp.53 ff., is also very useful in relating the surviving drawings to the written documentation.

18 Gaetano Pinali is hardly sympathetic to Selva's public gardens, as will be seen, and he seems to put the blame for their inadequacies on a mindless determination by the designer to follow French taste: his comments (Correr MS Cicogna 2427) are transcribed by Romanelli 1988, specifically pp.473-5.

19 See my *Picturesque Garden in Europe*, fig. 85, for a typical formula from c.1785 in which irregular ground is added to an existing, regular site. Selva himself referred to the final segment of the Public Gardens as designed with "irregolità Inglese" (cited Mezzalira [note 6 above], p.60).

20 *Le Venezie Possibili*, p.158.

21 This reservation and his related concern that Venice was not a mainland city are quoted by Romanelli 1988, p.55. Selvatico particularly criticized the lack of sensitivity shown to the lagoon setting by Selva. Zanotto, on the other hand, seems to have praised the views afforded by the setting, while keeping fairly silent on the gardens themselves (see below in this chapter, p.148).

22 There seems to have been some uncertainly as to whether they should be destroyed, although Selva categorically said they would be demolished: see Mezzalira dissertation pp. 69 & 75. One Venetian, Gaetano Pinali, distinctly anti-French in his sentiments, proposed the re-use of the mills for *trattoria* and café (transcribed Romanelli 1988, p.470). No image of the mills seems to exist.

23 Ruffo, pp.43ff., discusses the suppression of green space, mostly private, by reviewing the description of properties on the Napoleonic *catasto* (1807–09).

24 Correr Inv. 6333. The second (Correr 6333/b M42721), which surveys a larger segment of the proposed site is what is illustrated here. The Ughi plan from the 1720s also shows clearly what lay in the way of the new site.

25 Selva's remarks to this effect are quoted by Romanelli 1988, p.119, note 40.

26 Romanelli 1988, p.121 note 52.

27 See my *Picturesque Garden in Europe*, pp.94 & 99. Selections from Silva and Pindemonte are available in *L'Arte dei giardini. Scritti teorici e practici dal XIV al XIX secolo*, ed. Margherita Azzi Visentini, 2 vols (Milano, 1990), II, pp.215-73 and 155-77.

28 His comments on the garden projects are transcribed by Romanelli 1988, pp.469-72.

29 The *Descrizione* is included in the collection by various authors, *Venezia e le sue Lagune* (1847), II, pt II, pp.384-5.

30 Howells, pp.213-6. He went on patronizingly to describe some who did frequent the gardens and what they did there, ending with an unpleasant anti-semitic gibe.

31 His distinction between what is appropriate for private versus public gardens is quoted in Visentini 1988 (1), p.222; her book discusses some of the "new" gardening, mostly on the Venetian mainland. For Hirschfeld, see the abridged translation of his important and very influential five-volume treatise, *Theory of Garden Art*, edited and translated by Linda Parshall (Philadelphia, 2001).

32 Writing in 1847 Selvatico compared Selva's poor skills with those of Jappelli, who would not, he felt, have made such a terrible job of the public gardens; it is thought that Jappelli may have apprenticed in Selva's office.

33 Even Selva played with various possibilities: see Mezzalira dissertation, Fig. 42, for three variations of design. The Municipal Archives contain a considerable body of materials, as yet untapped, on the design, maintenance and redesign of these public gardens, suggesting the considerable investment of energy, time and money that was involved.

34 Based upon this proposal of Guignon, the city engineer subsequently drawn up a scheme for the re-modelling of the existing flowerbeds and for introducing a series of hillocks and bumpy elevations (depicted in many sections): the plan, accompanied by a detailed verbal explanation of the proposals, is held in the A.V.M. 1770 IX/6/6. The project seems to have been shelved for financial reasons.

35 Many of these Venetian proposals seem in the spirit of contemporary French publications, notably those by Gabriel Thouin, *Plans Raisonnés de Toutes Espèces de Jardins* (Paris, 1819, 1823 & 1828), Victor Jean Baptiste Petit, *Parcs et Jardins des Environs de Paris, Nouveau Recueil de Plans de Jardins et Petits Parcs...* (Paris, c.1861), and François-Joseph Duvilliers, *Les Parcs et Jardins* (Paris, 1871).

36 See Romanelli 1988, pp.47 and 123 note 60.

37 The manuscript account of his travels is held in the Biblioteca Querini Stampalia, MS. Cl.VIII/35, 1175, and it has been transcribed by Stella Randolph in *Labyrinthos*, 5/6 (1984), pp.218-49.

38 His drawings are held at the Accademia in Venice: a catalogue of their exhibition in 1996 was published as *Disegni di Giacomo Quarenghi. Vedute e capricci* (Milan, 1996).

39 See Pierre de la Ruffinière du Prey, "Giannantonio Selva In England", *Architectural History*, 25 (1982), pp.20-34, where the point is made, rightly, that the importance of the English visit to Selva and to his subsequent work has been overestimated.

40 On picturesque pattern books see my *Picturesque Garden in Europe*, pp.130-3, one such publication by the German, Grohmann, was published in Venice: see Chapter Eight in this book, p.164.

41 The drawing for this *tempietto* in the Correr Museum is illustrated in Visentini 1988 (1), p.224, and Selva's remarks are quoted p.225.

42 See Giandomenico Romanelli, "Due progetti di un arco per Napoleone", *Arte Veneta*, XXVII (1973), 286-9. On earlier invocations in Venice of triumphal arches, see Lina Padoan Urban 1969 and her (with other authors) *Venise en fêtes*, pp.152-4.

43 Brown 1996, p.6, a Venetian claim or boast that, of course, took no account of modern archaeological evidence for early Roman settlements. But a 16th-century proposal to rebuild the Rialto marketplace on the model of a Roman forum was also rejected: see M.Tafuri 1986, pp.5-8. On the city's skepticism and even hostility to Palladio's architecture, for the same reasons, see Tracy E.Cooper, *Palladio's Venice* (New Haven, CT, 2007).

44 It is an interesting engraving, too, in that is represents (correctly) the pavement in the Piazza, which in plan appears but a version of the parterre in the Royal Gardens.

45 For the engraving Correr Museum, Gherro 9.

46 See Romanelli 1988, pp.169 ff.

47 *Sulla Architecttura e sulla Scultura in Venezia*, pp.474-5 ("gretti e monotoni viali ordinati dal Selva"). Selvatico invoked the talents of Jappelli as being a potentially more able and inspired designer of the gardens that were needed.

48 Howells, pp.215-6.

49 Mezzalira reproduces (Fig. 64) a photograph by Tommaso Filippi from the late 1890s which shows the central *viale* completely and eerily empty. Yet she also quotes the enthusiatic response of Hippolyte Taine's 1866 *Voyage en Italie*, though admittedly he makes no mention of other visitors.

50 According to Alinari Archives, the caption to this illustration is "St. Mark's Square. The pigeons 1900 ca."

1 *The Works of John Ruskin*, The Library Edition, ed. E.T.Cook and Alexander Wedderburn, 39 vols (London, 1903-12), hereafter *Works*, vol. 10, p.65; Ruskin actually wrote that Venetians "had no gardens", *Works*, vol. 7, p.417. Zanetti, pp.158-9.

2 Another aspect of this cultural re-assessment in face of the fall of the Republic is considered by Martha Feldan, "Opera, Festivity, and Spectacle in 'Revolutionary' Venice: phantasms of time and history", in *Venice Reconsidered*, pp.217-260.

3 Ruskin's phrase about buildings (*Works*, vol. 10, p.143), but applicable here too.

4 Quoted by Tanner, *Venice Desired*, p.28.

5 "Un vieux jardin", in *Sous le ciel Vénitien* (Paris, 1911), pp.56-63. Hénard does not mention Eden, but the description follows in many ways Eden's own published account of some years earlier. Certain details are, however, changed: Eden did not (as far as I know) own a palace on the Grand Canal, as the Frenchman claims the English owner of this old garden did; rather Eden lived on site, and not in the "decrepit" buildings that form part of the account here, which means that the Frenchman has invented the decrepitude of the buildings where Eden in fact lived comfortably.

6 William Beckford, *Dreams, Waking Thoughts and Incidents*, ed. Robert J Gemmett (Cranbury, NJ, 1971), pp.105-6; whether Ruskin's is a deliberate echo, is not clear. For *The Stones of Venice* see *Works*, vol. 10, p.9.

7 The approach to Venice from the mainland forms the last chapter of the first volume of *The Stones of Venice* (Works, vol. 9). See also *Ruskin in Italy. Letters to his Parents 1845*, ed. Harold I.Shapiro (Oxford, 1972); the burden of much of these letters (see pp.198-223) is "fearful dilapidation", "total ruin" or "weeds, where gardens had been".

8 Published in Brussels, 1842, pp.53 & 2.

9 Respectively in this paragraph: Ruchinger, noted by Alessandro Marcello, "La Flora Urbica", p.123; *The Italian Journal of Samuel Rogers*, p.176; Chateaubriand, *Mémoires d'Outre-Tombe*, cited in *Venetian Views, Venetian Blinds*, p.108; Browning, "A Toccata of Galuppi's" in *Dramatic Lyrics* (1842); Valery, *Venise* (Brussels, 1842), pp.53 & 2; Lee, second edition, p.55; Thomson, first published in 1874; Régnier, pp.159 & 163; James, *Collected Travel Writings* (Library of America edition, 1984), pp.288, 314-5 & 330; 355-6 for the final quotation.

10 See many of the essays in *Venetian Views, Venetian Blinds*, to which I am indebted here, especially Weener von Koppenfels, "Sunset City – City of the Dead", who quotes the remark by Laconte on p.104, and Sergio Perosa, "Literary Deaths in Venice". Tony Tanner's *Venice Desired* has also been an invaluable resource. However, Cunico (p.37) is at least one Venetian voice that talks of the continuing "abbandoni e distruzioni" of the "patrimonio di verde storico".

11 On artists' visions of Venice see work by Margaretta M.Lovell and the volume, *Gondola Days*. On Whistler's Venice see Eric Denker's book, and both Alistair Grieve's article in *Print Quarterly* 1996 and his book, *Whistler's Venice*.

12 See Burdett Gardner, *The Lesbian Imagination (Victorian Style). A psychological and critical study of Vernon Lee* (New York, 1987), p.405.

13 *Giardini di Venezia*, facing p.72.

14 Ruchinger, *Cenni storici*, p.xii.

15 A. Quadri, *Huit jours à Venise*, p.238: Quadri lists it as one of half dozen places to walk in Venice (pp.419-20).

16 Gera, *I Principali Giardini di Venezia*.

17 P.419-20, where Quadri lists three public places (The Public and the Royal Gardens, and the Botanical Garden) and four private ones (Papadopoli, Galvagna, Zenobio, and Gradenigo). On the acquisition of these gardens by the city see Carlo Brandolini d'Adda, an article illustrated with photographs of its rich planting, of the Scuola Comunale open-air classrooms established where the green houses once stood and of a women's gardening class. See also the images in the article by Carlo Brandolini d'Adda, "Venezia e I suoi giradini", *Rivista di Venezia*, VIII, March 1929.

18 See Cecchetti 1885 for an effusive celebration of these plants persons' paradise.

19 Quadri, p.191.

20 Gera, *I Principali Giardini di Venezia*, p.13.

21 See Sergio Barizza, *Il Comune di Venezia 1806–1946*, (1982, second edition 1987), p.104, for an old photograph of a family group in this garden (in Municipal Archives); the man at the table may well be Signor Groggia himself. I am grateful to Professor Rosella Mamoli Zorzi for alerting me to this photograph.

22 She illustrated Eden's pergolas and lilies in two of her own publications.

23 *Giardini di Venezia*, facing p.92.

24 P.25. What may also lurk behind Eden's remark, perhaps, are both a pun (no Venetian *campi* are called squares or *piazze*) and an implicit assumption that, given the often labyrinthine *calli* and waterways of the city itself, the meandering paths of picturesque gardens were unnecessary and provided insufficient contrast.

25 Ruchinger, *Cenni Storici*, p.ix.

26 *Collected Travel Writings*, p.297.

27 See John Hall's account in *Hortus*, 67 (2003). The "Moorish kiosk" is mentioned by Ileana Chiappini di Sorio, in Albrizzi/Pool, p.44. The photographs I received in 2005 were kindly supplied by Andrew Crompton of Manchester University.

28 E.V.Lucas, *A Wanderer in Venice* (1914: ninth edition, 1930), p.116, notes that the Papadopoli gardens near the station "may be visited on application".

Chapter nine

Possible gardens: grounds for change

1 Spence, *Letters from the Grand Tour*, ed. Slava Klima (Montreal and London, 1975), p.392; Stokes, "Venice, an aspect of art", in *The Critical Writings*, ed. L.Gowing, 3 vols (London, 1978), II, p.297.

2 See Chapter One, note 38.

3 The nationalistic, indeed Fascistic, agenda, of the Florence exhibition is discussed by Raffaella Fabiano Giannetto, *Medici Gardens. From Making to Design* (Philadelphia, 2008), pp.5-8.

4 Cited Crouzet-Pavan, *Venice Reconsidered*, p.49; Corner's *Scritture sulla laguna* is reprinted in *Antichi scrittori d'idraulica veneta*, ed. G.Pavanello, vol. 1.

5 Sansovino, *Delle cose notabilii...*, quoted Tafuri 1985.

6 This first bizarre proposal was announced in the *Guardian* newspaper for 2l January 2005: see www.guardian.co.uk/worldlatest/story/0,1280,-5430194,oo.html. On the earlier proposal for a metro see *Fondamenta Nuovissime*, ed.Michele Lodola and Connie Occhialini (Venice: ILAUD, 2000) and *The Architectural Review* (Venice number), especially the introduction by A.Rogatnick. On the Moise project among other proposals, see John Keaney, *Venice against the sea. A city besieged* (New York, 2002).

7 The phrase is Doody's, p.14.

8 "Progetti di Strade e di Ponti in Venezia antica", *Le Tre Venezie*, 3 (1930), pp.12-6; see also Alberto Magrini in the same journal, 4 (1931), p.500.

9 A.-F.Sergent-Marceau, p.82.

10 Bettini's proposal is, alas, barely formulated and very faintly drawn: on a double opening (pp.60-1) of his folio sketch book, "Caos e Farragine", vol. III (captioned "Progetto del Bettini per pulire li canali di Venezia..."), in the Archivio Doria-Pamphili, Rome. On it he has outlined in red a map of the city and its waterways, then in faint pencil marked a long causeway from the Arsenal across the front of the existing Fondamenta Nuove, then to Murano (this portion clearly marked with an allée of trees) and circling round to the eastern end of the city stopping at another unnamed island. Bettini worked for the Mocenigo family in France and in Venice: this same volume contains a plan of their property at San Samuele [pp.217-8]). On Bettini's work, see Minna Heimbürger-Ravalli, *Disegni di giardini e opere minori di un artista del '700* (Florence, 1981).

11 As reported by M.Valery, who was much struck by the ruin of the city, *Venise et ses environs* (Brussels, 1842), p.4.

12 See Balistreri; also *Architectural Review* (Venice issue), pp.317-8.

13 Ibid, p.318.

14 See F.Bac, *Livre-Journal 1919*, ed. Lawrence Joseph (Paris, 2000), with good bibliography including the few articles on his garden designs.

15 Published in Paris in 1909, the tale of the American lady from Philadelphia turned Venetian countess is on pp.154 ff. and the brief put-down about Napoleonic gardens, pp.280-1. For other modernities, see Ruffo, pp.23 ff.

16 For some details and imaginative reconstructions of older waterways now covered over, see Zucchetta.

17 *The Works of John Ruskin*, vol. 27, p.328.

18 "Ancora del verde nell'urbanistica", *Proceedings of the IV National Congress of Planning* (Venice: Istituto Nazionale di Urbanistica, 1952), pp.113-8; I am grateful to Kimberley Stryker for this reference.

19 Cunico, p.37.

20 *Elenco degli Edifici Monumentali e dei Frammenti Storici ed Artistici della Città di Venezia* (1905). The section on the Giudecca, for example, has no mention whatsoever of any gardens.

21 On these housing projects generally see R.Vivante, *La Casa Salubre* (Venice, 1936) and "La casa a Venezia", *La Rivista Veneta*, 28-29 (December 1978).

22 On these roof gardens, see Giannino Omero Gallo, "Giardini sui Tetti", *Le Tre Venezie* (February 1932), pp.89-91, and Giorgiana Baccin Reale and Elisabetta Pasqualin, *Le Altane di Venezia* (Venice, 1989).

23 Following an ancient custom: see Tom. Giaccalone Monaco, "Vino e Pergola sulla Laguna", *Rivista di Viticoltura e di Enologia di Conegliano*, III (1954). Whistler records one of these among his Venetian etchings.

24 This essential point was made by Giorgio Bellavitis in arguing against the habit of seeing elite palaces as the only elements to be restored: *The Architectural Review* (Venice issue), p.290.

25 L.Halprin, *Notebooks 1959–71* (Cambridge, MA, 1972), p.57, from an annotation on his sketch of the Bacino.

26 Among the considerable literature on Scarpa, see *Carlo Scarpa alla Querini Stampalia. Disegni inediti*, ed. Marta Mazza (Venice, 1996).

27 Serlio, *The Five Books of Architecture* [1619], BK IV, pp.335-356. Similar flower-bed designs are offered in Giovanni Battista Ferrari, *De florum cultura* (1633), as well as in a variety of manuscript pattern books. Georgio Bellavitis said he took the geometry of the paving from the designation of gardens on the Giudecca in the map of Ludovico Ughi (personal communication from Dr. Philip Rylands)

28 Cosgrove, "The myth and the stones of Venice", *Journal of Historical Geography*, 8 (1987), pp.145-69; James, *Collected Travel Writings*, pp.290 & 292 (for the next remark).

29 Zorzi,*Venice*, p.26. On the other hand, there is a tradition for exhibiting exotic beasts, if we recall Longhi's painting of *The Rhinoceros* (c.1751).

30 I am grateful to Paula Deitz for sending me details of this Biennale garden, which I was unable to see for myself. I was also lucky to hear Kathryn Gustafson lecture on her work and specifically on this Venetian site at the University of Pennsylvania in September 2008. For the suppressed convent, Santa Maria in Gerusalemme, on the site of which this garden was installed, see Alvisi Zorzi, *Venezia Scomparsa*, II, pp.364-7.

31 Quoted, along with some of his sketches, in Trincanato, p.50. That Venice has been a touchstone of attitudes towards modernism is true equally in literary matters: see *Venezia nelle letterature moderne*, ed. Carlo Pellegrini (Venice and Rome, 1961), p.62.

32 Consequently I shall not dwell upon its slight garden-ist contributions: it is discussed by Guillermo Julian de la Fuente, *The Venice hospital project of Le Corbusier* (Houston, TX 1968) and Peter Eisenman, "Three Texts for Venice", *Harvard Design Review*, 3 (1984), previously published in *Domus* 611 (1980), by Baliesteri.

33 See plans in Amedeo Petrilli, *Il Testamento di Le Corbusier* (1999), specifically Fig. 28 where scattered trees and two "giardini" are marked.

34 The texts of these protests are to be found in the archives of the Assessorato all'Urbanistica del Comune di Venezia (along with a less considerable number of letters of support); I am grateful to arch. Chiara Ferro who photocopied this bulky material for me in 2006.

35 I have consulted the following for this brief excursus: *Venice for Modern Man*, catalogue for exhibition at Edinburgh, RIBA (London), Strasbourg, Paris and Venice, 1986; *Venezia. Il nuovo piano urbanistico*, ed. Leonardo Benevolo (Rome-Bari, 1996); Giovanni Battista Stefinlongo, Il "Giardino" del Doge. *I Giardini del Popolo. Studi sul restauro urbano* .... 1993–1998 (Chioggia, 1998); *Lavorare sui bordi*, ed. Francesco Benati and Laura Zampieri (Monfalcone, 2001); *Venezia Novissima*, catalogue of the exhibition "Edge of City" (Venezia Marghera, 2003); *Progetti per la Giudecca. Projects for the Giudecca*, ed. Arthur H.Chen and Francesco Calzolaio (Venice Lagoon Foundation, 2003); Gianfranco Pertot, *Venice. Extraordinary Maintenance* (London, 2004); and Leonardo Benevolo, Roberto D'Agostino and Mariolina Toniolo, *Quale Venezia? Trasformazioni urbane 1995–2005* (Venice, 2007).

36 This competition was published in a special issue of *G2*, *Concurso 2G Parque de la Lagune de Venecia / 2GCompetition Venice Lagoon Park* (2008), which illustrated the winning deisgns, some panels of runners-up, along with essays by members of the jury and essays on the Venetian situation. It is on this publication that I have drawn in these paragraphs, though the variety and scope of the competition is obviously not fully represented in the magazine and anyhow really requires a much more extended critique than can be attempted here.

37 Brandolini d'Adda's article is illustrated with photographs of these three efforts.

37a I am grateful to Philip Rylands who brought this project to my attention and supplied materials about it.

38 See Davis and Martin, specifically in their "Introduction: the city built on the sea".

39 This paragraph draws upon various newspaper articles in recent years: Elisabetta Povoledo, "Vanishing Venice: a city swamped by a sea of tourists", *The New York Times International*, 1 October 2006; Elisabeth Rosenthal, "Venice turns to Future to rescue the Past", *International Herald Tribune*, 22 February 2005. For some sober perspectives on the conservation problems that face Venice see Gianighian 2001.

40 Brusatin 1980, p.xxxiii.

41 Wigwam telephone 041 610791, and giardinistorici.ve@wigwam.it.

42 *The Architectural Review* (Venice issue), pp.290, 291 & 292, a careful and inspired argument.

43 It is a good choice of location, doubtless drawing upon the fact that San Francesco continues to boast extensive and fine green space, as do some other places in the Castello like the property of the Knights of Malta.

44 On the mythopoeic strategies of Venice there is a huge literature: but see, among others, the catalogue, *Venezia: Da Stato a Mito* and *Venice Reconsidered*.

45 It is worth quoting again the words of Professore Pier Luigi Cervellati (in Ruffo, p.7): "il recupero....non solo della storia dello stesso, ma anche del contesto urbano nel quale esso si iscrive" (the recovery.... not only of the history for its own sake, but for the urban context in which it is inscribed).

Bibliography

of the major published sources on Venice on which this book is based, with abbreviations used in the notes. Place of publication is Venice unless otherwise stated.

Casimiro **A**ffaitati, *L'Ortolano in villa e l'accurato giardiniere in città*, 3rd ed., Bassano, 1787.

Albrizzi / Pool: Alessandro Albrizzi (photographs) and Mary Jane Pool (text), *The Gardens of Venice*, with an introduction by Ileana Chiappini di Sorio, New York, [1989].

Alvise Cornaro e il suo tempo, exhibition catalogue, ed. Lionello Puppi, Padua, 1980.

Ammerman et al. 1999: A.J.Ammerman, C.E.McClennen, M.De Min and R.Housley, "Sea-level change and the archaeology of early Venice", *Antiquity*, 73, pp.303-12.

M.Andrieux, *Daily Life in Venice in the Time of Casanova*, trans. Mary Fitton, London, 1972.

Kerstin Appelshauser, *Die öffentliche Grünanlage im Städtebau Napoleons in Italien als politische Aussage*, Frankfurt am Main, 1994.

Architectural Review, special issue on "Venice: Problems and Possibilities", ed. J.M.Richards and Abraham Rogatnick, CXLIX, No.891, 1971.

L'Architettura per nostro secolo: L'Architettura per nostro secolo. Progetti Originali Italiani di fabbriche ordinate all'indole dei nostril bisogni...[etc.], 1834.

Aretino, *Lettere*: Pietro Aretino, *Lettere sull'arte*, ed. E.Pertile and E.Camesasca, 1957.

Aretino, *Ragionamento*: Pietro Aretino, *Ragionamento delle corti*, ed. Lanciano, 1914.

Atlas: An Atlas of Venice, ed. Edoardo Salzano [1989], Commune of Venice and New York 1990. (Also available on CD-Rom.)

Bagnara: *Il giardino e la scena, Francesca Bagnara 1784 – 1866*, exhibition catalogue, ed. P.Bussadori, Castelfranco Veneto, 1986.

Emiliano Balisteri, *Le Corbusier, Neutra, Samonà, Scarpa, Trincanato, Wright e Venezia*, Venezia-Mestre, 2002.

Balistreri-Trincanato & Zanverdiani: Corrado Balistreri-Trincanato and Dario Zanverdiani, with Anna Maria Ghion, *Jacopo de' Barbari. Il racconto di una città*, Venezia-Mestre, 2000.

Sergio Barizza, *Il Comune di Venezia 1806–1946. Guida-inventario dell'archivio municipale*, 2nd revised edition, 1987.

Basaldella: F.Basaldella, *Giudecca: storia e testimonianze*, 1986.

Basaldella 1991: F.Basaldella, *La Guidecca di Vervloet e cento immagine di un'isola*, privately printed.

Bassi: E.Bassi, *Palazzi di Venezia*, 1976.

Bassi 1962: E.Bassi, *Architettura del Sei-Settecento a Venezia*, Naples.

M.Battagia, *Delle academie veneziane*, 1826.

Giorgio Bellavitis and Giandomenico Romanelli, *Venezia*, in the series "Le città nella storia d'Italia", 1985.

Giorgio Bellavitis, *Palazzo Giustinian Pesaro*, Vicenza, 1975.

Berlèse: Abbé Berlèse [i.e. Lorenzo Bernado], *Venise et ses jardins*, Paris, 1842. (A ghostly book frequently cited, but nowhere to be found in Venetian libraries or in worldwide catalogue searches).

Berlèse 1843: Abbé Berlèse, "Report on the Orto Botanico to the IV Congresso degli Scienziati a Padova", *Gazzetta Privilegiata di Venezia*, 189/2, 21 August 1843.

Sergio Bettini, *Venezia. Nascità di una città*, Milan, 1978.

Bettoni: [Niccolò Bettoni], *Venezia e i suoi Giardini*, Portogruaro, 1826; reprinted in Stefinlongo 2000.

Piero Bevilacqua, *Venezia e le Acque. Una metafore planetaria*, Rome, 1995.

Marina Crivellari Bizio, *Campi Veneziani*, 2003, and *Campi Veneziani II*, 2004, both volumes with drawings by William Lombardo.

Giuseppe Boerio, *Dizionario del dialetto veneziano*, 2nd enlarged edition, 1856.

Ferdinand Boyer, "Napoleon I et les jardins publics en Italie", *Urbanisme et habitation: la vie urbaine*, 1 (1954), pp.1–8.

Carlo Brandolini d'Adda, "Venezia e i suoi Giardini", *Rivista di Venezia*, 8 (1929), pp.197–212.

Braunstein & Delort: Philippe Braunstein and Robert Delort, *Venise: portrait historique d'une cité*, Paris, 1971.

Brown 1988: Patricia Fortini Brown, *Venetian Narrative Painting in the Age of Carpaccio*, New Haven, CT, 1988.

Brown 1996: Patricia Fortini Brown, *Venice and Antiquity*, London and New Haven, CT, 1996.

Brown 2004: Patricia Fortini Brown, *Private Lives in Renaissance Venice*, New Haven, CT, 2004.

Brusatin: Manlio Brusatin, *Venezia nel settecento: stato, architettura, territorio*, Turin, 1980.

Marcello Brusegan, *I Palazzi di Venezia*, Rome, 2005.

Bussadori: Paola Bussadori, *Il Giardino e la Scena*, Castelfranco Veneto, 1986.

Cacciari: Massimo Cacciari, "Venezia possibile", *Micromega*, I (1989), pp.217–240.

Anna Caiana, "Un palazzo Veronese a Murano: note e aggiunte", *Arte Veneta*, XXII (1968), pp.47–59.

Annamaria Conforti Calcagni, *Bellissima è dunque la Rosa. I giardini dalle signorie alla Serenissima*, Milan, 2003.

A.Callegari, "Il giardino nell'Italia settentrionale e in particolare nel Veneto", *Dedalo*, XI, vol. XIII (1931), pp.1141 ff.

Martino da Canal, *Les histoires de Venise*, ed. A.Limentani, Florence, 1972.

Cartwright: Julia Cartwright, "The gardens of Venice", *Gardens of the Renaissance*, London, 1914, pp.102–34.

Casola: *Canon Pietro Casola's Pilgrimage to Jerusalem in the year 1494*, ed. Margaret Newett, Manchester, 1907.

G.Cassini, *Piante e Vedute Prospettiche di Venzia*, 1982.

Cassiodorus: *Opera*, ed. A.J.Frith, *Corpus christianorum*, ser. Latina, XCVI-XCVIII (Turnhout, 1958–72), vol. III (*Variae epistolae*).

Cornelio Castaldi, *Priolani ruris ad murianum delitiae*, with an Italian translation by Jacopo Bernardi, 1868.

I Castasti Storici di Venezia 1808–1913, ed. Italo Pavanelo, Rome, 1981. (This reproduces three different city surveys: Napoleonic, 1808–1811; Austrian, 1838–1842; Austro-Italian, 1867–1913.)

Catasto Napoleonico Mappa della citta di Venezia, Marsilio Editore reproduction for the Archivio di Stato di Venezia.

Cecchetti, "La vita": B.Cecchetti, "La vita dei Veneziani fino al secolo XIII", *Nuovo Archivio Veneto*, XXVII (1884), pp.5–54, pp.321–37, XXVIII (1884), pp.5–29, pp.267–96 &XXIX (1885), pp.11–48.

Cecchetti 1885: B.Cecchetti, *Del Giardino dei signori Luigi Borghi e Virginia Tabaglio in Venezia*.

Cecchetti 1887(1): B.Cecchetti, "A ricordo dell'Orto Botanico di Venezia", *Archivio Veneto*, 34 (1887/II), pp.237–43.

Cecchetti 1887(2): B.Cecchetti, *Una passeggiata nel giardino dei Conti Papadopoli*.

Mario Cermenati, "Un diplomatico naturalista del Rinascimento: Andrea Navagero", *Nuovo Archivio Veneto*, 1912.

R.Cessi and A.Alberti, *Rialto; l'isola, il ponte, il mercato*, Bologna, 1934.

André Chastel, "Ultima lezione di Le Corbusier", *L'Arcipelago di San Marco*, 1990, pp.55–62.

Emanuele Antonio Cicogna, *Delle vita e delle opere di Andrea Navagero: oratore, istorico, poetà Veneziana dal secolo decimosesto*, 1855.

Emanuele Antonio Cicogna, *Delle Iscrizioni Veneziane* [1842], modern photographic re-edition, Bologna, 1970.

Commines: *The History of Philip de Commines*, London, 1596.

Concina 1989: Ennio Concina, *Venezia nell'éta moderna*, 1989.

Concina 1995: Ennio Concina, *Storia dell'architettura di Venezia*, Milano, 1995.

Concurso 2G Competition. Parque de la Laguna de Venecia. Venice Lagoon Park, Barcelona, 2007.

Corti: Gianluca Aldegani and Fabrizio Diodati, *Le Corti. Spazi pubblici e privati nella città de Venezia*, with essays by Egle Renata Trincanato, 1991.

Denis E.Cosgrove, *Social Formation and Symbolic Landscape*, Totowa, NJ, 1984.

M.Costantini, *L'acqua de Venezia*, 1984.

Alberto Cosulich, *Venezia nell'800*, San Vito di Cadore, 1988.

M.Cristal, *Il giardiniere delle finestre, dei pogginoli e dei piccoli giardini*, 1870.

Giuseppe Cristinelli, *Cannaregio. Un sestiere di Venezia*, Rome 1987.

Crouzet-Pavan 1992: Elizabeth Crouzet-Pavan, "*Sopre Le Acque Salse". Espaces, Pouvoir er Société à Venise à la fin du Moyen Age*, 2 vols, Rome.

Crouzet-Pavan 1995: Elizabeth Crouzet-Pavan, *La mort lente de Torcello. Histoire d'une cité disparue*, Paris.

Crouzet-Pavan 1997: Elizabeth Crouzet-Pavan, *Venise: une invention de la ville, XIII–XV siècle*, Paris.

Crouzet-Pavan 1999: Elizabeth Crouzet-Pavan, *Venise triomphante. Les horizons d'un myth*, Paris. An English translation by Lydia G.Cochrane has been published by the Johns Hopkins Press, Baltimore, MD, 2007.

Crovato, A., "I pavimenti alla veneziana", *Venezia l'Altra Riva* (1989), pp.8–116.

M.T.Cruciani, "Il giardino Veneto", *Antichità Viva*, V/2 (1966), pp.41–52.

Cunico: Mariapia Cunico, *Il Giardino Veneziano. La storia. L'Architettura. La Botanica*, 1989.

Cunico 1996: Mariapia Cunico et al., *Nei giardini del Veneto*, Milan.

Gino **D**amerini, *Giardini sulla laguna*, Bologna, 1927.

Damerini: Gino Damerini, *Giardini di Venezia*, Bologna, 1931.

Damerini, *Scenografi:* Gino Damerini, *Scenografi veneziani dell'ottocento*, 1962.

Dami: Luigi Dami, *Il Giardino Italiano*, Milano, 1924.

Mariagrazia Dammicco, with photographs by Marianne Majerus, *Venetian Gardens*, New York, 2007.
Also published in French as *Jardins Secrets de Venise*, Paris 2007, in German as *Die geheimen Gärten von Venedig*, Munich 2007.

Robert C.Davis and Garry R.Martin, *Venice. The Tourist Maze. A cultural critique of the world's most touristed city*, Berkeley, CA, 2004.

Régis Debray, *Contre Venise*, Paris, 1995.

Françoise Decroisette, *Venise au temps de Goldoni*, Paris, 1990.

Eric Denker, *Whistler and his circle in Venice*, Corcoran Gallery exhibition catalogue, Washington, DC, 2003.

Difesa di Venezia. Contributi per una azione di conoscenza e di difesa di Venezie e della sua Laguna, ed. Giorgio Bellavitis, Milan and Venice, 1970 (publication to accompany the exhibition, "Una Venezia da Salvare", at the Centro Pirelli, Milan).

Documenti...: Documenti Relativi alla storia di Venezia anteriori al mille, 2 vols, Padua, 1991.

Margaret Doody, *Tropic of Venice*, Philadelphia, PA, 2007.

Dorigo 1983: Wladimiro Dorigo, *Venezia Origini*, 3 vols, Milan, 1983.

Dorigo 2003: Wladimiro Dorigo, *Venezia romanica. La formazione della citta medioevale fino all'eta gotica*, 2 vols, Venice and Sommacampagna.

Eden: Frederic Eden, *A Garden in Venice*, London, 1903, reprinted by Francis Lincoln Books, 2003. An Italian translation was issued by Pendragon Publishers, Bologna, 2008.

Ronnie **F**erguson, *A Linguistic History of Venice*, Florence, 2007.

Giacomo Filiasi, *Memorie storiche de' Veneti, primi e secondi*, Padua, 1811.

Luciano Filippi, *Vecchie Immagini di Venezia*, 3 vols, Venice, 1992, 1993.

Fontana 1865: Gianiacopo Fontana, *Cento Palazzi Fra I Più Celebri di Venezia sul Canalgrande*, 1865.

Fontana 1967: Gianiacopo Fontana, *Venezia, Monumentale, I Palazzi*, 1845–63 in fascicles; reprinted, 1967.

V. Fontana, *Costruire a Venezia nel cinquecento*, ed. Tullio Campostrini, 1993.

Caroline Fletcher and Jane Da Mosto, *The Science of Saving Venice*, Turin, 2004.

Umberto Franzoi and Dina Di Stephano, *Le Chiese di Venezia*, Milan, 1976.

R. Fulin, "Documenti per servire alla storia della tipografia veneziana", *Nuova Archivo Veneto*, 23 (1882).

Gardin, *Giardini*: Gianni Berengo Gardin, Cristiana Moldi-Ravenna and Trudy Sammartini, *Giardini Segreti a Venezia*, 1988.

Jean Georgelin, *Venise au siècle des lumières*, The Hague, 1978.

Francesco Dr. Gera, *I Principali Giardini di Venezia*, 1847.

Gianighian 2001: Giorgio Gianighian, "Venice, Italy", in *Management of Historic Centres*, ed. Robert Pickard, London.

Gianighian & Pavanini: Giorgio Gianighian and Paola Pavanini, *Dietro I Palazzi. Tre secoli di architettura minore a Venezia 1492–1803*, 1984.

Giardini Veneziani: Mariagrazia Dammicco, Gabriella Bondi, Letizia Querenghi, *I Giardini Veneziani*, Maserà di Padova and Venice, 2003.

Gondola Days. Isabella Stewart Gardner and the Palazzo Barbaro Circle, exhibition catalogue by Elizabeth Anne McCauley, Alan Chong, Rosella Mamoli Zorzi and Richard Linger, Isabella Stewart Gardner Museum, Boston, 2004.

Alistair Grieve, "The sites of Whistler's Venice etchings", *Print Quarterly*, 13 (1996), pp.20–39.

Alistair Grieve, *Whistler's Venice*, New Haven, CT, 2000.

Henry **H**arvard, *Amsterdam et Venise*, Paris, 1876.

Robert Hénard, *Sous le ciel Vénetien*, Paris, 1911.

Jean-Claude Hocquet, "Technologie du marais salant et travail du saunier dans la lagune de Venise au moyen age", *Studi Veneziani*, IX (1985), pp.15–41.

Hugh Honour and John Fleming, *The Venetian Hours of Henry James, Whistler and Sargent*, London, 1991.

Deborah Howard, *Venice and the East. The impact of the Islamic world on Venetian Architecture 1100–1500* , New Haven CT, 2000.

W. D. Howells, *Venetian Life* [1866, 1885], Marlboro, VT, 1989.

Hunt 1981: John Dixon Hunt, "L'idea di un giardino in bel mezzo del mare" (text also in English), *Rassegna*, 8 (October, 1981), pp.57–65.

Hunt 1986: John Dixon Hunt, *Garden and Grove. The Italian Renaissance Garden in the English Imagination: 1600–1750*, London.

Hunt 1999: John Dixon Hunt, "The garden in the city of Venice: epitome of state and site", *Studies in the history of gardens*, 19 (1999), pp.46–61.

Hunt 2000: John Dixon Hunt, "The garden in the city of Venice: some preliminary observations" (text also in Italian), in *Fondamenta Nuovissime*, ed. Michele Lodola and Connie Occhialini, ILAUD, 2000, pp.22–37.

Hypnerotomachia Poliphili, critical edition by Giovanni Pozzi and Lucia A. Ciapponi, 2 vols, Padua, 1980; there is a modern English version by Joscelyn Godwin, London, 1999.

Interpretazioni Veneziane. Studi di storia dell'arte in onore di Michelangelo Muraro, ed. David Rosand, 1984.

Isole Abbondonate: Isole Abbondonate della Laguna, exhibition catalogue by Giorgio and Maurizio Crovato, Padua, 1978; New bi-lingual edition, 2008.

Le Isole della Laguna di Venezia dalle incisioni del '700, with an introduction by Ugo Fugagnollo (n.d).

Janson and Bürklin: Alban Janson and Thorsten Bürklin, *Auftritte. Interaktionen mit dem architekonischen Raum: die Campi Venedigs / Scenes. Interaction with architectural space: the Campi of Venice*, Basel, Boston, Berlin, 2002.

A. Nicandro Jasseo [i.e. Mancel Azevdo], *Venete Urbis Descriptio*, 1780.

John **K**eahey, *Venice against the Sea. A city besieged*, New York, 2002.

La **L**aguna di Venezia 1933: *La Laguna di Venezia*, ed. Giovani Magrini, many volumes, 1933 ff.

Laguna di Venezia 1995: *La Laguna di Venezia*, ed. G. Caniato, E. Turri and M. Zanetti, Verona.

La Laguna di Venezia 2003: *La Laguna di venezia nell cartografia storica a stampa*, ed. G. Baso, M. Scarso and C. Tonini, catalogue for exhibition at the Correr Museum.

Lavorare sui bordi: Lavorare sui bordi. Paessaggi di margine nella laguna di Venezia, Studi e progetti corso di Arte dei Giardini Mariapia Cunico 1996–2000, ed. Francesca Benati and Laura Zampieri, University of Venice, 2001.
James Lees-Milne, *Venetian Evenings*, London, 1988.

Margaretta M. Lovell, *A Visitable past. Views of Venice by American Artists 1860–1915*, Chicago, IL, 1989.

Margaretta M.Lovell, *Venice. The American View 1860 –1920*, exhibition catalogue, Fine Arts Museum of San Francisco, 1984.

Alberto **M**agrini, "Gruppi Urbanistici e Piani Regolatori. Studio per un piano regolatore di Venezia e Mestre", *Le Tre Venezie*, 4 (1931), pp.500–505.

Charles Malagola, *Le Lido de Venise à travers l'histoire*, Paris, 1909.

S. Marceau, *Coup d'œil sentimental... sur Venise* [1805], ed. N.Zutti, Geneva, 1981.

Marcello, "Flora": Alessandro Marcello, "La Flora Urbica di Venezia", *Memorie di Biogeografia Adriatica*, IX (1973–4), pp.123–293.

Paolo Maretto, *La casa veneziana nella storia della città dalle origini all'ottocento, 1986*

Martinioni: Francesco Sansovino, *Venetia Città Noblissima et singolare* [1581], with additions by Giustiniano Martinioni, ed. Lino Moretti, reprint of 1663 edition, 1968.

Mask of Venice: The Mask of Venice. Masking, theater & identity in the art of Tiepolo & his time, exhibition catalogue, ed. James Christen Steward, Berkeley, CA, 1996.

Predrag Matvejevitch, *The Other Venice. Secrets of the City*, translated by Russell Scott Valentino, London, 2007 (originally published in French, 2004).

Mazzarotto, *Feste*: Bianca Tamassia Mazzarotto, *Le Feste Veneziane. I giochi popolari, le ceremonie religiose e di governo*, Florence, 1961.

Meneghini: G.Meneghini, *La farmacia attraverso i secoli e gli speziali di Venezia*, Padua, 1944.

Chiara Mezzalira, "Definire un margine. Il bordo sud-orientale di Venezia tra il fine della Repubblica e l'annessione all'Italia", doctoral dissertation, University of Venice, 2005.

William Mathewson Milliken, *Unfamiliar Venice*, Cleveland, OH, 1967.

Minio 1927: M.Minio, *I botanici veneziani*, Treviso, 1927.

Minio 1952–3: M.Minio, "Codice Rinio integralmente rivendicato al medico Nicolò Roccabonella", *Atti dell'Istituto Veneto di Scienze, Lettere ed Arti*, CXI (1952–53), pp.49–64.

Miozzi: Eugenio Miozzi, *Venezia nei secoli*, 3 vols, 1957.

Molmenti & Mantovini: P.Molmenti and D.Mantovini, *Calli e Canali in Venezia*, 1890–91 (except Preface is dated 1893); republished as *Calli e Canali di Venezia*, 1976.

Monaco: Tom. Giaccalone Monaco, "Vino e pergola sulla laguna", *Rivista di viticoltura e di enologia di Conegliano*, III (1954), unpaginated.

Paul Morand, *Venises*, Paris, 1971.

Dionisio Moretti, engravings of buildings along the Grand Canal, in A.Quadri, *Il Canal Grande di Venezia*, 1828–9.

L. Sormani Moretti, *L'orto sperimentale*, 1885.

Z. Morosini, *Murano, le sue officine e i suoi orti* [1500], 1882.

Enrico Motta, "*I Giardini di Venezia*", *Venice*, I (1925), pp.23–32.

Edward Muir and Ron Weissman, "Social and symbolic places in Renaissance Venice and Florence", in *The Power of Place. Bringing together geographical and sociological imaginations*, ed. John A.Agnew, Boston, MA, 1989.

Savero Muratori, *Studi Per Una Operante Storia Urbana di Venezia*, 2 vols, Rome, 1960.

F.Mutinelli, *Annali urbani di Venezia*, 1838.

Pasqual **N**egri, *I Giardini di Venezia. Poemetto*, 1818.

John Julius Norwich, *Paradise of cities. Venice in the 19th century*, New York, 2003.

Thomas **O**key, *The Old Venetian Palaces and Old Venetian Folk*, London, Dent, 1907

Origini: Origini – età ducale. Storia di Venezia, I, Rome, 1992.

Origini di Venezia: Le Origini di Venezia. Problemi, esperienze, proposte, proceedings of a symposium, 1980, 1981.

G.B.**P**aganuzzi, *Iconografie delle Trenta Parrocchie di Venezia*, 1821.

Paoletti: Ermolao Paoletti, *Il Fiore di Venezia*, 4 vols (I: 1841, II: 1839, III & IV: 1840).

Christopher J. Pastore, "Expanding antiquity: Andrea Navagero and the villa culture in the cinquecento Veneto", Ph.D. dissertation, University of Pennsylvania , 2003.

Charlotte Elfriede Pauly, *Der venezianische Lustgarten*, Strassburg, 1916.

Paola Pavanini, "Venezia verso la pianificazione? Bonifiche Urbane nel XVI secolo a Venezia", *D'une Ville à l'autre. Structures matérielles et l'organisation de l'espace dans les villes européennes*, Collection de l'Ecole Française à Rome, Rome, 1989.

F. Pellegrini, *Gli orti di Murano*, 1877.

Gianfranco Pertot, *Venice. Extraordinary Maintenance*, London, 2004 (original Italian edition, 1988).

Amedeo Petrilli, *Il Testamento di Le Corbusier. Il progetto per l'Ospedale di Venezia*, 1999.

Giannina Piamonte, *Venezia vista dell'acqua*, 1968.

Piani Particolareggiati: I Piani Particolareggiati del centro storico di Venezia 1974–1976, published by the Commune di Venezia, 1977.

T. Pignatti et al., *Palazzo Labia a Venezia*, Turin, 1982.

Magaret Plant, *Venice. Fragile City 1797–1997*, New Haven, CT, 2002.

F. Pona, *Il paradiso dei fiori ovvero l'archetipo de' giardini*, Verona, 1622.

R Protti, "La sacca della Misericordia e il giardino Contareno [sic]", *Emporium*, 23 (1932). (This essay has proved elusive and has not been consulted).

Puppi 1978: Lionello Puppi, "I Giardini Veneziani del Rinascimento", *Il Veltro*, XXII/3-4 (1978), pp.279–98.

Antonio **Q**uadri, *Huits jours à Venise*, [1831], 4th ed., 1847.

Amedeo Quondam, "Nel giardino del Marcolini, un editore veneziano tra Aretino e Doni", *Giornale storico della letteratura italiana*, 157 (1980), pp.75–125.

Giorgiana Baccin **R**eale and Elisabetta Pasqualin, *Le Altane di Venezia*, 1989.

Henri de Régnier, *La vie vénitienne* [originally *L'Altana ou la vie vénitienne*, 2 vols, 1928], Paris, 1986.

Harrison Rhodes, *Venice of Today and Yesterday*, privately printed, Daytona Beach, FL, 1936.

Ridisegnare Venezia. 10 progetti di concorso per la riconstruzione di Campo di Marte alla Giudecca, exhibition catalogue, 1986.

Samuel Rogers, *The Italian Journal of...*, ed. J.R.Hale, London, 1956.

Romanelli 1972: G.Romanelli, "Per G. A. Selva Urbanista", *Arte Veneta*, XXVI (1972), 263–71.

Romanelli 1988: G.Romanelli. *Venezia Ottocento*, 1977, 2nd edition, 1988.

G.Romanelli & S.Baldone, *Venezia Piante e Vedute*, supplement to *Bolletino dei Musei Civici*, 1982.

David Rosand, *Myths of Venice. The figuration of a state*, Chapel Hill, NC, 2001.

Vittorio Rossi, "Jacopo d'Albizzotto Guidi e il suo inedito poema su Venezia", *Nuovo Archivio Veneto*, V (1893), pp.397–451.

G.Ruchinger, *Cenni storici sull'Imperial Regio Orto Botanico di Venezia*, 1847.

Pierre de la Ruffinière du Prey, "Giannantonio Selvia In England", *Architectural History*, 25 (1982), pp.20–34.

Ruffo: Leonardo Ruffo, *Il Giardino Storico Veneziano: una metodologia d'intervento* (DAEST, Tesi di Laurea "Agostino Nardocci", no.6), 2000. An abridgement of his much longer doctoral thesis for the University of Venice.

Cristoforo **S**abbadino, *Discorsi sopra la laguna*, in *Antichi scrittori d'idraulica veneta*, ed. Roberto Cessi, II, pt 1 (1930).

Marc Antonio Sabellico, *Del Situ di Venezia Città* [1502], ed. G.Meneghetti, 1957.

P.A.Saccardo, *Della Storia e Letteratura della Flora Veneta*, Milan, 1869.

Sansovino: Francesco Sansovino, *Venetia Città Noblissima et singolare* [1581], see Martinioni.

Sanudo: Marin Sanudo, *De origine, situ et magistratibus urbis venetae ovvero la città di venezia (1473–1530)*, ed. A.C.Arico, Milan, 1980.

Marin Sanudo: *Venice. Città Exclentissima. Selections from the Renaissance diaries of Marin Sanudo*, ed. Patricia H.Labalme and Laura Sanguineti White, trans. Linda

L.Carroll, Baltimore, MD, 2008. A selection of key passages (though none concerns gardens) from the 58 volumes of the diaries published between 1879 and 1903.

Vittorio Scamozzi, *Idea dell'architettura universale*, 1615.

Schulz 1970: Juergen Schulz, "The printed plan and panoramic views of Venice (1468–1797)", *Saggi e Memoriedi storia dell'arte*, VII (Florence).

Schulz 1978: Juergen Schulz, "Jacopo de' Barbari's View of Venice: map making, city views and moralized geography before the year 1500", *The Art Bulletin*, LX/3.

Schulz 1982: Juergen Schulz, "The Houses of Titian, Aretino and Sansovino", in *Titian. His world and legacy*, ed. David Rosand, New York.

Schulz 1984 : Juergen Schulz, "Wealth in mediaeval Venice: the houses of the Ziani", in *Interpretazioni Veneziane*, ed. David Rosand, pp.29–36.

Schulz 1991: Juergen Schulz, "Urbanism in mediaeval Venice", in *City States in Classical Antiquity and Mediaeval Italy*, ed. Anthony Molho, Kurt Raaflaub and Julia Emlen, Ann Arbor, MI, pp.419–466.

Schulz 1993: Juergen Schulz, "The Houses of the Dandolo: a family compound in mediaeval Venice", *JSAH*, 52, pp.391–415.

Schulz 1999: Juergen Schulz, "Cà da Mosto", in *Mediaeval & Renaissance Venice*, ed. E.K.Kittell and Thomas F.Madden, Urbana, IL, 1999.

Schulz 2004: Juergen Schulz, *The New Palaces of Mediaeval Venice*, University Park, PA, 2004.

Selva, English diary: Stella Rudolph, "Dai diari inediti di Giannantonia Selva: il viaggio in Inghileterra", *Labyrinthos*, 5/6 (1984).

Pietro Selvatico, *Sull'archittetura e sulla scultura in Venezia*, Venice, 1847, modern reprint 1980.

Semplici: Semplici dell' Eccellente M. Luigi Anguillara, 1561. (Copy annotated by Giovanni Marinelli in Marciana Library [Rari V.632]).

A.-F.Sergent-Marceau, *Coup d'œil sentimental, critique et historique sur Venise*, ed. N.Zuffi, Geneva, 1981.

F.Hopkinson Smith, *Gondola Days*, New York 1899 (a smaller format edition of his folio, *Venice of Today*, New York, 1902 – copyrighted 1894 and with its Preface dated 1895).

Stefanutti 1958: U.Stefanutti, "Maestro Gualtieri, chirurgo della Repubblica Veneta nel XIV secolo", in *Quattro figure significative nella medicina del passato* (from *Giornale venento di Scienze Mediche*, 1959).

Stefanutti 1961: U.Stefanutti, *Documentazioni cronologiche per la storia della medicina, chirurgia e farmacia a Venezia dal 1258 al 1332*, 1961.

Stefinlongo 2000: Giovanni Battista Stefinlongo, *Per I Luoghi della Memoria*, Rome, 2000.

Stefinlongo 2005: Giovanni Battista Stefinlongo, *Architettura & Paessaggio. Architettura del Paesaggio*, Riccione, 2005.

Storia della Cività Veneziana, ed. Vittore Branca, 3 vols, Florence, 1979.

Tafuri 1985: Manfredo Tafuri, "Documenti sulle Fondamenta Nuove", *Architettura Storia e Documenti*, I (1985), pp.79–95.

Tafuri 1985(2): Manfredo Tafuri, *Venezia e il Rinascimento*, Turin, 1985; an English translation of this work by Jessica Levine was issued by MIT Press in 1989.

Tafuri 1986: Manfredo Tafuri, *Humanism, Technical Knowledge and Rhetoric: the Debate in Renaissance Venice*, Cambridge, MA.

Hippolyte Taine, *Venise, récit de voyage* (extract from his *Voyage en Italie*), Paris, 2006.

Tony Tanner, *Venice Desired*, Cambridge, MA, 1992.

Tassini *Curiosità*: Giuseppe Tassini, *Curiosità Veneziane*, 1863; edition cited revised with notes by Lino Moretti, 1990.

Tassini 1879: Giuseppe Tassini, *Alcuni Palazzi ed edifice antichi di Venezia, storicamente illustrate*, 1879.

Tassini 1885: Giuseppe Tassini, *Edifici di Venezia distrutti o volti ad altro uso da quello a cui furono destinati*, 1885; reprinted 1969.

Tassini 1890s: *Miscellanea. Il Veridico 1892–1893–1894*, 1970.

Tassini [1891] 1961: Giuseppe Tassini, *Feste Spettacoli divertimenti e piaceri degli antici Veneziani,* sec. ed., 1891, reprinted 1961.

TCI Guide: *Venezia*, Touring Club Italia, 3rd edition, Milan, 1985.

Toni 1904: Ettore de Toni, "Un codice-erbario anonimo", *Memoria della Pontificia Accademia Romana dei Nuovi Lincei*, XXII (1904).

Toni 1908 (i): Ettore de Toni, "Il codice erbario di P. A. Michiel", *Memoria della Pontificia Accademia Romana dei Nuovi Lincei*, XXII (1908).

Toni 1908 (ii): Ettore de Toni, [biography of P. A. Michiel], *Ateneo Veneto* (July-Sept., 1908), pp.69–103.

Toni 1919–25: Ettore de Toni, *Il libro dei semplici di Benedetto Rinio* [sic: see Minio 1952–3 above), Rome, 1919–25.

Toni 1940: Ettore de Toni, *I Cinque Libri di Piante*, 1940.

Alexandre Toursaint de Limojoin, sieur de Saint Didier, *La ville et la république de Venise*, Paris, 1680.

Bernardo Trevisan, *Della Laguna di Venezia* [1715], facsimile reprint, 1988.

Egle Renata Trincanato, *Venezia Minore*, 1948.

Egle Renata Trincanato, *Su Venezia e la Laguna. Veneta e altri scritti di architettura 1948–1993*, ed. Francesco Tentori, Rome, 1997.

Urban 1966: Lina Padoan Urban, "Teatri e 'teatri del mondo' nella Venezia del cinquecento", *Arte Veneta*, XX (1966), pp.137–146.

Urban 1969: Lina Padoan Urban, "Apparati scenograficinelle feste Veneziane cinquecentesche", *Arte Veneta*, 23 (1969), pp.145–155.
Urban 1980: Lina Padoan Urban, *Le feste sull'acqua a Venezia*, 1992.

Urban 1992: Lina Urban, Giandomenico Roamnelli and Fiora Gandolfi, *Venise en fêtes*, Turin.

Diego **V**aleri, *Guida sentimentale di Venezia*, 1942: modern edition, Firenze-Antella, 1997.

Venetia. Le Immagini della Repubblica, ed. Gino Moretto, Piazzola s/ Brenta, 2001.

Venetian Views, Venetian Blinds. English Fantasies of Venice, ed. Manfred Pfister and Barbara Schaff, Amsterdam, 1999.

Venezia e Istanbul: Incontri, confronti e scambi, ed. Ennio Concina, Udine, 2006.

Venezia da stato a mito, ed. Allessandro Bottagno, 1997.

Venezia Piante e Vedute, ed. G.Romanelli and Susanna Bidene, supplement to the *Bolletino* of the Museo Correr, 1982.

Le Venezie Possibile da Palladio a Le Corbusier, ed. Lionello Puppi and Giandomenico Romanelli, Milan, 1985.

Venezia nell'Ottocento, ed. G.A.Cibotto, Rome, 1975.

Venezia nell'Ottocento, Immagini e mito, ed. Giuseppe Pavanello and G.Romanelli, Milan, 1983.

Venice. A documentary history, 1450–1630, ed. David Chambers and Brian Pullan, with Jennifer Fletcher, Oxford, 1992.

Venice and the Islamic World 828–1797, catalogue for the exhibition at the Metropolitan Museum of Art, New York; published by Yale University Press, New Haven, CT, and London, 2007.

Venice Before San Marco. Recent studies on the origins of the city, ed. Albert J.Ammerman and Charles E.McClennen, published by Colgate University, Hamilton, NY, 2001.

Venice in Canaletto's Age, catalogue for the exhibition at the Brooks Museum of Art, Memphis, TN, and the Ringling Museum of Art, Sarasota, FL, 2009.

Venice Reconsidered, ed. J.Martin and D.Romano, Baltimore, MD, 2000.

Venise au fil du temps, atlas historique, complied by Egle Trincanato et al., Boulogne-Billancourt, 1971.

Venise entre les lignes, anthology of writings on Venice chosen by Éveline Schlumberger [1970], Hélène Demoriane and Roger Gouze, Paris, 1999.

R.Vianello and V.Giormani, "L'Orto Botanico di San Giobbe a Venezia", in *Atti e Memorie dell'Accademic Italiana di Storia Della Farmacia*, 12th year (1996), pp.3–14.

Visentini 1984: Margherita Azzi Visentini, *L'Orto Botanico di Padova e il giardino del Rinascimento*, Milan.

Visentini 1988 (1): Margherita Azzi Visentini, *Il giardino veneto. Tra sette e ottocento e le sue fonti*, Milan.

Visentini 1988 (2): *Il giardino veneto. Dal tardo medioevo al novecento*, ed. Margherita Azzi Visentini, Milan.

Gino Voltolina, *Le antiche vere da pozzo veneziane*, with historical research by Linda Mavian, Venice, 1981.

A. **W**irobisz, "L'attività edilizia a Venezia nel XIV e nel XV secolo [sic]", *Studi Veneziani*, VII (1965), pp.307 ff.

V. **Z**anetti, *Guida di Murano* (1866), facsimile edition, Milan, 1984, which includes the volume of corrections and supplements published by Zanetti in 1880.

Giorgio Zordan and Silvia Gasparini, *Repertorio di storiografica veneziana*, Padua, 1998.

Alvise Zorzi, *Venezia Scomparsa*, 2 vols, Milan, 1972.

Zorzi, *Venice*: Alvise Zorzi, *Venice 697–1797. A city, a republic, an Empire*, trans. Judyth Schaubhut Smith (revised English edition, Woodstock, NY, 2001).

Alvise Zorzi, *Venezia austriaca*, Rome 1985, augmented edition, 2000.

L.Zorzi, *Il teatro e la citta*, Torino, 1977.

Gianpietro Zucchetta, *Un' Altra Venezia*, 1995.

On the author

John Dixon Hunt is Professor of the History and Theory of Landscape at the University of Pennsylvania School of Design, Philadelphia, USA. He was a student at King's College, Cambridge, and took his Ph.D. at the University Bristol.

Professor John Dixon Hunt joined the University of Pennsylvania School of Design in 1994 and served as department chair through 2000. He was the former Director of Studies in Landscape Architecture at Dumbarton Oaks. He is the author of numerous articles and books on garden history and theory, including a catalogue of the landscape drawings of William Kent, *Garden and Grove, Gardens and the Picturesque, The Picturesque Garden in Europe* (2002), *The Afterlife of Gardens* (2004), and *Nature Over Again: The Garden Art of Ian Hamilton Finlay* (2008). He edits two journals, *Word & Image* and *Studies in the History of Gardens and Designed Landscapes*. Current interests focus upon landscape architectural theory, modern(ist) garden design, and ekphrasis. He is the inaugural series editor of the *Penn Studies in Landscape Architecture* (University of Pennsylvania Press), in which was published his own theoretic study of landscape architecture, *Greater Perfections: The Practice of Garden Theory* (1999). In 2000 he was named Chevalier of the Order of Arts and Letters by the French Ministry of Culture, and he was awarded an honorary degree of Doctor of Letters by the University of Bristol (UK) in 2006.

Acknowledgements

My work on Venetian gardens has been conducte inter- mittently, between other projects, for over thirty years, during which time I have had the advantage of much personal and institutional support. In Venice itself I have enjoyed the company and local assistance of good friends, Philip and Jane Rylands, Giorgio Gianighian and Paola Pavanini, Rosella Mamoli Zorzi, Clemente di Thiene, and Sergio and Alberta Perosa. I am also most grateful to the advice of both Juergen Schultz and Lillian Armstrong on matters Venetian, to Valentina Follo for help with translations, and to Mariagrazia Dammicco for getting me into the garden of the Contarini dal Zaffo. I am indebted to two colleagues who have carefully read and commented most productively on a final version of the book, enabling me to sharpen some arguments: David Leatherbarrow at the University of Pennsylvania and Edward Harwood at Bates College. Encouragement from an old friend and historian of Florence, Richard Goldthwaite, is also warmly acknowledged. Joseph Rykwert was the first to invite me to write an essay on Venetian gardens in a special issue of *Rassegna* in 1981, and since then I have tried out more and more of my overall project on various audiences at Rhode Island School of Design, the University of Pennsylvania, the 1999 summer school of ILAUD in Venice, the University of Western Australia, the University of Bristol, and in the pages of *Studies in the History of Gardens and Designed Landscapes*.

A Kress Senior Fellowship at the Center for Advanced Study in the Visual Arts, National Gallery of Art, Washington, D.C. in the spring of 1992 and subsequently two grants from the University of Pennsylvania – from the Salvatori Research Fund, and a University Research Foundation Award (this last helping to jump-start the final stage of the research) – have been invaluable. A final grant from the Gladys Krieble Delmas Foundation in 2007-08 allowed me to return to Venice for one last research visit and to conclude the writing of the book during a sabbatical year.

Staff at the Marciana Library, at the Correr Museum, at the Fondazione Querini Stampalia and at both state and municipal archives have been helpful, but, given the long duration of the work, I'd want also to acknowledge libraries at the University of London, the University of East Anglia, Dumbarton Oaks, and the Oak Spring Garden Library. Still, my best support and help has come in the last dozen years from my own colleagues in libraries at the University of Pennsylvania.

Finally, I would thank Andreas Müller and his colleagues at Birkhäuser for having confidence in this book and ensuring its handsome publication, and Thomas E. Beck for redrawing some essential plans. In Venice, Philip Rylands, Paola Pavanini and Giorgio Gianighian most kindly agreed to comb the proofs for errors and have, between them, saved me by their quite considerable labours from a multitude of Venetian *faux-pas*.

Illustration credits

All images not otherwise credited are from author's collection. Author's photos IX.9–11 with kind permission of the Fondazione Querini Stampalia, Venezia, and IX.14–17 of the Peggy Guggenheim Collection.

The Royal Collection © 2008, Her Majesty Queen Elizabeth II: IV.2

Alinari; Fratelli Alinari Archives – Alinari Archive, Florence; Alinari Archives, Florence: V.16 (ACA-F-020856-0000), 20 (ACA-F-020838-0000); VII.27 (ACA-F-012934-0000)

arch.CAMERAPHOTO epoche di Vittorio Pavan: IV.13

Architectural Review: IV.28, 31

Bergamo, Accademia Carrara: III.40 (n.435/08 prot. – n.67/08RDF)

Berlin, bpk/Kupferstichkabinett, SMB/Jörg P. Anders: VI.1

Chicago, The Art Institute of Chicago, Gift of Marian and Max Ascoll Fund, 1991.112, E24320, Reproduction, The Art Institute of Chicago, Photography © The Art Institute of Chicago: VI.3

Barbara David: Cover

Editorial Gustavo Gili: IX.22–23

Mariapia Cunico: IV.23

Giacomelli Fotografia: IV.33, VI.17

Gustafson Guthrie Nichol, Gustafson Porter: IX.18

Kansas City, Spencer Museum of Art, Museum purchase: Helen Foresman Spencer Art Acquisition Fund, 1990.0003: VIII.4

Lyon, Musée des Beaux-Arts de Lyon, © MBA Lyon: III.38

Andreas Müller: IV.10a; VII.1, 20; VIII.1a; IX.1a, 12 (with kind permission of Fondazione Querini Stampalia), IX.19–21 (with kind permission of Gustafson Guthrie Nichol and Gustafson Porter)

Murano, Glass Museum, Fondazione Musei Civici di Venezia: VI.7

New York, The Pierpoint Morgan Library, 1966. 11:10, Bequest of Junius S. Morgan and Gift of Henry S. Morgan, Photography David A. Loggie, © The Pierpoint Morgan Library, New York. 2009: VI.6

New York, Private Collection. Image © The Metropolitan Museum of Art: VI.5

Oxford, Ashmolean Museum, University of Oxford: VI.4

Philadelphia: University of Pennsylvania, Anne and Jerome Fisher Fine Arts Library (Gift of G.Holmes Perkins): III.24, 25

Private collections: III.16–23, 26–30, 37; IV.5; VI.20

St. Louis Art Museum: II.15, left (museum accession number 545:1957)

Treviso, Musei Civici di Treviso, inv. P 110: III.41

Venice, Correr Library and Museum: V.11, 17–19, 23; VI.2, 9–12; VII.2–5, 8–13, 21–23; VIII.6–7, 12

Venice, Daniele Hotel: I.4

Venice, Gallerie dell'Accademia, Venice: II.17, III.39

Venice, Marciana Library: II.3 (Lat.XIV, 77 [=2991]); III.31 (It.II,30 [=2991] f.36r), 32 (ibid f.14r), 33 (ibid f.89r), 34 (ibid f.128r), 35 (ibid f.129r), 36 (ibid f.5r); V.14 (Di Rari Veneti 111)

Venice, Commune di Venezia, Archivio Storico: VII. 16–19

Venice, State Archives: Courtesy of the illustration department of the Archivio di Stato in Venezia, concession /2009: II.2 (Misc Mappe, dis. 1216), 5 (Scuola Grande di San Rocco, Il consegna, reg. 26, Tomo I, num. antica 31, num. moderna 63); III.7 (Savi ed esecutori alle acque, serie Laguna, dis. 4), 43 (Savi ed esecutori alle acque, b. 55, dis. 10), 44 (Misc Mappe, dis. 705); IV.1 (Misc Mappe, dis. 618), 34 (Archivio Grimani, busta 7); V.1 (Corporazioni religiose, San Domenico di Castello, b.4), 2 (Misc Mappe, dis. 171), 3 (Misc Mappe, dis. 77/1), 4 (Misc Mappe, dis. 1293), 5 (Misc Mappe, dis. 595), 6 (Savi ed esecutori alle acque, serie Laguna, dis. 148), 7 (Genio Civile, serie I, dis. 20), 8 (Genio Civile, serie I, dis. 32), 9 (Corporazioni religiose, San Domenico di Castello, b.4), 10 (Savi ed esecutori alle acque, Relazioni 945/3), 12 (Provv.Agg.sopra Monasteri 3), 15 (Savi ed esecutori alle acque b. 367 bis, dis. 1), 21 (Savi ed esecutori alle acque, b. 650, dis. 2), 22 (Savi ed esecutori alle acque, serie Laguna, dis. 109); VI.23 (Provveditori in Zecca, b. 1217, dis. n.n.)

Washington, D.C., Library of Congress: II.15, right

Washington, D.C., Rosenwald Collection, images courtesy of the Board of Trustees, The National Gallery of Art, Washington, 1500, woodcut on two sheets pasted together : II.7-9; III.1-6, 8-14

Frank Lloyd Wright Foundation, Scottsdale, Arizona/Artists Right Society (ARS) New York © 2009: IX.1

Worcester, Massachusetts, Worcester Art Museum, Museum Purchase, Sustaining Membership Fund: II.14

Figure II.1 is reproduced from *Venise au fils du Temps* (1971); II.10, from *Paolo Maretto, La casa veneziana nella storia della città dalle origine all'ottocento* (1986); II.11, from E.R.Trincanato, *Venezia minore* (1948); II.16 from Gianpietro Zucchetta, *Un'altra Venezia* (1995); and IX.1 from the review *Metron Architettura* (IX, 1954), as illustrated in Emiliano Balisteri, *Le Corbusier, Neutra, Samonà, Scarpa, Trincanato, Wright e Venezia* (2002)
Plans IV.10 and IV.35 redrawn by Thomas E.Beck

Every effort has been made to trace the copyright holders of images. We apologise in advance for any unintentional omission and would be happy to insert the appropriate acknowledgements in any subsequent edition.

Index of selected sites

as listed in the Gazetteer, Chapter Four